The Diefenbaker Legacy

The Diefenbaker Legacy

Canadian Politics, Law and Society Since 1957

edited by
Donald C. Story
and
R. Bruce Shepard

Canadian Plains Research Center
University of Regina

Diefenbaker Canada Centre
University of Saskatchewan

1998

Canadian Plains Research Center
University of Regina
Regina, Saskatchewan S4S 0A2
Canada

Canadian Cataloguing in Publication Data

Main entry under title:

The Diefenbaker legacy
    (Canadian plains proceedings, 0317-6401 ; 30)

Proceedings of a conference held at the University of Saskatchewan, March 6-8, 1997.

    Includes bibliographical references.
    ISBN 0-88977-091-3

1. Canada - Politics and government - 1957-1963 - Congresses.*   I. Story, Donald C. (Donald Clarke), 1947- II. Shepard, R. Bruce. III. University of Saskatchewan. Right Honourable John G. Diefenbaker Centre for the Study of Canada.   IV. University of Regina. Canadian Plains Research Center.   V. Series.

FC615.D544 1998   971.064'2   C98-920029-9
F1034.2.D544 1998

Cover Design: Alexander Angelov, Ishtar Publishing and Design
Cover photographs courtesy the Diefenbaker Canada Centre and the Saskatchewan Archives Board

Printed and bound in Canada by
Hignell Printing Limited, Winnipeg, Manitoba

Printed on acid-free paper

Contents

Acknowledgements

This book brings together selected papers presented at a conference held at the University of Saskatchewan on March 6-8, 1997 in honour of the fortieth anniversary of the advent to power of John Diefenbaker as Prime Minister of Canada. The conference and this publication received generous financial support from: the Saskatchewan Heritage Foundation; the Diefenbaker Society; and the College of Law, the Office of the Vice-President (Academic), the Diefenbaker Canada Centre, and the Publications Fund Committee of the University of Saskatchewan. Their support is gratefully acknowledged.

Thanks are extended as well to the conference organizing committee, comprised of R. Bruce Shepard, Director, Diefenbaker Canada Centre (Chair), Professor D. De Brou, Department of History, Professor Donald C. Story, Department of Political Studies and Professor D. Schmeiser, College of Law, University of Saskatchewan. The staff of the Diefenbaker Canada Centre also deserve acknowledgment for services that they provided the Conference, as does Russell Isinger who was an inspiration behind the scenes in the conceiving of the Conference.

We also wish to thank the Heads of the Departments of Political Studies and History, Professors Hans J. Michelmann and W.A. Waiser, respectively; the Dean of the College of Arts and Science, David Atkinson; and the Dean of the College of Law, Peter MacKinnon and the Acting Dean, Dan Ish for their encouragement and support.

Finally, thanks to Don Ward, the copy editor, for his careful hand, good judgement and infinite patience in helping prepare the manuscript.

Donald C. Story
University of Saskatchewan
February 1998

Introduction

Donald C. Story

This volume commemorates the fortieth anniversary of the ascent to power of John Diefenbaker as Prime Minister of Canada. The book is an anthology comprised of papers presented at the conference, "The Diefenbaker Legacy: Law, Politics and Society Since 1957," held at the University of Saskatchewan on March 6-8, 1997. The authors evaluate the influence of Diefenbaker's prime ministership on Canada's public policies, political institutions and political culture through an approach that reassesses the major policies and decisions of the Diefenbaker government and re-examines its political and administrative operation.

Making use of recently opened archival documents and papers, the authors re-examine an era that most Canadian historians characterize as difficult for Canada. It was a time when the international system was being transformed by the decline of Britain (and the Commonwealth) and the strong assertion of power by the United States as leader of the Western world.

When accompanied by the decline of Canadian market prospects in Britain and the accelerated integration of the Canadian and American trade and investment economies and defence establishments, this power shift had the effect of isolating Canada in North America. As a result, the Canada-US relationship would become more concentrated, complicated and contentious; this would in turn impose constraints on Canada's pursuit of a middle power role in the world.

Canada was moving into the next stage of its maturity as a political society and was experiencing the attendant growing pains — now brought to the attention of Canadians themselves by the new medium of television. The early 1950s had been a period of rapid growth for Canada: its secondary manufacturing and natural resource industries expanded exponentially; at the same time its population was increasing and becoming more ethnically diverse on account of a large influx of immigrants from war-ravaged Europe and the beginnings of immigration from Asia. But the latter part of the 1950s brought a slowing of the Canadian economy that descended into a recession. Accordingly, pressure was put on government to develop policies and initiatives to meet emerging demands for social, economic and political change. While public finances became strained, Canadians called for enhanced social programs and new financial arrangements to mitigate growing regional disparities. Meanwhile, other demands grew out of a political culture in Canada which was in its own state of evolution, influenced by forces such as the dawning of the Quiet Revolution in Quebec; demands for constitutional change; a new and expanding awareness among Canadian citizens of their rights; growing provincial opposition to federal policies; the increased regionalization of Canadian politics; new and revitalized federal and provincial political parties; the emergence of the administrative state; an increasingly aggressive and influential media; and the emergence of new political actors such as aboriginal peoples and women.

The book attempts to capture this era of change and cast new light upon the attempts made by Diefenbaker and his government to meet the challenges that the era posed. The authors, both established and new scholars in the fields of history, political science and law, have as their common purpose the identification of elements of Canadian policy, process and culture that were affected or shaped in an enduring way by Diefenbaker's response to the issues and events of his time.

The volume's first two sections, "Canada-US Relations" and "Canadian Defence and Security Issues" are devoted to Diefenbaker's legacy to what by the 1950s had become the central preoccupation of Canadian foreign policy — relations with the powerful continental neighbour. Essentially the legacy is a relationship in which Canada was more assertive towards the US on matters that were of critical importance to Canadians, while supportive of the larger strategic goals of the US as leader of the Western world. Ann Flanagan provides an account of the new assertiveness in her study of the Diefenbaker government's position on the control of exports to Communist China. Trade was one of those critical aspects of foreign policy to which Canadians had always believed there should be no impediments. Diefenbaker's assertiveness on this policy, when applied to the China case, lay in his indication that his government would follow, in the first instance, the wishes of the Canadian people. This would be a troublesome inference to US officials who were aware of the Canadian practice of keeping Cold War diplomacy and trade in separate watertight compartments.

Another of the major foreign policy issues on which Canada would assert its position *vis-à-vis* the Americans during the Diefenbaker years would be nuclear weapons. Erika Simpson's paper shows how Diefenbaker would eventually come to argue publically for joint Canadian-American control of nuclear weapons stationed on Canadian soil, and against employing nuclear weapons in the international system as a "universal deterrent." According to Simpson, Diefenbaker's concerns about the spread of nuclear weapons were caused partly by his strong "personal sense of the responsibility for the survival of millions of Canadians." Again, Diefenbaker's position seemed to be that his government would be guided by the Canadian people, in this case by their growing concerns expressed to him in many letters about the dangers of nuclear war. Diefenbaker's assertiveness turned to insistence when the issue was Canadian control over nuclear weapons on Canadian soil; for, according to Diefenbaker, there was nothing more critical to Canadians than the sovereignty of Canada. Especially given the fears that Canadians had of a looming nuclear war, Diefenbaker argued that it was absolutely necessary that Canada be able to bring influence to bear on any plan to use nuclear weapons.

The assumption underlying the new self-assertion by Canada during the Diefenbaker years was continuing Canadian support for the larger security and strategic goals of the United States. This support is underlined in both Kevin J. Gloin's and Russell Isinger and Donald C. Story's reassessments of aspects of the Diefenbaker government's foreign and defence policies. The conventional view of Canada-US relations during the Diefenbaker years is that they were contentious and conflictual. Gloin's work brings to light rather a basic harmony in the Canada-US relationship during most of this period (i.e., the pre-Kennedy years) predicated on Canadian support for US foreign policy goals of opposing communism and promoting a stable and prosperous world.

Isinger and Story retell the story of the cancellation of the Avro CF-105 Arrow, disputing the argument long made by Arrow advocates that Diefenbaker in fact failed to defend Canadian interests in allowing the United States to effectively kill the technologically superior interceptor. The "plane truth" is instead that the US government supported the project all along, even offering in the end to buy several squadrons of the aircraft and have them deployed in Canada as part of the NORAD forces. Diefenbaker doubted whether vital Canadian interests were sacrificed in the

Arrow's cancellation, which was entailed by the Diefenbaker government's support of the US strategic rationale developed for the coming age of guided missiles.

The authors who explore Diefenbaker's legacy to Canadian domestic politics focus on both policy and process. Examining the Diefenbaker government's relations with the provinces, the press and the federal bureaucracy respectively, P.E. Bryden, Patrick H. Brennan and Ken Rasmussen are inclined to view the Diefenbaker legacy more critically — as basically a lesson about failed political leadership. Bryden views the Diefenbaker government as having failed to provide leadership in defining and articulating the national interest with respect to Canada's finances and the economy. In the event of the resulting leadership vacuum, Ontario's Premiers Leslie Frost and John Robarts, sensing the "centrality of Ontario's place in the nation," moved towards defining and defending the national interest themselves.

Brennan's study of the relationship between Diefenbaker and the press disputes a popular notion that prominent political commentators, in this instance at *Maclean's*, were partisans bent upon damaging the Diefenbaker government. But Brennan also shows that Diefenbaker's public dismissal of particular media people as Liberal partisans was counterproductive to his leadership, "angering and disillusioning a broad spectrum of opinion" in Canadian society. Nor did Diefenbaker help his leadership and that of his government, according to Rasmussen, by clinging to an outdated Whitehall notion of political-bureaucratic relations. Insisting that a clear line be kept between cabinet ministers and senior bureaucrats, Diefenbaker failed to take advantage of the bureaucracy's policy expertise and knowledge and, moreover, to institute needed reforms to the policy-making process. "The art of leadership in the era of the administrative state," says Rasmussen, "involves harnessing the policy capacity of the bureaucracy so that it works toward a partisan agenda."

The section of the volume whose heading is "Political Leadership" includes three papers by Patrick Kyba and Wendy Green-Finlay, Richard Sigurdson, and David Stewart, which cast the legacy left by Diefenbaker's leadership in a more positive light. Kyba and Green-Finlay make the case that Diefenbaker's extraordinary rise to and fall from power has overshadowed his achievements as Prime Minister. The achievements have been ignored as well because, with some exceptions, they tend to be of a regional nature. A proper rendering of Diefenbaker's legacy, the authors maintain, should cite the lasting effects of legislation passed by the Diefenbaker government in crucial functional policy areas such as agricultural pricing, crop survival, grain exports, land use, natural resource development particularly in power generation, northern (including Arctic) development, road infrastructure and natural conservation.

Sigurdson sees one of Diefenbaker's important lasting achievements to be the impact of his political beliefs and ideas upon the Canadian political culture. In particular, Diefenbaker brought into sharper focus values and principles, for example, freedom from prejudice, freedom of speech, equality, minority rights, aboriginal freedoms, and civil liberties, that would dominate Canadian political and societal discourse in the latter part of the twentieth century. Sigurdson acknowledges that Diefenbaker's idea of "individual equality" was an "impediment to the national unity issue," holding little appeal for Quebec secessionists and First Nations. Yet he proposes that if individual equality can be made to encompass respect for individuals as "members of identity-conferring groups" such as First Nations and new peoples, it might serve as a basis of a political nationality for a future Canada (with or without Quebec).

Diefenbaker's legacy to Canadian party politics is the subject of David Stewart's paper. Essentially Stewart's argument is that Diefenbaker carved out a permanent place on the Canadian political landscape for a "progressive conservative" party. One of Diefenbaker's early achievements was to turn the old, narrowly based, "minority" Conservative party into the dominant party in English Canada, supported by various ethnic groups, different regions, and people from all walks of life. Diefenbaker was defeated in 1963, but he had infused Canadian conservatism with a vital populist or progressive strain that would help bring the Progressive Conservative party to power again in 1983. Moreover, when the Conservatives strayed too far from the grass roots later in the 1980s, western supporters of Diefenbaker-styled populism would move to, and play an instrumental role in the success of, the new Reform party. Diefenbaker serves as a reminder that modern conservatism cannot survive in Canada without populism.

The book contains two papers under the heading "Human Rights" in recognition of not only Diefenbaker's landmark Bill of Rights but his particular contribution to the Canadian success of marrying rights to parliamentary democracy. In the first paper, Robert M. Belliveau fixes his attention on the Bill of Rights, clarifying its content as a clear expression of Diefenbaker's beliefs and intentions. The Bill was to be an authoritative instrument to help Parliament protect those civil liberties that were under attack in Canada by the executive branch of government. "The intent of the pledge [in the Bill of Rights]," says Belliveau, "was to force the executive to govern through Parliament." This emphasis on enhancing Parliament's protection of rights through judicial means, Christopher MacLennan point outs in the companion paper, was insufficient for Canadian rights advocates, who would continue their fight to have human rights fully entrenched in the Constitution. MacLennan's conclusion is that the true significance of the Bill of Rights lies in the "awareness of human rights issues that it generated in Canada," which in turn paved the way for Canadians' eventual adoption of the Charter of Rights and Freedoms. What MacLennan might have added is that Diefenbaker's influence could be clearly discerned in the Charter — not only in the rights provisions which came right out of the Bill, but in the "notwithstanding clause" which maintained a balance between Diefenbaker's two cherished ideals of rights and parliamentary government.

Canada-US Relations in the Diefenbaker Era: Another Look

Kevin J. Gloin

John Diefenbaker was a fierce Canadian nationalist and an unapologetic patriot. During his successful campaign for Prime Minister in 1957, he accused the previous government of jeopardizing Canadian interests by becoming too closely associated with the United States. By the time he was voted out of office in 1963, there was a palpable public tension between his government and the administration of John F. Kennedy, and he is often remembered as an anti-American crusader.

Knowlton Nash, a prominent Canadian journalist has written that the Diefenbaker period included "the sharpest Canada-US confrontation since the War of 1812." The interpretation of leading scholars has been only slightly less sensational, with historians J.L. Granatstein and Norman Hillmer noting that "Canada's relations with the United States had reached their nadir" during the Diefenbaker-Kennedy period, while Michael Bliss wrote that Diefenbaker wallowed "in a crude anti-Americanism" that was "demagogic."[1]

Many such interpretations have been "Canada-centric," utilizing mainly Canadian sources and Canadian opinions. A different picture of Canada-US relations emerges when more attention is given to the American perspective and official documents. In fact, Diefenbaker's government was on close and friendly terms with Washington during most of his time as Prime Minister. When considered within the larger background of American foreign policy and the Cold War, Diefenbaker's anti-communism and support of American international initiatives emerge as important factors in the maintenance of good bilateral relations. Furthermore, Diefenbaker's counterpart in Washington for nearly four of his almost six years as Prime Minister was President Dwight D. Eisenhower, and there was little animosity between the two

---

1   Knowlton Nash, *Kennedy and Diefenbaker: Fear and Loathing Across the Undefended Border* (Toronto: McClelland & Stewart, 1990), 242; J.L. Granatstein and Norman Hillmer, *For Better or For Worse: Canada and the United States to the 1990s* (Toronto: Copp Clark Pitman, 1991), 193; Michael Bliss, *Right Honourable Men: The Descent of Canadian Politics from Macdonald to Mulroney* (Toronto: Harper Collins, 1994), 211.

leaders. Serious conflicts emerged only after John F. Kennedy was elected, and there is evidence that the President was more responsible than the Prime Minister for the changing tone of bilateral relations.

Our memory of the Diefenbaker period in Canada-US relations should pay more attention to Diefenbaker's defence of Canadian interests, his relationship with Eisenhower, the general contours of American foreign policy, and the larger picture of the ongoing Cold War.

THE COLD WAR CONTEXT

Examinations of Canadian foreign policy in the second half of the twentieth century place a heavy emphasis on relations with the United States. The intimate links of geography, politics, and trade, not to mention cultural connections such as television, radio, and magazines, have affected every foreign policy decision made in Ottawa as well as the daily lives of virtually every Canadian resident. Analysis of American foreign relations since 1945, on the other hand, does not begin with Canada. This latter reality, though obvious, seems too often neglected in studies of the bilateral relationship. From 1945 onward, the primary factor in American foreign policy was what became known as the Cold War, alternatively characterized as the ideological struggle between the world's strongest democracy and the world's strongest dictatorship, or the economic struggle of the free-market system against the centralized state-planning system of communism. There ensued a long period of dangerous shadowboxing by the two most powerful countries on the globe — powerful enough to defend themselves to the last person, and eventually powerful enough to annihilate each other (or any part of the globe) in a matter of minutes.

In its foreign relations, the United States thought first and foremost about the Cold War with communism. This was the context for Canada's relations with the United States after 1945, including the 1957-1963 period when Diefenbaker was Prime Minister. American foreign policy in the Cold War had two main thrusts. One was the policy of containment against the spread of communism in international politics.[2] The other was the promotion of a healthy international community, which largely consisted of trying to prevent another economic depression like that of the 1930s (American policy makers felt that desperate economic circumstances had propelled the rise of Hitler, Mussolini, and Japanese militarists).[3] These policy thrusts, in turn, were the stick by which the foreign policies of other countries were measured. From this perspective, the foreign policy of the Diefenbaker government usually measured up. For most of Diefenbaker's administration, Canada proved as reliable an ally in the Cold War as it had been before and would be after Diefenbaker's time.

DIEFENBAKER AND EISENHOWER

When Diefenbaker was elected Prime Minister in 1957, Dwight D. Eisenhower was roughly five months into his second term as President of the United States. By the standard of national leaders who meet on the international scene, Eisenhower and

---

2   The seminal study is John Lewis Gaddis, *Strategies of Containment: A Critical Appraisal of Postwar American National Security Policy* (New York: Oxford University Press, 1982).

3   John Lewis Gaddis, *The United States and the Origins of Cold War, 1941-1947* (New York: Columbia University Press, 1972), 11; Diane B. Kunz, *Butter and Guns: America's Cold War Economic Diplomacy* (New York: Free Press, 1997).

Diefenbaker had an uncommonly friendly relationship, characterized by genuine affection and mutual respect. They continued corresponding even after Eisenhower had retired to his farm at Gettysburg.[4]

There were many personal similarities which allowed the two leaders to be at ease with each other. They were of the same generation ("Ike" was only five years older than "Dief"), and they had both been raised in rural areas. Basil Robinson, the Prime Minister's personal advisor on External Affairs, has observed that Diefenbaker "felt completely at home with Eisenhower ... and with Diefenbaker so much was personal."[5] Meanwhile, the President also placed great value on "face-to-face, friendly discussions"[6] with other state leaders. In a press interview after his return from Ottawa, Eisenhower dutifully outlined many of the topics which had been discussed, but ended by insisting "the big value of the visit was, I think, the development of the personal relationship."[7]

DIEFENBAKER THE ANTI-COMMUNIST ALLY

Diefenbaker's personal traits were not as important to Eisenhower, however, as were his positions and opinions in foreign affairs. Diefenbaker's anti-communism was instrumental in developing a positive relationship between Canada and the United States. There has been a tendency among writers to portray Eisenhower as an affable fellow who was friendly with everyone, and it is true that Eisenhower was skilled in personal diplomacy. But it should also be noted that he did not tolerate much divergence from US policy on critical issues. American uncertainty about the position of India regarding communism, for example, was an impediment to Eisenhower striking up a close relationship with Jawaharlal Nehru, and he was not pleased with French President Charles de Gaulle's ambivalence toward NATO.[8]

Eisenhower's Secretary of State, John Foster Dulles, went to Ottawa for a weekend in July 1957, a month after the Canadian election. "I had an immensely interesting two days in Ottawa," Dulles wrote back to Eisenhower, reporting that Diefenbaker "is, I think, the kind of person we can get along with.... There is no doubt but what they are much more Commonwealth minded than was the prior administration, but Diefenbaker shows a real awareness of the vital importance of working closely with the United States."[9] In the President's briefing book for his trip to Canada in May 1958, the biographical sketch of Diefenbaker said: "Although critical of certain

4   Diefenbaker Canada Centre (DCC), Personal and Confidential Series (P&C), vol. 83, XII/D/76, "Eisenhower, General Dwight: 1957-62"; vol. 7, XII/A/232, "Diefenbaker, J.G. — Correspondence — V.I.P. — Eisenhower, Dwight D.: 1957-1961"; Dwight D. Eisenhower Library (DDEL), Papers as President of the United States, Ann Whitman File (AWF), International Series, "Canada (1)-(6)."

5   H. Basil Robinson, *Diefenbaker's World: A Populist in Foreign Affairs* (Toronto: University of Toronto Press, 1989), 318.

6   Dwight D. Eisenhower, *The White House Years: Waging Peace, 1956-1961* (New York: Doubleday, 1965), 485.

7   DDEL, Records as President, White House Office Files, Office of Staff Secretary, International Trips and Meetings Series, ADDE Trip to Canada, Chronology, July 11, 1958). Transcript of radio interview, 11 July 1958.

8   Eisenhower, *The White House Years*, 106-7, 426-28.

9   DDEL, AWF, Dulles-Herter Series, "Dulles, John Foster — July 1957," Secretary of State to President, 29 July 1957.

Informal shot of Olive and John Diefenbaker and Dwight Eisenhower, waving his hat in the air, standing on the front steps of the Parliament Buildings, 22 July 1958 (courtesy the Diefenbaker Centre, MG01/XVII/JGD 615).

United States policies ... he is believed to be basically friendly toward this country. He urges closer economic as well as defence cooperation... ."[10] Dulles and Eisenhower quickly recognized the difference between Diefenbaker's electioneering rhetoric and his government's policies, and their initial impression that they could work with the Prime Minister proved correct.

Diefenbaker may have been periodically apprehensive of Washington, but he was perpetually suspicious of the Kremlin. Robust anti-communism was a hallmark of his foreign policy. Many examples can be cited throughout his political career, but perhaps the boldest and most significant denunciation of communism came during his speech to the United Nations on 26 September 1960. That meeting of the UN General Assembly came at the end of a summer which ranked among the lowest in Soviet-US relations. Angry recriminations had been issued by Nikita Khrushchev after an American U-2 spy plane was shot down over the USSR. The Soviet leader walked out of the May disarmament talks, and Eisenhower cancelled his trip to Moscow. With diplomatic tensions mounting, Khrushchev announced that he would lead his country's delegation at the General Assembly. Once in New York, Khrushchev exploited the occasion for all it was worth. In his two-hour address to the General Assembly on the second day, he tried to play on the anxiety of neutral countries by describing the UN peacekeeping proposal for the Congo as the handiwork of Western "colonialists," and he directly attacked UN Secretary-General Dag Hammarskjöld as their accomplice. He interrupted speeches by British Prime Minister Harold Macmillan and the representative from the Philippines by shouting from his seat and banging his shoe on the desk. He confirmed the worst fears of Americans when he was seen giving Cuban leader Fidel Castro a bear hug.[11]

Eisenhower and Macmillan tried to be constructive in their speeches, but Diefenbaker chose to make what he later called "a frank, direct answer" to Khrushchev's tirade.[12] He turned Khrushchev's own words against him, outlining the Soviet style

10   DDEL, Records as President, White House Central Files, Confidential File, "Canada, Trip of President, 1958 (Briefing Book)."

11   Michael R. Beschloss, *Mayday: Eisenhower, Khrushchev and the U-2 Affair* (New York: Harper & Row, 1986); Robert E. Quirk, *Fidel Castro* (New York: Norton, 1993), 334-38; Nikita Khrushchev, *Khrushchev Remembers: The Last Testament* (Boston: Little, Brown, 1974), 451-55, 477-79; see photo of Khrushchev and Castro by Wide World Photos in Robert D. Schulzinger, *American Diplomacy in the Twentieth Century*, 3rd ed. (Oxford University Press, 1994), 257.

12   John G. Diefenbaker, *One Canada: Memoirs of the Right Honourable John G. Diefenbaker*, vol. 2 (Toronto: Signet, 1978), 106.

of colonialism and calling Khrushchev "the master of the major colonial power in the world today." He challenged the Soviet leader to allow free elections in the nations of Eastern European being held under Soviet domination.[13]

The September 1960 meeting was probably the most memorable General Assembly session in the history of the UN. The Prime Minister met with Eisenhower soon after his speech. Basil Robinson was with him, and described the American reaction as "appreciative," and Eisenhower as "happy to find Canada so unconditionally on his side."[14] We now know that Eisenhower, privately, had given up hope of finding any common ground with the Soviets before his presidency finished at the end of the year. He harboured a secret desire to launch a verbal attack on Khrushchev,[15] but he knew the diplomatic risks were too grave to do this directly. He had taken the high road with his UN speech, trying to create "an atmosphere of conciliation."[16] Once Khrushchev had slammed any door that the President had tried to open, however, he found Diefenbaker's upbraiding of the Soviet leader gratifying. He made special note of the Prime Minister in his report back to his Cabinet about the 1960 UN meeting. "Dief was very hard indeed on the Communists," the President said. "Many of the delegates were offended by Khrushchev's behaviour during Macmillan's speech."[17]

URANIUM AND NON-PROLIFERATION

Canadian support of American Cold War policies went beyond Diefenbaker's rhetorical flourishes. In a number of key areas, the Progressive Conservative government continued the policies that had been established by the Liberals under Mackenzie King and Louis St. Laurent. For example, it effectively balanced the protection of Canadian interests against American objectives regarding sensitive topics such as nuclear non-proliferation and the sale of uranium for non-military uses.

Washington was seriously committed to the policy of nuclear non-proliferation, which had been first enunciated formally after Franklin Roosevelt's meeting with Winston Churchill at Quebec in 1943.[18] A measure of the American government's commitment can be seen in the fate of Julius and Ethel Rosenberg: found guilty of conspiracy to steal and pass on atomic secrets to the Soviets, they were executed in 1953.[19] Canada had a tangential role in the case. The Rosenbergs had been uncovered on the trail leading from the German scientist Klaus Fuchs, who had been unmasked

13   National Archives of Canada (NA), "Statement to UN General Assembly," 26 September 1960, MG31 E83, vol. 7); John Hilliker, "Diefenbaker and Canadian External Relations," in J.L. Granatstein (ed.), *Canadian Foreign Policy: Historical Readings* (Toronto: Copp Clark Pitman, 1986), 188-89.

14   Robinson, *Diefenbaker's World*, 155.

15   Stephen E. Ambrose, *Eisenhower: Volume Two — The President* (New York: Simon and Schuster, 1984), 589.

16   Eisenhower, *The White House Years*, 581.

17   DDEL, AWF, Cabinet Series, "Cabinet Meeting, October 7, 1960."

18   Arnold Kramish, "Four Decades of Living with the Genie: United States Nuclear Export Policy," in Robert Boardman and James F. Keeley (eds.), *Nuclear Exports and World Politics: Policy and Regime* (New York: St. Martin's Press, 1983), 18.

19   Ronald Radosh and Joyce Milton, *The Rosenberg File: A Search for Truth* (New York: Holt, Rinehart, and Winston, 1983); for a dissenting view on the Rosenbergs' guilt, see Walter Schneir and Miriam Schneir, *Invitation to an Inquest* (Garden City, NY: Doubleday, 1983).

as a spy in 1945 by Igor Gouzenko, a code clerk at the Soviet embassy in Ottawa.[20] Canada's central importance to American nuclear policy was not, however, espionage rings, but its huge quantities of uranium, an irreplaceable element of nuclear fission.

Since World War II, the United States had pursued a policy of purchasing all Canada's available uranium. This had served the dual purpose of meeting American needs for weapons production while restricting the international dissemination of uranium. But Washington's policies toward uranium changed under Eisenhower. Guaranteed purchase programs ended, and controls on distribution were relaxed. This was partly because the world supply of uranium and other strategic materials had gone from a situation of "scarcity to plenty."[21] By the late 1950s, proven global uranium reserves were large, and the United States military had stockpiled a sizable cache. The policy shift was also a response to Eisenhower's "Atoms for Peace" initiative, which had urged that global technological research be directed less at weapons than toward the peaceful uses of nuclear power. In May 1958, the United States Atomic Energy Commission (AEC) announced that it would allow sales of uranium by private American companies to domestic and "friendly nation" consumers, for the purpose of non-military power. The following year, the AEC informed Ottawa that it would honour the remainder of its purchase contracts with Canada, but would not buy any Canadian uranium after 1962.[22]

Uranium was not a minor matter during the Diefenbaker era. In 1958, Canada and the United States each produced about 13,000 tons of uranium, amounting to some 75 percent of the free world's production. Virtually all the Canadian uranium was sold to the United States. In 1958, uranium led all Canadian mineral exports (including crude oil), with a trade value of almost $300 million.[23] Only newsprint, wheat, and timber products were worth more among Canada's exports during the Eisenhower-Diefenbaker era.[24]

The cessation of US government purchases, to be offset by private sales for non-military uses, sounded simple in principle, but created new difficulties. A major problem arose from the desire to ensure that the uranium would neither be used for military purposes nor resold to Communist countries. For a number of years during the Diefenbaker era, this was a type of diplomatic Gordian knot, as various interest groups, both in and out of government, tried to decide on enforcement procedures for safeguarding uranium sales. The Canadian government found itself whipsawed between Washington, which remained adamant about preventing the development of a "fourth nuclear power,"[25] and private Canadian companies such as Rio Tinto that

20   J.L. Granatstein and David Stafford, *Spy Wars: Espionage in Canada from Gouzenko to Glasnost* (Toronto: Key Porter Books, 1990); Robert Chadwell Williams, *Klaus Fuchs, Atomic Spy* (Cambridge, MA: Harvard University Press, 1987).

21   Alfred E. Eckes, Jr., *The United States and the Global Struggle for Minerals* (Austin: University of Texas Press, 1979), 230.

22   NA, RG 25, Acc. 86-87/414, Box 220, A#14002-2-6-40 pt. 2, "Uranium Procurement"; Ted Greenwood with Alvin Streeter, Jr., "Uranium," in Carl E. Beigie and Alfred O. Hero (eds.), *Natural Resources in US-Canadian Relations*, vol. 2 (Boulder, CO: Westview Press, 1980), 324.

23   NA, RG 25, Acc. 86-87/414, Box 220, A#14002-2-6-40, pt. 8, "Canada's Leading Minerals in the North American Market — Uranium."

24   J.W. Griffith, *The Uranium Industry — Its History, Technology and Prospects* (Ottawa: Department of Energy, Mines and Resources, 1967), 20.

25   For example, "Paper Agreed Upon at the Conference at Bermuda (Agreed Note on Military Nuclear

were convinced government regulations on after-sale use of the uranium was affecting the industry's ability to find customers.[26]

During the summer of 1957, the Diefenbaker government approved a uranium export policy which instituted safeguards on a bilateral basis. It amounted to little more than a gentleman's agreement between states, wherein a foreign government would make a promise to Ottawa on behalf of the companies within its borders that the uranium would not be resold or used for the development of weapons.[27] Canada did this reluctantly, and the Cabinet agreed that it would be responsible for safeguards only until such time as "a suitable international authority" could be established.

But indecision and infighting in Washington precluded the possibility of an international agreement. The two key policy players on the uranium issue, the AEC and the State Department, were at odds. The former favoured an extensive and powerful system of safeguards, including random examinations of the purchaser's facilities and detailed accounts for every pound of uranium purchased. State Department proposals, on the other hand, were more flexible, and relied more heavily on the honour of the purchasers.[28]

Throughout 1957 and 1958, the Canadian and American governments maintained close contact on the uranium issue, and exchanged information. Diefenbaker's Cabinet had decided to permit the sale of uranium to Germany and Switzerland in 1957, but refused to sell to France.[29] The Americans were aware of the awkward position of Ottawa. Officials from Canadian uranium companies were constantly pressuring Ottawa to allow unregulated sales, and had taken their case south of the border to lobby the Americans.[30] There was also alarm in both Ottawa and Washington in 1958 regarding rumours that South Africa had made an unregulated sale of uranium to Japan. Washington recognized that its own paralysis was obstructing the creation of an international accord, and in late October 1958 it asked Canada to help guide the uranium exporters to agreement. "[S]ince their own position was so unsettled," a message from the Washington Embassy read: "the USA authorities could hardly take the initiative in convening even a working level meeting. The State Department officials wondered if Canada could not take the lead."[31]

Ottawa immediately accepted the challenge. Government officials drew up an international safeguard program, circulated it to the four other major uranium exporting nations — the United States, the United Kingdom, South Africa, and Australia — and produced a signed agreement within four months.[32] This was done

Programmes of Fourth Countries)," 23 March 1957, in *Foreign Relations of the United States, 1955-1957* 28 (doc. 292): 766.

26 NA, RG 25, Acc. 86-87/414, Box 220, #14002-2-6-40 pt. 5, Uranium Producers' Committee (Canadian Metal Mining Association), "Markets for Canadian Uranium," January 1959.

27 DCC, P&C vol. 28, XII/A/739, "Uranium-Export Policy-Secret [1957]," Cabinet Document 177/57, "Export of Uranium from Canada," 15 August 1957.

28 NA, RG 25, Acc 86-87/414, Box 220, #14002-2-6-40 pt. 4, see the series of notes from the Embassy in Washington to Ottawa.

29 NA, MG32 B9, vol. 21, Cabinet Document 315/57, 3 December 1957; ibid., RG 25, Acc. 86-87/414, Box 220, #14002-2-6-40 pt. 2, Telegram 1806, 21 August 1957, Washington Embassy to Ottawa.

30 Ibid., pt. 5, Robert Winters to R.B. Bryce, 20 November 1958.

31 Ibid., pt. 4, Telegram 2557, 21 October 1958, Washington to Ottawa.

32 Ibid., pt. 6 and pt. 7, Minutes of Five Power Meetings in London, 26-27 February 1959.

secretly, but other uranium exporters were soon quietly informed,[33] and the agreement became the basis for a comprehensive deal under the aegis of the International Atomic Energy Agency in early 1961. Asking Canada to "take the lead" in carving out such a critical agreement was an example of the deep American trust in the beliefs and abilities of Canadians, confirming that Canada-US relations during this period were positive and productive, at least on one issue.

THE KENNEDY ADMINISTRATION

In January 1961, John F. Kennedy took Eisenhower's place in the White House. He was the opposite of Eisenhower in many ways. Young and brash, he preferred to talk while Eisenhower had tended to listen. This, of course, was part of Kennedy's widespread popular appeal. He consciously projected the image of an active, vigorous President, full of idealism and determination. He campaigned on the theme of change, and promised to get the country moving again. At his inauguration, he triumphantly declared that "the torch has been passed to a new generation of Americans."

The Kennedy administration increased the power of the White House and further separated its activities from party politics, the Cabinet and regular executive departments, and Congress.[34] This was evident in its conduct of foreign relations, which was at times profoundly different from the Eisenhower administration.[35] Structurally, Kennedy's utilization of an extensive team of "the best and the brightest" meant more advisers to the President, and the creation of new jobs with new titles. Officials in Ottawa noticed the change. Under Eisenhower they had known to communicate with Dulles or Christian Herter, but Kennedy relied less exclusively on Dean Rusk, his Secretary of State, and frequently turned to people like Walt Rostow or McGeorge Bundy, who occupied new presidential advisory positions.

The awkward "sofa memo" affair — also referred to as the "S.O.B." memo, from an incorrect story that the writer had scrawled this insult on it, referring to Diefenbaker — can be attributed to this proliferation of advisers, some of whom were not trained in diplomacy (Bundy was a dean at Harvard, Rostow a professor of economics). The memo was left behind after a meeting in Diefenbaker's office in May 1961, and outlined issues that the President should "push" with the Prime Minister. Kennedy's decision to formalize the meetings and travel with an entourage of advisers increased the chances of unfortunate accidents like this occurring.[36]

More importantly, the tone of the infamous memo was an example of the change in style that the Kennedy administration would adopt in dealing with Canada and the rest of the world. Where the Eisenhower group had been congenial, respectful,

---

33   For example, Belgium; see ibid., pt. 7, Telegram 1531, 14 May 1959, London to Ottawa.

34   Sidney M. Milkis and Michael Nelson, *The American Presidency: Origins and Development, 1776-1990* (Washington, DC: Congressional Quarterly Press, 1990), 295-302.

35   John Herd Thompson and Stephen J. Randall, *Canada and the United States: Ambivalent Allies* (Athens, GA: University of Georgia Press, 1994), 214-19; now the best survey of Canadian-American relations, this book makes a distinction between Diefenbaker's pre-Kennedy and Kennedy years.

36   Nash, *Kennedy and Diefenbaker*, 121-22; Michael R. Beschloss, *The Crisis Years: Kennedy and Khrushchev, 1960-1963* (New York: Harper Collins, 1991), 163; the memo itself does not have "S.O.B." or any other markings on it, except for the initials W.W.R. (Walt W. Rostow, the author) in pen; see DCC, P&C vol. 88, XII/D/204, "US and Kennedy."

Close-up of John F. Kennedy and John Diefenbaker chatting, Ottawa, 16 May 1961 (courtesy the Diefenbaker Centre, MG01/XVII/JGD 1399).

and sensitive to Canadian concerns, the Kennedy group was aggressive, and sometimes arrogant. Dean Rusk was a professional diplomat and veteran of the State Department, but he brought an attitude to the position of Secretary of State which was different than either that of Dulles or Herter. Thirty years later, in his memoirs, he was still complaining that the European allies of the United States did a lot of "carping," that they had "tended to sit like a pouting dowager," and that they had become "comfortable and fat" by the 1960s.[37]

Other aspects of Kennedy's conduct signalled a change during his visit to Canada in May 1961. The Department of External Affairs had long been sceptical about the advantages of Canada joining the Organization of American States (OAS). Diefenbaker shared this scepticism, and made his feelings clear to Kennedy in their initial private meetings. Later, however, the President tried to circumvent Diefenbaker with a direct appeal to the Canadian people during his speech to Parliament.[38] Many in Ottawa, as well as a few American advisers, were unimpressed by Kennedy's tactics.

The Eisenhower administration had not operated this way in foreign relations with its allies. When Clarence Randall, Eisenhower's chairman of the Council on Foreign Economic Policy, proposed opening discussions on "US-Canadian economic integration," Dulles quickly shut him down. Although both nations believed in liberal trade policies, the Secretary explained, "there might be a Canadian concern that the

37   Dean Rusk, *As I Saw It: A Secretary of State's Memoirs* (London: I.B. Tauris, 1991), 234.

38   Nash, *Kennedy and Diefenbaker*, 114-16.

economic integration of both countries would in effect subject Canada to preponderant United States economic influence." If any initiative on the matter were to come, Dulles thought it was better to wait until the Canadians proposed it.[39]

There is no record that Kennedy regretted his comments to Parliament regarding Canadian membership in the OAS, and no reason to suppose that he even thought twice about them. His administration had little compunction about interfering in the affairs of other nations. The most famous examples include active support for an attempt to overthrow the government of Cuba, and silent support for the coup in Vietnam that toppled Ngo Dinh Diem. Nothing as violent or dramatic happened regarding Canada, of course. But consider the Kennedy administration's reaction to Diefenbaker's speech in the House of Commons on 25 January 1963 on defence issues and, more particularly, the utilization of nuclear weapons. Diefenbaker, ostensibly trying to clarify his government's position, ended up clarifying nothing — which may have been his intention all along.[40] The American embassy in Ottawa took it upon itself to clarify Diefenbaker's clarifications. US Ambassador W.W. Butterworth sent out his own press release on 30 January 1963, outlining point by point the failings of Canadian defence policy: "The Canadian government has not yet proposed any arrangement sufficiently practical to contribute effectively to North American defence."[41] Butterworth's extraordinary action, and the wording of the statement, had been approved by the White House and the State Department, including Acting Secretary of State George Ball, and National Security Adviser McGeorge Bundy.[42] The *New York Times* called it "hamhanded, ill-conceived and undiplomatic."[43] It was a direct and blatant interference in Canada's affairs, which the Kennedy people privately acknowledged and accepted.

THE CUBAN MISSILE CRISIS

Kennedy's tendency to focus only on American concerns and categorize allies perfunctorily, or simply assume they would be supportive, was illustrated by his handling of the Cuban Missile Crisis in 1962. The principal details of the crisis are well known. The President made a dramatic television speech on 22 October 1962, announcing a naval quarantine around Cuba, and ordering Soviet ships to refrain from delivering nuclear missiles to the island. They did. On 27 October, Washington demanded that Moscow dismantle and remove all existing missiles in Cuba within forty-eight hours. They did. Canadian historians have tended to vilify Diefenbaker for his actions during the crisis, portraying him as the weak link in an otherwise united front behind the Americans. The Prime Minister refused to put Canadian forces on military alert without a Cabinet vote, then sat through several days of Cabinet indecision before finally agreeing to mobilize. On the advice of senior officials at External Affairs, Diefenbaker's speech in the House of Commons on the evening of

---

39   DDEL, Council on Foreign Economic Policy, Office of Chairman, Randall Series, Subject Subseries, "Canada [5]," John Foster Dulles to Clarence B. Randall, 25 July 1957.

40   "One of the most baffling and controversial speeches to be found in the Parliamentary record," wrote Peyton V. Lyon, *Canada in World Affairs, 1961-1963* (Toronto: Oxford University Press, 1968), 146-53; Basil Robinson called it "an indigestible stew," *Diefenbaker's World*, 306.

41   Lyon, *Canada in World Affairs*, 157-58; Nash, *Kennedy and Diefenbaker*, 243-44.

42   Nash, *Kennedy and Diefenbaker*, 238-46.

43   Granatstein and Hillmer, *For Better or For Worse*, 209.

22 October suggested that a United Nations committee be sent to investigate the situation in Cuba.[44] "The Canadian military had been mortified at their inability to act in support of their allies," wrote J.L. Granatstein and Norman Hillmer. "The United States' other allies — Britain, France, and West Germany," asserts Robert Bothwell, "received word of Kennedy's intentions calmly and promised support."[45]

When examined from a broader perspective, however, Diefenbaker's response during the Cuban Missile Crisis was not extraordinary. He was not the only one offended by the American style of unilateral diplomacy. The White House had not consulted Canada — Diefenbaker was officially informed of the American actions two hours before Kennedy's televised quarantine speech on 22 October — but simply demanded that the nation put its military forces on alert. Kennedy's failure to communicate with the other NATO partners was also noted abroad. The President of France, Charles de Gaulle, complained about "being informed, but not consulted" when an envoy from the White House arrived to brief him.[46] And Britain's Harold Macmillan rejected the entreaties of NATO supreme commander General Lauris Norstad to place British forces on a higher state of readiness. As Alistair Horne, the British Prime Minister's biographer wrote, "Macmillan, with his own personal memories, pointed out that mobilization sometimes led to war."[47]

Like Diefenbaker, Macmillan was concerned about an aggressive showdown with the Soviets. Both Prime Ministers tried to delay the confrontation, and urged the President to augment his efforts to assess public opinion. Macmillan was critical of Kennedy, and urged caution at key moments. The difference was that he was able to make suggestions and offer criticism privately while maintaining public support for the United States, because of Kennedy's daily telephone calls to him. Diefenbaker's only recourse was the public forum.

After the Cuban showdown, Macmillan noted in his diary that the French "were anyway contemptuous, the Germans *very* frightened, though pretending to want firmness; the Italians windy; the Scandinavians rather sour."[48] Indeed, there were widespread concerns about the American actions, and the Western alliance began to experience serious difficulties soon after the crisis. Western Europe openly balked when Kennedy proposed a "grand design" to integrate US-European economic and political policies; they quickly realized that Washington wanted the partners to pay more of the defence costs, but had no intention of allowing them to shape nuclear decisions.[49] Charles de Gaulle shifted from being perturbed during the Cuban Crisis to a state of obstinacy. When the United States offered Polaris submarines to Britain after declining requests from France, he vetoed British membership in the Common Market, calling the United Kingdom an American "Trojan horse," and signed a Franco-German Treaty of Friendship the following week. From then on, Western

---

44   J.L. Granatstein, *Yankee Go Home? Canadians and Anti-Americanism* (Toronto: Harper Collins, 1996), 131.

45   Granatstein and Hillmer, *For Better or For Worse*, 205; Robert Bothwell, *Canada and the United States: The Politics of Partnership* (New York: Twayne Publishers, 1992), 83.

46   Beschloss, *The Crisis Years*, 477-78.

47   Alistair Horne, *Harold Macmillan*, vol. 2 (New York: Viking, 1989), 365-66.

48   Ibid., 380 (emphasis in original).

49   Frank Costigliola, "The Failed Design: Kennedy, de Gaulle, and the Struggle for Europe," *Diplomatic History* 8, no. 3 (Summer 1984): 227-52.

John Diefenbaker, John Kennedy, and Harold Macmillan at Nassau in the Bahamas, 21 December 1962 (courtesy the Diefenbaker Centre, MG01/XVII/JGD 1454).

Europe, dominated by the Franco-German alliance, prospered and grew distinctly apart from the Anglo-American community.[50] And France developed its own nuclear arsenal.

With the collapse of the Soviet Union and the end of the Cold War, more information about life inside the Communist sphere is becoming available. It seems that even those nations in the Communist bloc normally considered the "satellite" states were no more pleased with Moscow during the Cuban Missile Crisis than the Western allies had been with Washington. Khrushchev's reckless unilateral actions opened fissures within the Warsaw Pact. The Soviets had not informed their East European satellites of Operation Anadyr (code name for the installation of the Soviet missiles in Cuba), and the crisis was long over before Moscow explained its motives for deployment and withdrawal. Documents which reveal expressions of dissatisfaction from the governments of Poland, East Germany, and Hungary are now available.[51] Romania was so upset by the whole affair that, in a stunning breach of the central obligation of Warsaw Pact membership, its Foreign Minister travelled to the United States and secretly informed Washington officials that his government wanted to dissociate itself from Khrushchev's actions. (The other NATO governments were not informed of the Romanian Foreign Minister's mission; it was only publicly

---

50   Martin Walker, *The Cold War: A History* (New York: Henry Holt, 1993), 181.

51   Janos Radvanyi, *Hungary and the Superpowers: The 1956 Revolution and Realpolitik* (Stanford: Hoover Institution Press, 1972), 137; the testimony of this defector can now be supported with documents; for example, see Mark Kramer, "The 'Lessons' of the Cuban Missile Crisis for Warsaw Pact Nuclear Operations," *Cold War International History Bulletin* 5 (Spring 1995): 59.

revealed in January 1993.[52]) Further east, the People's Republic of China criticized Khrushchev's policy as moving "from adventurism to capitulationism."[53]

Fidel Castro was outraged, and felt betrayed. He had gladly accepted the missiles, and the gift of Soviet bombers, for his own air force. Once the United States had issued its challenge, Cubans worked alongside the Soviet troops stationed there to prepare for an American invasion. The Havana government learned of the Soviet decision to withdraw the missiles the same way the United States did — through Khrushchev's Radio Moscow announcement on the morning of 28 October.[54]

Cold War historians Vladislav Zubok and Constantine Pleshakov have said that the Cubans ended up as "impotent onlookers in the superpowers' deadly waltz."[55] Afterward, Khrushchev sent his closest associate, Anastas Mikoyan, to smooth the ruffled Cuban feathers, and Mikoyan endured a storm of questions and criticisms. Castro's associate, Ernesto "Che" Guevara, complained bitterly that the Soviet actions had dismayed many Latin American Communists and undercut some promising possibilities of "seizing power in a number of Latin American countries."[56] Castro thought the Soviets had given up too much by agreeing to take back the planes they had given the Cubans, and was upset that the Americans were still flying over Cuban air space. He was also angered that the Soviet negotiating tactic had been to demand American withdrawal from bases in Turkey, instead of from the Guantanamo base in Cuba.[57] In the middle of a long-winded explanation by Mikoyan, an irritated Castro interrupted with: "Why explain the rationale? Just say bluntly what the Soviet government wants."[58]

It is not difficult to see that both major alliance systems were undermined by the actions of the United States and the Soviet Union. The making and handling of the crisis tarnished Khrushchev's reputation among well-informed members of the Soviet élite, and certainly among his allies. He held on as leader for another two years, but movement against him in the Politburo quickened after the Cuban Missile Crisis.[59] For his part, Kennedy left the Western alliance weaker than he had found it. France developed an independent nuclear arsenal — which the United States had always opposed — and eventually pulled out of NATO in 1966. After Cuba, there was a general pattern of apprehensive reactions to American foreign policies by its allies. Diefenbaker was not the only one to question the tactics and wisdom of the superpowers.

---

52   Raymond L. Garthoff, "When and Why Romania Distanced Itself From the Warsaw Pact," *Cold War International History Project Bulletin* 5 (Spring 1995): 111.

53   Walker, *The Cold War: A History*, 179.

54   Philip Brenner and James G. Blight, "The Crisis and Cuban-Soviet Relations: Fidel Castro's Secret 1968 Speech," *Cold War International History Bulletin* 5 (Spring 1995): 81.

55   Vladislav Zubok and Constantine Pleshakov, *Inside the Kremlin's Cold War: From Stalin to Khrushchev* (Cambridge, MA: Harvard University Press, 1996), 268.

56   "Memorandum of Conversation: A.I. Mikoyan with Oswaldo Dorticos, Ernesto Guevara, and Carlos Rafael Rodriguez," 5 November 1962, in *Cold War International History Project Bulletin* 5 (Spring 1995): 108.

57   "Memorandum of Conversation: A.I. Mikoyan with Fidel Castro...," in *Cold War International History Project Bulletin* 5 (Spring 1995): 98-99; see also General Anatoli I. Gribkov and General William Y. Smith, *Operation Anadyr: US and Soviet Generals Recount the Cuban Missile Crisis* (Chicago: Edition Q, Inc. , 1994), 189-99.

58   Zubok and Pleshakov, *Inside the Kremlin's Cold War*, 269.

59   Ibid., 268; Walker, *The Cold War: A History*, 178-89.

CONCLUSION

There has been a tendency to portray John Diefenbaker as incorrigibly anti-American, and a thorn in the side of Canada's southern neighbour. This perspective neglects Diefenbaker's role as a Cold War ally, and the good relations with the United States that characterized most of his time in office. For almost two-thirds of his time as Prime Minister, Diefenbaker's relationship with the United States was personified in his warm and cordial relationship with Dwight D. Eisenhower.

Diefenbaker was a strong nationalist, and fought to protect Canadian interests. He was periodically suspicious of American motives, and he watched the powerful neighbour closely; but his foreign policies were usually in accord with American diplomatic objectives. His decisions helped promote a healthy international economy while still containing communism. He made anti-Communist speeches, supported American initiatives in international forums like the United Nations and, despite the protests of domestic business interests, continued to place restrictions on the sale of strategic materials such as uranium and nickel. Bilaterally, Canada signed a Defence Production Sharing Agreement, established NORAD, and continued to add to the Distant Early Warning (DEW) defence system. The two governments held regular joint Cabinet meetings and leadership summits in each other's countries, and treated each other preferentially in trade matters.

Diefenbaker's time has been described as "the crisis years," a time of "fear and loathing" in Canada-US relations. A closer examination reveals that severe difficulties between the two nations only began to emerge after John F. Kennedy came to the presidency. The United States was undeniably the leader of the free world, and it was engaged in a potentially fatal struggle with the Communist bloc. Kennedy's conception of how to lead the democratic alliance was, ironically, to act like an autocrat. Important decisions were made in Washington, and he became irritated if the allies did not fully support him. He chose Dean Rusk as Secretary of State, an expert in Asian affairs who quickly developed a low opinion of the European allies. Kennedy surrounded himself with advisers who were answerable not to Congress but to him. Many were academic experts from the eastern establishment, familiar with economic theories and models of political development, but not trained in diplomacy.

Diefenbaker's legacy in Canadian-US relations, and indeed his general foreign policy, should not be drawn solely from his final six months in office, when relations with the Kennedy administration were so unstable. Rather, we should remember his relationship with Eisenhower, his strong but reasonable defence of Canadian interests, and his steady, but not foolish, performance as a Cold War warrior.

THE CHINA SYNDROME: EXTERNAL ECONOMIC IRRITANTS IN THE CANADA-US RELATIONSHIP

Ann Flanagan

John Diefenbaker perhaps lacked the imagination to undertake a fundamental reappraisal of Canadian diplomacy in the changing world of the late 1950s. He remained a staunch Cold War warrior, giving expression to his well-known Soviet-focussed anti-communism in his famous speech to the United Nations General Assembly in 1960. But his anti-communism had certain limits, for during his period in office, Canada joined other Western allies in challenging certain aspects of American strategic policy, even where the United States had declared an essential security interest.

Export controls on Communist China were a clear example. In Washington's view, the external threat China posed to the West was expanding, as Mao Tse-tung moved his régime away from the Soviet Union and the Chinese prepared to detonate their own atomic device. Yet Diefenbaker's government was reluctant to adopt American definitions of security against the Chinese. Diefenbaker's Cold War was political and rhetorical, not economic. His government broadened the spectrum of goods sold to China, and deepened the Canada-China trade relationship, particularly through lucrative grain sales.

Trade with China was hardly the focal point of Diefenbaker's international diplomacy, but its significance in postwar Canadian foreign policy should not be minimized. If the issue of trade with China is seen as an aspect of Canada-US relations, some important themes of the Diefenbaker period can be neatly tied together: the relationship between the Diefenbaker government and successive American administrations, the tightening web of Canada-US bilateral relations, and growing concern about US control of the Canadian economy.

Canada, it turned out, had less freedom to manoeuvre on China trade than its leaders had thought it might, owing to its US-dominated economic structure. High-level personal diplomacy between Ottawa and Washington could only go part way toward resolving the issue. Congress and individual export firms could not always be brought along on the matter. In this atmosphere, China moved away from the margins of Canadian foreign policy and relocated itself at the centre of the Canada-US relationship.

DIEFENBAKER AND NON-STRATEGIC TRADE WITH CHINA

The Korean War had solidified the American image of China as a dangerous adversary. In the early 1950s, Western allies adopted their own China trade controls, inspired by the war and by US prodding. The first multilateral trade controls on China emerged at the United Nations. More modest controls were adopted in 1952 by the China Committee (CHINCOM), a low-profile, consultative Western export-control organization. CHINCOM was initially effective in influencing its member states; for example, in 1953, Canada, a CHINCOM member, exported no goods to China at all.[1]

However, the China trade controls soon began to cause problems in allied relations.[2] A controversial "China Differential" opened in 1954 when multilateral trade reforms permitted the export to the Soviet Union and Eastern Europe of non-strategic items which could not be exported to China, suggesting that China was now the more dangerous enemy. The European allies argued against the China Differential, maintaining that Soviet bloc countries could easily trans-ship goods to Peking. But the United States administration feared public and congressional hostility toward China, and stalled further multilateral attempts to cut back on non-strategic trade restrictions on China.

By May 1957, Britain had decided unilaterally to cut the China restrictions back to the Soviet level. Most Western allies followed suit. By July, only the United States, Turkey, and Canada were maintaining the Differential. Extensive publicity on the issue expanded Western interest in China trade, and increased commercial pressures for the relaxation of controls. Attitudes in the United States Congress, however, were clear: Republican senators such as William Knowland and Charles Potter were horrified at the possibility of trade with China. Such trade would augment China's war potential; it would bring "strong, unflagging pressure" for diplomatic recognition, and it would ease the régime's economic difficulties. Prewar trade with the Nazis and the Japanese, they argued, demonstrated that one could not safely conduct business with tyranny. Not surprisingly, the strict US embargo remained in place, despite President Dwight Eisenhower's own doubts about the efficacy of blunt economic weapons.

This is how matters stood as John Diefenbaker took office. One of the first policy questions for the new government was what position to take on trade with China: should Canada follow the British lead in liberalizing trade, or the American lead in maintaining a strict embargo? In July 1957 Davie Fulton, Acting External Affairs Minister, asked his department to consider the issue. External Affairs brought in the Department of Trade and Commerce, whose officials were more familiar with the situation. Precise economic intelligence about China was lacking, and the political considerations governing Chinese trade were difficult to assess. The joint evaluation of the two departments, however, was that the Chinese market did not appear promising. Even diplomatic recognition of China would only lay the groundwork for a slow increase in trade.[3] This might have been considered pessimism or merely

---

1   1953 was the first year in which Canadian trade statistics differentiate between Communist China and Nationalist China, thus creating a handy benchmark year.

2   US export control policy, and the ensuing controversy with the allies, is documented in *Foreign Relations of the United States*, 1955-57, vol. 10, *Economic Defence Policy*, 205-495. A Canadian summary is in National Archives of Canada (NA), RG 25, vol. 7606, file 11280-1-40, part 1.1, Memorandum for the Minister, "Review of Strategic Controls," 14 January 1958.

3   NA, RG 25, vol. 7606, file 11280-1-40 part 1.1, Acting Undersecretary of State for External Affairs to Deputy Minister, Trade and Commerce, 1 August 1957.

realism; the point is that American fears that the allies were salivating over potential Chinese markets did not hold in the Canadian case.

Nevertheless, Ottawa felt that the China Differential had little strategic value, and that its continued enforcement would amount to "economic warfare."[4] US sensitivity was insufficient justification to continue to maintain it. Thereafter, although there was no formal announcement, Trade and Commerce began to broaden the categories of non-strategic goods which exporters could send to China. It was originally so quiet a policy that Liberal Opposition Leader Lester Pearson was puzzled, the following summer, as to whether the China Differential still existed.[5] As it turned out, the abandonment of the Differential had some immediate effect — for instance, some immediate expansion

John Diefenbaker (right) standing in wheat field during the 1958 election (courtesy the Diefenbaker Centre, MG01/ XVII/JGD 481a).

occurred in metal exports — but having a greater impact on Canada-China trade in the coming years would be the internal Chinese grain production shortfalls which would result in an exponential increase in Canadian grain exports, particularly wheat and barley.

The Canadian public responded very positively to the large-scale grain deals with China announced in 1960. The sales were a triumph for Diefenbaker's government, which had been preoccupied both with the western Canadian farmers' lot and with the vast surpluses of prairie grain stored at great expense. A November 1962 poll indicated that more than 80 percent of Canadians supported the sale, while non-strategic trade with China enjoyed the support of some three-quarters of the Canadian population in the immediate wake of the first grain deal.[6]

Diefenbaker did receive numerous letters criticizing him for providing China an escape from its economic and agricultural difficulties, but equally, many saw the grain sales as a positive development, opening a door to China. Agriculture Minister Alvin Hamilton's desire to increase two-way trade provided another possible opportunity for East-West engagement.[7] Thus, despite Diefenbaker's anti-Communist attitudes, his government was willing to pursue limited economic engagement with China and

4   Ibid.

5   Canada, House of Commons, *Debates*, 18 July 1958, 2371; ibid, 2407-08.

6   See Paul Evans and Daphne Gottlieb Taras, "Canadian Public Opinion on Relations with China: An Analysis of the Existing Survey Research," Working Paper #33, University of Toronto-York University Joint Centre on Modern East Asia, March 1985, 11.

7   See Patrick Kyba, "Alvin Hamilton and Sino-Canadian Relations," in Paul Evans and B. Michael Frolic (eds.), *Reluctant Adversaries:Canada and the People's Republic of China* (Toronto: University of Toronto Press, 1991), 168-86.

reap the benefits of non-strategic trade. This would be one of the Diefenbaker government's legacies in foreign policy.

While Canadians' reaction to the grain sales were positive, the political risks of angering the United States were always a consideration. China trade was not only about China; it was about Canada-US relations. Following a January 1961 suggestion by External Affairs, Washington was thus kept informed of impending China grain sales. Yet the new US President, John F. Kennedy, seemed unconcerned about the matter in his early meetings with Diefenbaker.[8] Kennedy, in fact, seemed attracted to the idea of American grain sales to the Chinese in March 1961.

There would be some problems with the Americans. Negotiations between Ottawa and Washington ensued when US officials attempted to crack down on possible Chinese imports arriving by way of, or on the way to, Canada. Diefenbaker intervened personally in the first case: "Communist shrimp" and soya sauce had been barred from traversing western US roads, the trucking route to central Canadian markets. In a second case, a Windsor exporter found that its Chinese-style frozen entrées were shut out of US markets. American national security, it was argued, might be compromised if Chinese products found their way into the country. Such cases received wide publicity in both Canada and the United States. Yet ad hoc solutions to these problems were almost invariably reached. Canada had an ally in the US State Department, which overrode Treasury reservations for the purpose of preserving friendly Canada-US relations. Nuisance cases did exist, but on the whole Washington did not react adversely to non-strategic Canadian trade.[9]

DIEFENBAKER AND EXTRATERRITORIALITY

A greyer area emerged where Canadian subsidiaries of US corporations were concerned. Early in the Korean War, the US had applied its strict Foreign Assets Control (FAC) regulations — better known as the Trading with the Enemy Act — to China. These regulations prohibited trade with China, and applied equally to subsidiaries of American firms operating in other countries.[10] As early as 1954, Trade and Commerce recognized that such restrictions might lead to bilateral problems, but Canada's Commercial Counsellor in Washington decided to let the matter rest. He felt that the chances of a major dispute with the United States were "remote." Indeed, the FAC regulations were moot through most of the 1950s, as the CHINCOM allies had adopted controls on China trade that closely paralleled those of the United States. But when Canada decided to abolish the China Differential in 1957, the level of strategic controls came to differ. In December 1957 the issue that had been dormant for so long came to life.

Late that year, Ford of Canada received an inquiry about motor vehicles from the East-West Export Import Company on behalf of Communist China. Normally, a permit for this type of sale could be issued readily under Canadian export regulations, but Ford of Canada's assigned sales territory did not include China. It thus consulted

---

8   Kyba, "Alvin Hamilton and Sino-Canadian Relations," 173.

9   A number of such cases are described in NA, RG 25, vol. 7606, parts 1.1 and 1.2, beginning in early 1959. The Oriental Commerce foodstuffs story can be found in RG 19, vol. 4223, file 8780/U58 part 1, beginning September 1959.

10   A good summary of US Foreign Assets Control history and its effect on allied relationships can be found in FRUS 1958-60, vol. 4, 721-23.

with its parent company. Here complications arose, for Ford Motors was American, and subject to American laws which forbade trade with China. The American parent decided that its subsidiary should not pursue the matter. Ford of Canada subsequently confirmed that the inquiry had been just that — there had never been a solid offer — and Canadian files later revealed that the principals in the export-import company were known members of Communist front organizations, and therefore suspect in motive.[11] But these distinctions meant little when the matter became public.

Beginning in December 1957, the Ford case stirred up controversy in Parliament and the press. The magnitude of the proposed sale lent the issue a significance it might not otherwise have had, and it was a worry for a minority government concerned about public opinion, unemployment and economic stagnation. Trade and Commerce officials were aware of interventions by US parent companies,[12] but the high profile of the Ford case presented it as a new issue in bilateral relations. To the extent that US export control law prevailed over Canada, the issue was one of extraterritoriality, and there were troublesome implications not only for Canadian sovereignty but for the bilateral relationship with the United States.

Canada was not alone in its concerns about US extraterritoriality. Britain and Japan were also being hurt by FAC regulations. Their trade policies, too, differed from the policy of the United States, and exports were vital to their economic health. But the problem was developing on a different scale in Canada. Canadian representatives abroad were instructed to look into the broader international subsidiary effect. The Canadian High Commission in London found only two cases in which British sales had been blocked; ironically, one of those cases involved Ford's British affiliate.[13] Indeed, Canada's situation was unique because of its branch-plant economy. Judging from inquiries received by Trade and Commerce, China was interested in many of the manufactured and processed products of these branch plants.

Extraterritoriality arose where foreign relations met domestic economic structure. US direct investment in Canada had grown during the postwar years. Its disadvantages, including the loss of economic control by Canadians, were becoming apparent. As economic growth slowed, public questioning about the benefits of this form of economic structure sharpened. Did US investment conduct itself in the economic interests of Canada? Did it conduct itself as Canadian investment would? For Diefenbaker, the investment/sovereignty issue was irresistible. In his 1957 and 1958 election campaigns he delighted in nationalistic appeals, eliciting and propelling Canadian nationalism along with a darker anti-Americanism. The Americans, he protested, were meddling in Canadian affairs.

The forces of nationalism that were fed by Diefenbaker's personal focus on the subsidiary issue were arrayed against the strident anti-communism of the Americans. Was the bilateral relationship destined to be unhinged by peripheral economic irritants?

---

11   NA, Pearson Papers, MG 26, N3, vol. 240, file 722/C539-1, James A. Roberts (Dep. Minister, Trade and Commerce) to Michael J. McCabe (Exec. Asst. to Minister of Trade and Commerce), 25 June 1963.

12   NA, RG 25, vol. 7606, file 11280-1-40, part 1.1, C.J. Small to R.E. Collins, "Canadian Cars for Communist China," 24 January 1958; ibid., Denis Harvey to USSEA, 2 April 1958.

13   Ibid., London to External Ottawa, no. 681, 8 April 1958.

SOLUTIONS

The problem was easily recognized, but difficult to deal with. Trade and Commerce guidelines issued in late June 1957 stressed that no initiative should be taken in warning subsidiaries about FAC regulations; if a subsidiary seemed concerned, it might be counselled about different ways of avoiding US shipping and US dollar payment.[14] But External Affairs felt that these guidelines did not "come to grips with the problem." Subsidiaries could not be expected to export against the directives of their head offices, and any action to "protect" them might adversely affect foreign investment in Canada. It appeared to be "merely one more example of USA action with which we cannot agree and from which we suffer economically, but against which our only recourse is to seek to persuade the USA to change its ways."[15]

But American susceptibility to persuasion was doubtful. United States Treasury officials felt that the regulations were reasonable; they ensured equitable treatment for American firms wherever they operated.[16] In both Washington and Ottawa, the Ford case dragged on through the first half of 1958. State and Treasury briefly took the initiative to examine types of exemptions where the bulk of industry was under American control.[17] But their interest seemed to have slackened by mid-June. On 2 July, the Canadian Cabinet reviewed the export control situation, and was of the view that Congress seemed unlikely to legislate change. It decided that Diefenbaker himself should press the matter at his impending meeting with Eisenhower.

Fortunately, the Eisenhower administration was prepared to work around the existing legislation in order to satisfy Canadian concerns. This willingness may seem somewhat surprising. After all, the Cold War was raging, the United States had labelled China as possibly a more dangerous enemy even than the Soviets, and passionately demanded allied political support on the issue. However, there were several reasons why US Secretary of State John Foster Dulles recommended an accommodation with Canada on subsidiaries.

First, some officials in the United States administration philosophically disliked the notion of challenging Canadian sovereignty. Diefenbaker's nationalist rhetoric occasionally caused annoyance in Washington, but at the highest levels of the Eisenhower administration, Diefenbaker's views about Canadianizing subsidiaries found some sympathy. Dulles indicated as much when Canadian officials pursued the issue at a ministerial meeting in the fall of 1957.[18] Meanwhile, at a meeting of the National Security Council, Eisenhower reflected on his own experiences as a Coca-Cola stockholder; local subsidiaries were more successful, he felt, when they exercised greater control over their own operations. Intra-firm relations may have been an irritant in Canada-US transborder relations, but on the whole, they were not an issue in official relations. Extraterritoriality had awakened a similarly sympathetic response in Eisenhower and Dulles.

---

14   Ibid., Denis Harvey, "Trade with China" (Branch Memorandum, Commodities Branch, T&C), 25 June 1957.

15   Ibid., Economic Division to USSEA/Far Eastern Division, "Exports to Communist China," 27 February 1958.

16   Ibid., Washington D.C. to External Ottawa, no. 785, 2 April 1958.

17   NA, RG 19, vol. 4223, file 8780/U58-8, part 1, Denis Harvey to S.S. Reisman, 13 May 1958.

18   NA, RG 25, vol. 7606, file 11280-1-40, part 1.1, London to External Ottawa, no. 681, 8 April 1958.

A second reason to find a solution for the extraterritoriality issue was that, for the Americans, it really was not very important. Dulles doubted that an exemption for subsidiaries would make much difference in the extent of trade. He later disparaged potential Chinese sales as "phantom orders," intended only to sow discord between allies.[19] The Canadians may even have agreed with this assessment. According to the American account of their meeting with Dulles in July 1958, Canadian ministers Sidney Smith and Gordon Churchill felt that many of the Chinese orders had not been *bona fide*,[20] but were merely intended to stir up political trouble between the United States and its allies. No doubt the joint evaluation of China trade undertaken by External Affairs and Trade and Commerce the previous summer enhanced the ministers' scepticism.

Diplomatic considerations also suggested that some accommodation was desirable. Dulles wrote to Eisenhower that his forthcoming Ottawa visit was intended to improve relations with the Diefenbaker government, and the subsidiary issue seemed a good place to begin. "Vocal" and "widespread" criticism of American policies impeded close working relations with the Canadians, and the Canadian election campaign and the recession had added to a growing sense of Canadian nationalism. Some Canadian ministers, indeed, had tried to make the United States the "whipping boy for many of Canada's ills."[21] Extraterritoriality was a classic example of American offences against Canadian sovereignty. Hence, the political significance of making a timely concession to a friendly country might well outweigh any strategic considerations. Dulles recommended that it "might be deemed in the national interest to relax policy" and to facilitate trade by subsidiaries.

Canada's political cooperation seemed as important to Dulles as Canada's economic cooperation. In the briefing memo recommending the exemption, he added: "We assume in this connection the Canadian government will not recognize Communist China, and will continue to support the moratorium formula in the United Nations."[22] Indeed, Eisenhower and Diefenbaker focussed on the political aspects of China in their two official meetings in Ottawa in July 1958. Diefenbaker hedged a little. At their first meeting, Eisenhower vehemently urged no change in Canadian policy on recognition, warning that if Canada recognized China, it would "wreck" the United States and possibly the UN.[23] Diefenbaker responded that there would be no change. But at a second meeting two days later, Diefenbaker and Smith suggested that "very considerable" political pressures in Canada might lead to a reassessment of the recognition policy. Eisenhower became agitated; after all, Diefenbaker had recently won a whopping parliamentary majority.[24] Evidently, Canadian sensibilities on China were less important than the political pressures with which Eisenhower was confronted back home. But responding to a little flattery and showing a little

19   Memorandum of Discussion at the 393rd meeting of the National Security Council, 15 January 1959, reprinted in FRUS 1958-60, vol. 4, 755.

20   Memorandum of Conversation, 9 July 1958, reprinted in FRUS 1958-1960, vol. 7, part 1, 707.

21   Memo from Secretary of State Dulles to President Eisenhower, 3 July 1958, reprinted in FRUS 1958-60, vol. 7, part 1, 687.

22   "Specific topics for discussion by the President at Ottawa," memo from Dulles to Eisenhower, 3 July 1958, reprinted in FRUS 1958-60, vol. 7, part 1, 690.

23   Memorandum of Conversation, President's Visit to Canada, 8 July 1958, reprinted in FRUS 1958-60, vol. 7, part 1, 696.

24   Memorandum of Conversation, 10 July 1958, reprinted in FRUS 1958-60, vol. 7, part 1, 710-11.

forbearance in the face of the determination of the Americans, Diefenbaker eventually reassured Eisenhower that there would be no change in Canadian policy.

However, for Diefenbaker, the politics of China trade involved crucial sovereignty issues, and he did not hesitate to bring up the extraterritoriality issue with the Americans. American accounts of the conversation suggest, unflatteringly, that Diefenbaker had not grasped the complexity of the export control issue.[25] The substantive Ford matter was left to Smith's meeting with Dulles the following day. There, Dulles asked the Canadians not to press the matter publicly, although he hesitated to open the door to American-based companies to export. But he assured Smith that in cases of great economic impact, if a US subsidiary in Canada was the only company available to take the order, the American administration would give responsive treatment.[26]

SUCCESS?

Diefenbaker was both surprised and gratified that the discussions with the Americans had clarified the license exemption issue, but he was concerned with implementation. Would Congress have to approve each case? How long would each case review take? Dulles indicated that each case would have to be judged on its merits, but Treasury would issue the license, avoiding Congress, and the process would likely take only twenty-four to forty-eight hours. Ever concerned about appearances, Diefenbaker also obtained permission to use the term "exception," rather than the more loaded term "license," to describe what a subsidiary would be requesting of the US administration; the latter term implied that Canadian commercial policy was being made in the United States.[27] An *ad hoc* solution had evidently been reached on the major subsidiary irritant.

On the working level, however, follow-through on the agreement was less clear. The Canadian embassy in Washington lacked any notes on the Ottawa meeting.[28] The vague joint statement issued at the end of the talks had been intended more to forestall Canadian criticism than to outline a procedure. Canada's Commercial Secretary even had to consult the appropriate American export control authorities for guidelines. Eventually, an informal but slightly cumbersome application process emerged. A subsidiary receiving an order from China would notify its parent, which would then file for a license. The subsidiary would also notify the Canadian government, which could determine if an order was *bona fide*, whether it met security requirements, and whether its rejection would harm the Canadian economy. These conditions satisfied, the Canadian government would then notify Washington, and the American license would be issued.

American officials expected the procedure to be invoked only rarely.[29] As it turned out, Canadian subsidiary cases turned up early and often. If anything, the Ford

---

25   The American account of the conversation can be found in FRUS 1958-60, vol. 7, part 1, 696.

26   Memorandum of Conversation, 9 July 1958, reprinted in FRUS 1958-60, vol. 7, part 1, 707.

27   Memorandum of Conversation, 10 July 1958, reprinted in FRUS 1958-60, vol. 7, part 1, 710. Nonetheless, A.F.W. Plumptre admitted to "some misgivings about the formula when it was proposed, fearing that it might involve an uncomfortably detailed examination of Canadian affairs by US authorities." See NA, RG 19, vol. 4223, file 8780/U58, part 1, Plumptre to Minister, 22 July 1958.

28   NA, RG 25, vol. 7606, file 11280-1-40, part 1.1, Washington to Trade and Commerce, 19 July 1958.

29   Ibid.

experience had heightened awareness and sensitivity in Canada; almost anything dealing with China trade was assumed by the public, press, and Opposition to be "extraterritoriality." Given these sensitivities, it is not surprising that Diefenbaker publicly expressed his own concerns about restrictions on China trade, and repeatedly pressed External Affairs on the issue.

There was no "typical" outcome as the procedure was applied, but several cases show both its pitfalls and its limited success. As Dulles had foreseen, inquiries did not guarantee orders; "phantom orders" often vanished once an export permit was approved, either going elsewhere or never having existed at all. The first test case of the July agreement, a long-standing attempt by a subsidiary of Rayonier to provide a quote on sulphate pulp, fell into this category. Treasury issued a permit after a two-week delay, but the Rayonier subsidiary never shipped the goods. Canadian officials, attempting to make sense of these events, heard only rumours that the order had been pursued in seven different countries, and was ultimately placed in Sweden.[30]

The restrictive terms of the agreement served to cut down political controversy in the United States, but they also cut down the usefulness of the agreement as well. One condition, for instance, was that there be "no other Canadian company available" to take the order. Thus, Lee Textile Company and Robin Hood Milling found that the procedure could not be invoked when they hoped to ship to China, since purely Canadian companies apparently existed which could fill their orders.[31] Another requirement was that the goods be "non-strategic," but the term was left undefined. American and Canadian strategic definitions differed, and no ultimate arbiter of the differences was provided. In one notable case, the Americans questioned whether reconditioned locomotives should be considered "strategic," thus nullifying a large potential contract.[32]

Other cases rested within the often-closed domain of the firm. US government officials sometimes strongly suggested to a firm's directors that they might share the administration's strategic judgement that trade with Communist China was undesirable. Interviews by Canadian officials of representatives from International Nickel and Alcan Aluminum suggested that American citizens on company boards continued to fear individual prosecution under FAC regulations.[33] Institutional barriers persisted, including the denial of American shipping services and insurance, which made trade difficult to carry out. The prospects of consumer pressure or blacklisting were also a deterrent. Some orders, for undetermined reasons, were never pursued after preliminary inquiries by Trade and Commerce. One involved a possible sale by Chrysler Corporation, originating in August 1958. Diefenbaker himself had pressed the order forward, overriding External Affairs' concerns about American sensitivity, given the ongoing offshore islands crisis.[34] But ultimately, decisions would have to be

---

30   NA, RG 19, vol. 4183, file 8522/U585-2 (59), "Draft Minutes of Joint US-Canadian Committee on Trade and Economic Affairs," 5-6 January 1958, Ottawa.

31   Ibid., Briefing Paper, "United States Foreign Assets Control," Bilateral … Committee Agenda, 1959.

32   NA, RG 25, vol. 7606, file 11280-1-40, part 1.2, Washington D. C. to External Ottawa, 16 April 1959 ff.

33   NA, RG 25, vol. 7606, file 11280-1-40, part 1.1, Economic Division I to USSEA, "Alcan's Refusal to Supply Aluminum to China," 22 January 1959; Ibid., T & C Ottawa to T & C Washington, no. TC-131, 6 February 1959.

34   Ibid., J. Leger, "Exports to Chrysler Vehicle Engines to Communist China," Memorandum to the Minister, 19 August 1958; H.B. Robinson to Economic Division, 29 August 1958.

made by company directors. When a firm refused to go forward, Canadian options were limited. The Minister of Justice, Davie Fulton, felt it would be inappropriate for the government to apply for an exemption to a law whose validity and jurisdiction it did not officially recognize.[35]

The US government, at different levels, proved to be another roadblock. On the legislative level, a volatile Congress was able to put pressure on parent firms. In January 1959, Alcan refused to supply aluminum to China, even when the Treasury Department indicated it would be disposed to grant a license. Company representatives explained that Congress might retaliate by altering the tariffs on aluminum.[36] Blocs within Congress continued to feel strongly about Communist China, and Congress possessed constitutional powers over trade.

US officials also had to be reminded of the spirit of the agreement. Canadian officials at the Washington embassy felt that the State Department was a powerful ally against the more protectionist and legalistic views of Commerce and Treasury.[37] However, disturbing attitudes persisted in these latter departments. Gordon Churchill was concerned about the possibility of pre-emptive moves by Commerce or Treasury officials; pressure might be put on American businesses even before they made an application for an exemption. In a January 1959 ministerial meeting with the Canadians, the US Secretary of the Treasury denied that there had been political pressure on parent firms; he acknowledged, however, that it was a "possibility" in a government "the size of the US."[38] It seems that at least some members of the US administration felt that such pressure was a legitimate foreign policy tactic.

The lesson of the extraterritoriality issue seemed to be that limited concessions could be secured informally at high levels in the name of broader bilateral peace. The modest success of high-level bilateral cooperation between Canada and the United States in the China trade case is perhaps surprising, given Diefenbaker's reputation for anti-Americanism, and given the potential for a clash between an issue of sovereignty and the anti-Communist principle. But the China case shows that the Eisenhower administration was willing to engage in quiet compromise. Canada's diplomatic support was seen as more important than the marginal strategic benefits of halting subsidiary trade. The Kennedy administration came to office also apparently willing to work with Diefenbaker on this matter. And after the Prime Minister's personal appeal at their first meeting, Kennedy stepped in to solve FAC-related problems in shipping grain to China.

China trade was a rare, but not an isolated case. The lessons of China did have an impact when an extraterritoriality controversy arose in Fidel Castro's Cuba. When the Kennedy administration began to consider the application of Foreign Assets Control to Cuba in early 1961, Diefenbaker's vehemence over the need to respect Canadian sovereignty was taken into account. US Secretary of State Dean Rusk

---

35   Ibid., Washington to External Ottawa, no. 246, 29 January 1959.

36   Ibid., Economic Division 1 to USSEA, "Alcan's Refusal to Supply Aluminum to China," 22 January 1959; RG 20, vol. 1461, file 18-1-14, vol. 1 (T-18-979), C.M. Forsyth-Smith to Director, Trade and Commerce Service, Ottawa, 20 July 1959.

37   NA, RG 25, vol 7606, file 11280-1-40, part 1.2, Washington to External Ottawa no. 1621, 26 June 1959.

38   NA, RG 19, vol. 4183, file 8522/U585-1 (59), "Draft Minutes of Joint US-Canadian Committee on Trade and Economic Affairs," 5-6 January 1959, Ottawa.

offered a subsidiary exemption, asking only that Canada consider forbidding the export to Cuba of three specific categories of machinery. Cooperation on extra-territoriality had limits, however. It did not soften bilateral difficulties over the politics of Cuba, nor those over continuing trade in specific Canadian-produced nonstrategic goods. In fact, American anger over these factors intensified in time, to the point where Washington began to question Canada's ultimate trustworthiness as an ally.

It would always be difficult for the Diefenbaker government to celebrate victory on the extraterritoriality issue. Canada could win only limited, non-legislated, quiet concessions. Domestic pressures in the United States militated against a definitive solution. The US administration only saw limited room on the margins of existing legislation. The eventual resolution was case by case, rather than an agreement of principles.

Diefenbaker was correct to pursue the Americans on the principle that Canadian companies should operate under Canadian laws. Yet he did not vanquish extra-territoriality. The limits of his success were evident while he was still in office. Other instances of extraterritoriality, including anti-trust policy and balance of payments issues, would emerge in the coming years. Two years after Diefenbaker's fall from power, Arnold Heeney and Livingston Merchant studied extraterritoriality as a case of still-unresolved economic irritants in the bilateral relationship. Today we might look at the ongoing Helms-Burton controversy as a spiritual legacy of the extraterri-toriality issues of the Diefenbaker years. Some exercises in American power have neither died nor gracefully faded away. The vestiges of the Cold War mind-set continue to throw up third-party irritants in the Canada-US relationship. One should not be surprised that even an economic nationalist like Diefenbaker settled for a less than definitive solution at the height of the Cold War.

Note

The author gratefully acknowledges the support of the Social Sciences and Humanities Research Council.

New Ways of Thinking About Nuclear Weapons and Canada's Defence Policy

Erika Simpson

Canada is unique in that it has both the technological capability and the resources to develop its own nuclear weapons, or to acquire them from the United States, but has chosen not to. This paper analyzes the legacy of John Diefenbaker's government with regard to this aspect of Canadian defence policy, and the onset during the Diefenbaker years of new thinking about nuclear weapons. It explores how Diefenbaker and other key decision makers came to question whether Canada should assume a nuclear role; it examines their beliefs about nuclear weapons and the nature of the nuclear threat, and their assumptions about deterrence and about the nature of Canada's allied military commitment and involvement.

Between 1957 and 1960, the Diefenbaker government undertook to acquire five different nuclear weapons systems: Bomarc missiles; CF-l01B Voodoo air defence interceptors, to be deployed in Canada; CF-104 Starfighters, to be deployed in Europe as part of NATO's strike force; Lacrosse atomic missiles (which were eventually replaced by Honest John missiles), also to be deployed in Europe; and the rarely mentioned nuclear depth charges and torpedoes for Canada's maritime forces in the North Atlantic.[1] For a number of different reasons, the government had decided to commit itself to purchasing nuclear weaponry.[2] By 1961, however, the government

---

1   For an in-depth discussion of the nature and timing of these commitments, see Erika Simpson, "Canada's Contrasting NATO Commitments and the Underlying Beliefs and Assumptions of Defenders and Critics" (Ph.D. dissertation, University of Toronto, 1995), 247-66.

2   The major factors that seem to have impelled the government to embrace nuclear weapons include new technological developments such as the development of the Russian Sputnik in 1957 and the successful testing of the Bomarc B in 1959. Bilateral pressures, including the Congressional debate in the United States against acquiring a full complement of Bomarcs and the American transfer to Canada of the Voodoos, incited military advisers such as General Charles Foulkes, Chairman of the Joint Chiefs of Staff, to favour acquiring these nuclear-capable weapons systems. NATO directives, including MC 14/2 and MC/48/2 recommending defence preparations premised on using nuclear weapons from the outset, appeared to sway Diefenbaker and his first Defence Minister, George Pearkes. Financial imperatives such as the cancellation of the Avro Arrow, and its substitution with the relatively inexpensive Bomarc missile, also seemed to affect Diefenbaker's attitude. In fact,

Diefenbaker receiving poppy from Douglas Harkness, 1 November 1957 (Art Smith, MP, stands at left) (courtesy the Diefenbaker Centre, MG01/PHAL 003).

began to change its mind on the nuclear acquisition issue, and by the end of the following year high-level decision makers, including the Prime Minister himself, finally expressed outright opposition to fulfilling Canada's nuclear commitments. This paper attempts to explain this change in government policy and outlook, not so much by exploring the international and domestic factors that prompted it,[3] but rather by analyzing the beliefs and assumptions of the senior decision makers which lay behind it. The paper argues that the underlying attitudes and beliefs of key policy makers were an important influence on Canadian defence policy making during the Diefenbaker years.

The policy makers involved fall into two groups, who are identified here as Defenders (pro-nuclear) and Critics (anti-nuclear). In the first group were Diefenbaker's first Minister of National Defence, George Pearkes; Pearkes's successor,

---

military recommendations such as General Lauris Norstad's briefing to Cabinet seemed to have a considerable influence on members of Cabinet and the Chiefs of Staff. For further discussion of the impact and timing of these different factors, see Simpson, "Canada's Contrasting NATO Commitments," 246-98.

3   International crises such as the Cuban Missile Crisis led some decision makers such as Secretary of State for External Affairs Howard Green to question the necessity of acquiring nuclear weapons more forcefully. Canada's high-profile position in the UN's eighteen-nation Disarmament Committee influenced the Cabinet's debate. Cabinet was also influenced by: President John Kennedy's failure to consult during the Cuban Missile Crisis; the publication of the US State Department's press release criticizing Canada's nuclear policy; increasingly divided public opinion in Canada; Opposition Leader Lester Pearson's unexpected volte-face regarding the nuclear issue; as well as domestic criticism in the form of an outpouring of letters and complaints from groups like the Voice of Women. For further discussion of the impact and timing of these different factors, see ibid.

Douglas Harkness; the Chairman of the Chiefs of Staff, General Charles Foulkes; the Canadian Ambassador to the United States, Arnold Heeney; and other high-level military officials, such as the Chief of the Air Staff Hugh Campbell and Air Chief Marshal Frank Miller. Cabinet Ministers George Hees and Pierre Sevigny and Secretary to the Cabinet Robert Bryce may also be included in the group. The views espoused by this group were predominant in the Canadian government through the latter part of the 1950s, and represented traditional assumptions about nuclear weapons and Canada's responsibilities and involvement in nuclear deterrence. The group was instrumental in convincing Diefenbaker early in his prime ministerial leadership that Canada should acquire nuclear weapons. However, Diefenbaker became less certain about the nuclear option after he appointed his good friend and nuclear opponent Howard Green as Secretary of State for External Affairs in 1959.

Green, Undersecretary of State for External Affairs Norman Robertson, who also strongly opposed the acquisition of nuclear weapons, and George Ignatieff, who was appointed special adviser to Diefenbaker on nuclear issues in January 1961, indeed played a key role in eventually getting Diefenbaker and his government to rethink the nuclear acquisition issue. This group, and Critics more generally, articulated new ways of thinking within the government about the nuclear threat and the suitability of a nuclear deterrence strategy. Theirs was an outlook that would be influenced by the Canadian public's increasing anti-Americanism and a growing Canadian peace movement, and which years later would reach full expression in the policies of the government of Pierre Trudeau.[4]

This paper is framed as an analysis of the beliefs and assumptions of these two main groups, first the Defenders and then the Critics, and it describes the legacy that was left by the triumph of the latter, and particularly John Diefenbaker, over the former.

BELIEFS AND ASSUMPTIONS OF DEFENDERS

The main elements of the classical (i.e., Defenders') thinking about nuclear weapons and Canada's nuclear commitments, which prevailed strongly in the Canadian government through most of the 1950s, were as follows.

Defenders feared abandonment

Defenders feared that, if Canada weakened or reneged on its military commitments, the nation would be in danger of deserting its closest allies and finding itself abandoned and isolated. George Pearkes, Douglas Harkness, and other defence officials such as Charles Foulkes and Frank Miller argued that if the government failed to acquire nuclear systems, the country would be neglecting its allies and perhaps even running the risk of American retaliation.

Defenders believed Canada should pursue closer ties to the allies through established military commitments

Canadian decision makers had done a variety of things to signal Canada's close military ties to Europe and the United States, but the tendency among Defenders was to advocate traditional and established means of fostering such ties. In the early 1960s,

---

4   For an in-depth analysis of Trudeau's views on, and the attitude of some of his advisers toward, nuclear weapons, see ibid, chs. 3-4, 107-237.

these involved: commitments to maintain or increase the number of Canadian military forces personnel earmarked for NATO, particularly those deployed in Europe; promises to modernize or earmark more weapons systems and equipment for NATO, again particularly in Europe; and commitments to maintain or increase the percentage of the federal government's defence budget and the percentage of Gross National Product directed toward supporting the alliance.

Defenders believed the external threat to the allies was self-evident and imminent

Another core belief of Defenders related to their perceptions of the threat to the allies. Their discussions of the nature of the threat in fact were infrequent because the threat was accepted without critical reflection. For example, rather than consider whether the Communist world was monolithic or divided, Defenders focussed their intellectual energy on analysing the other allies' — particularly the Americans' — reactions to and positions toward the Communists.

Defenders assumed Canada's and the allies' weapons were defensive and non-threatening

Defenders tended to downplay Canada's capabilities, characterizing its weapons systems and intentions as defensive, not offensive. Although some commentators criticized select NATO weapons for being potentially first-strike systems, Defenders portrayed Canada's and the allies' weapons systems as part of a second-strike deterrent; the CF-104s in Europe, for example, were considered defensive until Trudeau began questioning this basic assumption in 1969. Whereas Defenders such as Harkness referred to Canada's Bomarcs and CF-101s as defensive, they avoided discussing the potentially offensive role of Canadian weapons systems such as the CF-104s. Indeed, the records of Cabinet meetings and high-level debates show that most Canadian leaders assumed that Canada's weapons systems were defensive, and did not consider whether the Soviet Union might perceive those systems as somehow provocative.

Defenders believed in the deterrence doctrine

Defenders premised their support for maintaining, if not strengthening, Canada's nuclear commitments on the doctrine of deterrence. Most expressed considerable faith in deterrence, a faith they retained as nuclear strategy evolved from "massive retaliation" in the 1950s to "flexible response" in the 1960s. Before 1957, for example, most Defenders believed deterrence was provided by the American monopoly on ballistic nuclear missiles.[5] By the late 1950s, the deterrence doctrine was, for them, based on the idea of massive retaliation.[6] In the 1960s, they believed that a credible deterrent was necessary so as to ensure a "flexible" response.[7] Despite the continuing

---

5   Until 1949, only the United States had developed thermonuclear weapons. The first Soviet explosion of an atomic device in 1949 was followed four years later by the development of a hydrogen bomb. But it was not until 1957, with the launch of Sputnik, that military strategists in the United States and Canada generally recognized that there now existed a "balance of terror" between the United States and the USSR. This balance had attendant implications for deterrence strategy — implications that came to be appreciated around 1959-60.

6   US Secretary of State John Foster Dulles first promulgated the doctrine of massive retaliation in 1954. It suggested that the United States would defend its interests in the world with considerable force, possibly including nuclear weapons.

7   The strategy of "flexible response" was officially adopted by NATO in 1967; however, it had been

changes in strategy, Defenders continued to accept that Canada had to fulfil its nuclear commitments or run the risk of undermining deterrence.

It is clear that, in the 1957-60 period, most Cabinet ministers and senior advisers were Defenders who recommended modernizing Canada's weapons systems with nuclear weapons because of their beliefs about the dangers of abandonment, the nature of the threat, the utility of nuclear weapons, and the reliability of deterrence. Foremost among these advisors were Defence Minister George Pearkes and his senior military adviser Charles Foulkes. The Prime Minister initially relied a great deal on their assessments. Whereas Diefenbaker seemed unsure of himself at the 1957 NATO Council meeting, and perhaps confused about the nature of the military commitments he was undertaking, there can be no doubt that between 1957 and 1960 he favoured acquiring nuclear weapons. Meanwhile, behind the scenes and in private conversations, Ambassador Arnold Heeney, Air Chief Marshal Frank Miller, Chief of the Air Staff Hugh Campbell, Associate Defence Minister Pierre Sevigny, senior Cabinet minister George Hees, and Secretary to the Cabinet Robert Bryce were also vigorous advocates of fulfilling Canada's nuclear commitments.

In fact, within the inner circle of senior decision makers at this time, there was no one who was clearly opposed to, or even critical of, Canada acquiring nuclear weapons. The views of Diefenbaker's first Secretary of State for External Affairs, Sidney Smith, had not yet crystallized, and, until Green replaced Smith, Undersecretary Norman Robertson would feel uncomfortable about articulating his growing concerns about nuclear weapons.[8] As for the Prime Minister, he did not encourage debate and discussion of defence issues among his senior advisers; indeed, in defence matters he initially relied solely on his own opinions and the advice of Pearkes[9] and Foulkes. He had no interest in discussing these issues with External Affairs or having them debated in Parliament. Thus, defence decision making was dominated during these early years by Defenders. That it might not be necessary to acquire nuclear warheads in order to demonstrate Canada's continued commitment to NATO and NORAD was an idea yet to be countenanced.

But as Canada moved into the 1960s, the Prime Minister and the nuclear

---

unofficial doctrine since the early 1960s. According to Canada's Ad Hoc Committee on Defence Policy in 1963, "Flexible response is in a sense a generalization of the concept of a limited war. It is based on the proposition that the Western Alliance as a whole and the United States in particular should not be placed in a position of excessive reliance on nuclear weapons or, more generally, of requiring to employ force in a manner incompatible with Western aims and objectives. The principle of flexible response places increased emphasis on the provision of conventional forces. It involves reduced dependence on strategic and tactical nuclear weapons although it does not reduce the requirement for these capabilities." See DND, Directorate of History (DHist), R.J. Sutherland (Chairman), et al., "Report of the Ad Hoc Committee on Defence Policy," p. 14 [SECRET CANADIAN EYES ONLY].

8   Interview with Basil Robinson, 14 September 1992. See also Basil Robinson, *Diefenbaker's World* (Toronto: University of Toronto Press, 1989), 108; Knowlton Nash, *Kennedy and Diefenbaker* (Toronto: McClelland and Stewart, 1990), 84; and J.L. Granatstein, *A Man of Influence: Norman Robertson and Canadian Statecraft, 1929-1968* (Ottawa: Deneau, 1981), 336-63.

9   Pearkes was appointed Lieutenant-Governor of British Columbia in 1960 and Douglas Harkness became the new Minister of National Defence. Whereas Diefenbaker had accorded Pearkes much authority and influence, Harkness was not as close to the Prime Minister nor as highly esteemed. Although he proved to be a vigorous Defender who argued in favour of acquiring nuclear weapons with conviction and energy, Harkness was not able to convince the Prime Minister and the Cabinet of his views.

proponents within the government began to face a challenge to their policies and positions. The challenge came from the Critics, both senior government officials and other elements of society who had different attitudes toward and beliefs about nuclear weapons.

BELIEFS AND ASSUMPTIONS OF CRITICS

Critics feared entrapment

In contrast to the Defenders, the Critics were preoccupied with the dangers of entrapment rather than abandonment. They tended to be suspicious of the likelihood and possible consequences of the allies drawing Canada into an armed confrontation. They worried about NATO undertakings, particularly American military objectives.

From the time Howard Green was appointed External Affairs Minister in June 1959, Prime Minister Diefenbaker became increasingly suspicious of the United States and fearful that the alliance leader would draw Canada unwillingly into a dangerous international confrontation. His suspicions reached a climax during the Cuban Missile Crisis, when the Cabinet debated whether or not to alert the Canadian military forces. In the emergency Cabinet meetings during the crisis, Diefenbaker and Green voiced their fears that the country was in danger of becoming entangled in American domestic affairs. Green argued that "there were great dangers in rushing in at this time." Furthermore, Canada should not be "stampeded" by Washington.[10] In particular, Diefenbaker's and Green's fears about entrapment led them to recommend that the Canadian government try to behave normally and deliberately, that the troop rotation to Europe be deferred, and that the government delay its decision to alert the Canadian military forces.[11]

Underlying their arguments was the assumption that alerting the military forces would only increase the likelihood of war. In one emergency Cabinet meeting, Diefenbaker's concerns about war impelled him to caution his colleagues that "Canadian mothers did not want their sons to be killed in any foreign war," and "the Cuba business was no affair of Canada's."[12] Indeed, his fear that the United States would drag Canada unwillingly into an armed confrontation, possibly a nuclear war, was such that when British Prime Minister Harold Macmillan sent an urgent message to Diefenbaker, the Canadian Prime Minister reported that Macmillan thought that the Soviet Union was "balanced on the knife's edge of indecision" and "any hostile

---

10   Privy Council Office (PCO), Cabinet Conclusions, 23 October 1962, pp. 4-5; 25 October, p. 16 [SECRET]. The Cabinet Conclusions were obtained under the Access to Information Act from the PCO, but are now also on deposit at the National Archives of Canada (NA). The records of Cabinet meetings, usually written by Robert Bryce, often attribute points made by Ministers not to specific individuals but to "some Ministers" or to "the Cabinet." However, comments made by the Prime Minister, the Secretary of State for External Affairs, and the Minister of National Defence were usually specifically attributed. Further evidence that it was Diefenbaker and Green who made these arguments in Cabinet is confirmed by other accounts of Cabinet meetings. See NA, Douglas Harkness Papers, MG 32, B19, vol. 57, "Unnumbered series on 'The Nuclear Arms Crisis'"; Patrick Nicholson, *Vision and Indecision* (Don Mills, ON: Longmans Canada, 1968), 158-59; Nash, *Kennedy and Diefenbaker*, 199; and Pierre Sevigny, *This Game of Politics* (Toronto: McClelland and Stewart, 1965), 256.

11   PCO, Cabinet Conclusions, 23 October 1962, pp. 4-5; 24 October 1962, p. 5 [SECRET]; and NA, Douglas Harkness Papers, MG 32, B19, vol. 57, "Unnumbered series on 'The Nuclear Arms Crisis'."

12   See Patrick Nicholson, *Vision and Indecision*, 159.

act might precipitate a Russian attack." Diefenbaker took Macmillan's message to mean that alerting Canada's defence might be just enough to precipitate the outbreak of war.[13] Significantly, it was not Diefenbaker's fears about Khrushchev's intentions that provoked the Prime Minister to oppose alerting the armed forces, but rather his beliefs about the escalatory tendencies of American military leaders.[14]

Immediately following the Cuban Missile Crisis, Diefenbaker ordered Harkness and Green to conduct secret negotiations with the United States to acquire nuclear warheads based on either the "joint control" or "missing parts" concepts.[15] He seemed to accept the necessity of accepting nuclear warheads but only so long as the United States consented to his concept of "joint control." As early as 1961, Diefenbaker had been saying that Canada preferred joint control of Canada's nuclear weapons systems, and this would require that President Kennedy use his executive powers to reinterpret the existing US law in such a way as to permit the "necessary agreement" of Canada.[16] Even during his first meeting with Kennedy, before their relationship became embittered, Diefenbaker referred to the imperative of obtaining joint control and joint custody over the nuclear weapons.[17]

In later years, Diefenbaker's close aide, Basil Robinson, explained that the Prime Minister's reason for seeking joint control seemed to be "to satisfy himself" that nuclear weapons located in Canada would not be used, except with the agreement of the Canadian government. According to Robinson, Diefenbaker was motivated not simply by "crass politics," but rather believed it was his "political responsibility"[18] to acquire and maintain joint control. Indeed, the Prime Minister was afraid of being accused of not having ensured Canada an equal say in the decision to use nuclear weapons.[19] Diefenbaker's memoirs also seem to confirm this assessment: "It was essential that the Canadian government be in as strong a position as possible to bring its influence to bear on any decision to use nuclear weapons, and perhaps to deter the United States from any possible ill-considered decisions in this respect."[20]

Diefenbaker's own belief that Canada was in danger of entrapment stemmed from his experiences in dealing with the Americans since coming to office, and his growing anti-Americanism. Privately, Diefenbaker referred to "the avalanche of anti-Americanism" in Canada, which stemmed from the widespread impression that the

---

13   Ibid., 165; Nash, *Kennedy and Diefenbaker*, 199.

14   PCO Cabinet Conclusions, 24 October 1962, p. 7, [SECRET].

15   PCO, Cabinet Conclusions, 30 October 1962, p. 10, [TOP SECRET].

16   PCO, Cabinet Conclusions, 21 February 1961, p. 1, [SECRET].

17   PCO, Cabinet Conclusions, 25 August 1961, p. 6, item k), [SECRET]. Diefenbaker also told the Cabinet after this meeting with Kennedy in 1961: "The President had said he would go as far as possible to meet the Canadian position in the matter, and there had been reliable reports in the last few days that members of the US Senate Foreign Relations Committee would agree to joint control with Canada over nuclear weapons stockpiled in this country for Canadian use. It would not have been possible two years ago to obtain US agreement to this principle. A change in US law might not be required to give effect to an agreement to share with Canada joint control over nuclear weapons stockpiled in Canada." These comments do seem to indicate that some measure of Canadian joint control, as Diefenbaker conceived it, was being seriously discussed in the United States in 1961.

18   Diefenbaker told Cabinet in 1961 that not to obtain joint control "would be an abandonment of responsibility on the part of Canada." PCO, Cabinet Conclusions, 25 August 1961, p. 4, [SECRET].

19   Basil Robinson interview, 14 September 1992.

20   John Diefenbaker, *One Canada 1962-1967*, vol. 3 (Scarborough, ON: Macmillan-NAL Publishing, 1977), 92.

United States was pushing other people around, from distrust of the American military, from the aggressiveness of American economic interests — and, he added almost as an afterthought, from the adverse Canada-US trading relationship.[21]

The Prime Minister's suspicions about US leaders began to affect his decision making in 1960, well before Kennedy became President. His growing impression was that the Americans were overly aggressive and that US military leaders were untrustworthy. For example, he came to regard the NORAD agreement of 1957 as having been presented to him under false pretences.[22] He was also frustrated about his unsuccessful effort to sell the Avro CF-105 Arrow to the United States, doubly so because he later had to acquire American-made interceptors.[23] He was also embarrassed to have been obliged to intervene personally to secure the Bomarc program.[24] With the inauguration in 1961 of a new, young, and seemingly impetuous President, Diefenbaker's suspicions of the Americans grew. They were reinforced by the Bay of Pigs incident in April 1961 and came to preoccupy him once he found the infamous "sofa memo": "What We Want from Ottawa Trip."[25] By 1963, according to George Ignatieff, the Prime Minister's distrust of the United States had grown to the point that he truly believed he had been tricked into accepting a defence policy which was subordinated to a certain type of weapons program and to the interest of a foreign government.[26] By contrast, it is notable that Diefenbaker — for example, during the Berlin crisis in September 1961 — harboured no suspicions whatever that the other NATO allies might seek to draw Canada unwillingly into an armed confrontation.

Critics believed Canada's established military ties to the allies should be restructured and de-emphasized

Critics sought to alter Canada's military support for the allies. In particular, they opposed increasing the number of Canadian military forces for NATO purposes. They were critical of the government's promises to modernize and deploy more

---

21   NA, Arnold Heeney Papers, MG 30, E 144, vol. 2, file "Memoir, 1960, Chapter 15, diary, #2," 30 August 1960 entry; see also Nash, *Kennedy and Diefenbaker*, 58.

22   Interview with George Ignatieff by Roger Hill, Senior Research Fellow, Canadian Institute for International Peace and Security, "Canadian Institute for International Peace and Security Transcripts" (CIIPS Transcripts), unpublished transcripts (Ottawa, 1987), 104. These are verbatim transcripts of interviews conducted by Roger Hill, David Cox, Nancy Gordon, et al. Excerpts are cited with the permission of Roger Hill.

23   According to Ignatieff, "he [Diefenbaker] was told by National Defence after he had signed NORAD, there was no need for such an aircraft, because the United States would take care of all that and they would not buy the Arrow in any shape or form; they had all kinds of aircraft and missiles and we were going into the missile age anyway. And in his fury, I think, Diefenbaker not only made the decision to scrap the Arrow, but he said that every Arrow plane, even the few models that had been made, had to be destroyed." CIIPS Transcripts, p. 118.

24   John Diefenbaker, *One Canada: The Years of Achievement 1956-1962*, vol. 2 (Toronto: Macmillan, 1976), 51-52, 60.

25   For a detailed account of Diefenbaker's growing suspicions once Kennedy came into power, see Nash, *Kennedy and Diefenbaker*. Nash argues that Diefenbaker's perception of the United States shifted because he strongly disliked Kennedy. In fact, Diefenbaker's "anti-American" impulses began to affect his decision making in 1960, well before Kennedy became President.

26   As Ignatieff recalled, "It affected his whole attitude in relation to the United States. I mean a lot has been said about his personal antipathy to a young President such as Kennedy. But it had this background in the defence issues, where he felt he had been cornered into a subordinate position and contrary to all his convictions." CIIPS transcripts, p. 118.

weapons systems and equipment to NATO, and they were generally intent on limiting the percentage of both the federal government's defence budget and the nation's GNP directed toward the Western alliance.

Between 1957 and 1963, most high-level decision makers, including Diefenbaker and Green, steadfastly rejected the concept of a complete severing of Canada's association with NATO — what they called "neutralism." In fact, Diefenbaker claimed that he could not abide neutralists, and heaped scorn on James Minifie, "the reigning advocate of neutralism," a "Washington-based journalist and expatriate for whom Canada wasn't good enough."[27] But Green, Robertson, and Ignatieff all believed the government should restructure its nuclear commitments to NATO. It was this small group that, at the beginning of 1960, played a central role in changing Diefenbaker's mind on the nuclear question. It was just after Ignatieff became a special advisor to Diefenbaker on nuclear issues that the Prime Minister began to embrace new ideas such as "joint control" and "missing parts" — propositions which seemed designed to delay decision making.[28] High-level military advisers, such as Foulkes, argued that negotiations with the United States to acquire nuclear weapons would need to be based on the principle that the warheads for the Canadian military forces in Europe, and the interceptors in Canada, would be supplied by the United States and remain American property. They also maintained that nuclear weapons stockpiled in Europe would be guarded by NATO soldiers, and custody and maintenance would remain with the United States.[29] But Diefenbaker now espoused "joint control." He explained: "We have made it equally clear that we shall not in any event consider nuclear weapons until, as a sovereign nation, we have equality of control — a joint control."[30]

Green, Robertson, and Ignatieff were the formulators of the joint control approach. Ignatieff later explained:

> We came up with our own formula for defusing the government's nuclear dilemma.... To the beleaguered Prime Minister, this compromise solution was a welcome peg on which to hang his own indecision, and he clung to it even after it became obvious that it wasn't strong enough to save his government.[31]

The missing parts approach also grew out of the trio's conversations.[32] Their suggestion that nuclear warheads be stored on American territory and delivered quickly in the event of emergency seemed designed to bridge gaps among opposing viewpoints

---

27   NA, Arnold Heeney Papers, MG 30, E 144, vol. 2, file "Memoir, 1960, Chapter 15, diary, A#2," 31 August 1960 entry. James Minifie was the author of a book which argued for Canadian neutrality, *Peacemaker or Powdermonkey: Canada's Role in a Revolutionary World* (Toronto: McClelland and Stewart, 1960).

28   For instance, the missing parts idea was based on the condition that the United States would consent to store the nuclear warheads, or parts of the warheads, on American soil and, in the event that Canada authorized their deployment during an emergency, the United States would undertake to transport the parts to Canada and install them in the Bomarc missiles and Voodoo interceptors.

29   For example, see General C. Foulkes on CBC TV, "Citizen's Forum," 6 November 1960, transcribed in *News and Views* 92, no. 22 (November 1960): 11.

30   For Diefenbaker's own reference list of his statements referring to joint control, see Diefenbaker Canada Centre (DCC), Prime Minister's Office, vol. 74, file 10385, "Public Statements by Members of the Government Regarding the Acquisition and Storage of Nuclear Weapons," 24 November 1960.

31   George Ignatieff, *The Making of a Peacemonger* (Toronto: Penguin Books, 1985), 189.

32   According to Nash, *Kennedy and Diefenbaker*, 152.

in Cabinet. It sought to satisfy Diefenbaker's desire for joint control while moderating US escalatory tendencies; and it endeavoured to satisfy Green, who was fervently opposed to having nuclear weapons on Canadian soil. Ignatieff later admitted: "We knew all along that the [joint control] proposal was no more than a holding action, that the Americans would never accept joint control with regard to the use of nuclear weapons. But in the meantime it did enable Howard Green to wage a number of successful campaigns on behalf of the one cause, which, in his mind, overshadowed all others in importance, namely arms control."[33] The missing parts approach also sought to mollify Defence Minister Douglas Harkness, who worried about Canada's defence of the deterrent.

Critics believed the external threat was exaggerated and misunderstood

While Defenders believed the Soviet threat was self-evident and imminent, Critics tended to believe that the threat was exaggerated and the intentions of the Soviet Union were being misinterpreted. During the Cuban Missile Crisis, Diefenbaker took the position that the Americans were exaggerating and misinterpreting the threat by Khrushchev. In fact, he had taken a similar view of the Soviet threat back in 1961 when, during the Berlin crisis, he had observed that it should not be overlooked that the Soviet Union had fears, too. Although Soviet policies sometimes defied reason, it was important to understand their interests, objectives, and concerns.[34] A few months later, Diefenbaker referred to Khrushchev as a "realist" who supported "a course of peace — a course of realism — a course in keeping with the choice of the Canadian people."[35] By October 1962, Diefenbaker was so preoccupied with the motives of Kennedy and other American military leaders that he barely bothered during Cabinet meetings to assess Khrushchev's intentions, and when he did so, he took a relatively benign view of Soviet motives. Indeed, many years later, Diefenbaker still argued that Khrushchev's approach during the crisis was cautious and moderate. As he wrote: "Khrushchev went out of his way to cultivate a moderate and reasonable image."[36]

Whereas Diefenbaker perceived the Soviet threat to be overstated, his impression of the United States as a threat to international peace and security intensified. Instead of criticizing Khrushchev for secretly deploying missiles to Cuba, he lambasted American officials for first telling him that the substance of their photographic evidence was secret, and then shortly afterward revealing it to the press.[37] Although the depth of Diefenbaker's suspicions was quickly evident to Kennedy owing to the Prime Minister's impromptu proposal for an on-site inspection team, Diefenbaker openly revealed his distrust of American intentions when he told reporters during the crisis that, if his on-site inspection proposal was implemented, "the truth will be revealed."[38]

Diefenbaker was concerned that certain American leaders were bent on inciting war. His Cabinet had come to the conclusion that there were "domestic political

---

33   Ignatieff, *The Making of a Peacemonger*, 189.

34   DCC, Speech Series Collection, vol. 65, file 996, "Partial Notes for an address to the Canadian Bar Association," Winnipeg, 1 September 1961, p. 22.

35   DCC, Speech Series Collection, vol. 87, file 1122, 28 May 1962, p. 2.

36   John Diefenbaker, *One Canada 1962-1967*, 71.

37   PCO, Cabinet Conclusions, 24 October 1962, p. 2, [SECRET].

38   Nash, *Kennedy and Diefenbaker*, 189.

overtones in the US decision" to confront the Soviet Union over Cuba. Instead of focussing on Khrushchev's provocative intentions, the Cabinet concluded that the United States could be responsible for provoking war by imposing a selective block-ade on Cuba.[39] As the Prime Minister explained to Cabinet, certain military leaders in the United States appeared determined to fight the USSR — indeed, three years before, some of them had told him that the United States could defeat the Russians any time before the autumn of 1962, but that the outlook thereafter was less certain.[40]

Diefenbaker's gradual change of heart regarding the Soviets, which seemed to occur in 1961, stemmed in part from his belief that, as a matter of survival, it was essential for freedom-loving nations to seek, through the processes of diplomacy, to build on the hope of international peace. He came to the view that, although Soviet foreign policy would not be transformed, it was possible "to identify and to welcome certain modifications in the Soviet approach to international problems." For exam-ple, he emphasized that the Soviet Union's participation in the UN's Special Disar-mament Committee should not be disregarded.[41]

The Prime Minister's altered perception of the Soviets also stimulated changes in the way he processed information about Soviet actions. During the Cuban Missile Crisis, for instance, he suggested to his colleagues that Khrushchev's attempt to deploy nuclear missiles in Cuba was understandable given the Americans' prior deployment of nuclear missiles in Turkey, within striking distance of the Soviet Union. Whereas in 1958 Diefenbaker likely would have condemned Khrushchev, by 1962 he was trying to see the situation from the adversary's viewpoint.

For Diefenbaker and other Critics, the main threat to Canada's security came to be not the Soviet bloc but the threat of nuclear war arising out of both sides' stockpiles of nuclear weapons. In their view, the greatest threat to Canadians was not the danger of armed attack, but the possibility of miscalculated or accidental war escalating uncontrollably. The threat of nuclear war was much more dangerous and salient than the threat from Russian missiles in Cuba.

Critics believed both sides' weapons were unnecessarily threatening

Critics viewed the weapons and weapons structures of both the allies and the Soviet bloc as problematic. Many of NATO's weapons systems, they pointed out, were unnecessary, and potentially threatening. Critics worried in particular that both sides would regard the other's forces and doctrine as provocative, prompting a spiralling arms race and uncontrollable escalation.

As more information circulated in the late 1950s about the dangers of nuclear war, some key policy makers in Ottawa, including Howard Green and Norman Robertson, became increasingly vocal on the matter of Canada's nuclear acquisition policy. Arnold Heeney wrote in his diary: "My judgement is that this instinctive repulsion for nuclear involvement of any kind is at the base of Mr. G's [Green's] own negative attitude over all defence matters, espec. [especially] where the United States, the great nuclear power is involved."[42] Like his minister, Norman Robertson was also "absolutely horrified that mankind would seriously contemplate using the nuclear

---

39   PCO, Cabinet Conclusions, 23 October 1962, p. 4, [SECRET].

40   Ibid., 24 October 1962, p. 7, [SECRET].

41   For early evidence of his changing perceptions, see DCC, Diefenbaker Speech Series Collection, vol. 30, file 779, speech to Michigan University, Lansing, USA, 7 June 1959, pp. 6, 18, 20.

42   NA, Arnold Heeney Papers, MG 30, E 144, vol. 2, file "Memoir, 1960, Chapter 15, diary #2," 20 September 1960 entry.

weapon."[43] As Basil Robinson explains, both Green and Robertson were affected by the anti-nuclear arguments propounded in the mid-1950s by the peace movement, first in the United Kingdom and later in Canada. Robertson, particularly, took the anti-nuclear viewpoint to heart, believing that once one understood the effect of a nuclear explosion, one's only course could be to oppose nuclear weapons and contribute to efforts to put them outside humankind's experience.[44]

There is no doubt that the peace movement beginning in Britain in the 1950s and spreading throughout Western Europe and North America in the 1960s caused many Canadians to think about the dangers of nuclear war and to question the assumptions undergirding the policy of deterrence. Letters, marches, and appeals drawing attention to the dangers of nuclear war had an overwhelming impact on some leaders. For some, the dismantling and destruction of nuclear, conventional, biological, and chemical weapons became the only option.

Diefenbaker's own beliefs were profoundly influenced by impressions he received in the early 1960s as more people began to discuss the dangers of nuclear war.[45] His assertions in January 1963 that "nuclear war is indivisible" and "nuclear weapons as a universal deterrent are a dangerous solution" were purportedly based on his reading of the Nassau Communiqué and ideas expressed by George W. Ball, the US Under-Secretary of State.[46] But the Prime Minister was also influenced by the personal mail he received from anti-nuclear groups such as the Voice of Women.[47] Although very much swayed by Green,[48] Diefenbaker claimed to be considerably affected by the thousands of letters he received from ordinary Canadians which reflected changes in the general climate of opinion.[49] Even though he reasoned that people rarely wrote letters except to express their opposition to something, he regarded his letters to be a most useful cross section of the public's understanding — or even sometimes misunderstanding — of the goals the government had set for itself.[50]

An examination of his personal jottings reveals that, by 1961, Diefenbaker believed that he himself would somehow be responsible if nuclear weapons were used

---

43   Interview of Basil Robinson, 14 September 1992.

44   Ibid. Robinson also speculates that Robertson's comparatively early exposure to the peace movement stemmed from his strong interest and close reading of developments in British politics. See also Granatstein, *A Man of Influence*, 338-39.

45   Nicholson, *Vision and Indecision*, 159; Sevigny, *This Game of Politics*, 259.

46   *Hansard*, 25 January 1963, 3128.

47   See Nicholson, *Vision and Indecision*, 159; Sevigny, *This Game of Politics*, 259.

48   By 1962, Diefenbaker referred to Green as "one of the greatest leaders in the field of disarmament and world peace" and someone who had achieved for Canada "an undisputed place in the field of international affairs and the pursuit of peace for all mankind." DCC, Prime Minister's Papers, vol. 87, file 1122, "International Affairs-Defence Policy," 28 May 1962, p. 3.

49   Generally speaking, Diefenbaker relied on letters but not on public opinion polls to detect shifts in public opinion. This is confirmed by Pierre Sevigny's remarks in Peyton Lyon, *Canada in World Affairs: 1961-1963* (Toronto: Oxford University Press, 1968), 71, and Harkness's comments in Peter Stursberg, *Leadership Lost 1962-1967*, 25.

50   DCC, Diefenbaker Speech Series Collection, vol. 59, file 967, "Notes for an Address on 'The Nation's Business'," 21 June 1961, p. 1. According to Arnold Heeney's diary, Diefenbaker was powerfully affected by the shift toward anti-Americanism which he detected in his letters beginning in 1959. See NA, Arnold D.P. Heeney Papers, MG 30, E 144, vol. 2, file "Memoir 1959, Chapter 15, diary #1," 29 March 1959 entry.

in a third world war. As he scrawled on his notes for a radio speech: "the thought of a third world war, especially one in which nuclear weapons would be used, is a constant companion of one who has the responsibility and trust which rests on me."[51] It may have been this sense of responsibility and trust which prompted him to begin cautioning that many of NATO's weapons were unnecessary and might be perceived as provocative, thus posing a threat to all. Certainly by 1963 he felt compelled to explain to the House of Commons that acquiring more nuclear weapons was a mistake and would add nothing materially to Canadian defences. He indeed argued that there should be no further development of nuclear power anywhere in the world, and that having nuclear weapons as a universal deterrent would be a dangerous situation.[52]

Diefenbaker's view that the stockpiling of nuclear weapons by both sides was unnecessarily threatening seems to have been prompted partly by his personal sense of responsibility for the survival of millions of Canadians. But it probably also grew out of his regular weekend conversations with Green, who believed fervently that nuclear weapons were threatening and dangerous. Indeed, the acquisition of nuclear weapons by Canada might lead, Diefenbaker thought, to a spiralling arms proliferation in other regions of the world, including the Middle East, and to heightened dangers of unintentional escalation.[53]

The belief that nuclear weapons were dangerously offensive sometimes prompted new lines of reasoning. In Diefenbaker's case, he no longer refrained from referring to the possibility of nuclear war, but began to put forward vivid and grisly references to its consequences. Due in part to his rhetorical skills, Diefenbaker excelled at using vivid metaphors — the Pentagon intended to make Canada a "burnt sacrifice"; the Liberal party wanted to make Canada a "nuclear dump."[54] With great effect, the Prime Minister calculated the destructive capacity of nuclear weapons. "The present day bomb, with the dimension of 100 million tons of TNT," he announced, "would equal the explosive content of 10 million aircraft in the last war. That is why those of us who have the responsibility of leadership — this responsibility that remains with us day and night — carry this fear that through error or mistake we bring about a war that will destroy all mankind."[55]

Critics believed the deterrence doctrine was misleading

Critics generally believed that relying on NATO's nuclear forces would increase, not reduce, the likelihood of war, and they drew attention to threatening scenarios which they feared could not be averted by deterrence. As early as 1961, an unidentified

---

51   DCC, Diefenbaker Speech Series Collection, vol. 56, file 950, "Speech on CBC Radio International," 5 May 1961, p. 2.

52   *Hansard*, 25 January 1963, 3129-3130.

53   For example, see PCO, Cabinet Conclusions, 23 August 1961, p. 6, item c), [SECRET]. The Cabinet Conclusions did not directly attribute this argument to Howard Green but to "some" Cabinet ministers. It is highly probable that it was Green, however, as it is accompanied by other arguments typical of his reasoning (e.g., "It would be a tragic policy for Canada to stockpile nuclear weapons at this time . . . the Canadian example might result in a dozen or more powers, some of them, like the United Arab Republic, in tense and dangerous parts of the world, following the example... .").

54   Peter C. Newman, *Renegade in Power* (Toronto: McClelland and Stewart, 1963), 388, 392.

55   DCC, Diefenbaker Speech Series Collection, vol. 87, file 1122, "International Affairs — Defence Policy," 28 May 1962, p. 2.

minister argued during a Cabinet meeting that it would be misleading to give Canadians the impression that Bomarc missiles and Voodoos could actually defend them against nuclear weapons.[56] While Diefenbaker initially subscribed to the view that making preparations for civil defence against nuclear attack was necessary, by 1960 he stated there would almost surely be "total destruction" and "a shattered world" if nations drifted into nuclear war. One year later he considered there could be "no margin for doubt about the devastation which could be wreaked on mankind either by intent or by miscalculation," and by 1963 he made even stronger references to nuclear war, stating: "The day the strike takes place, eighteen million people in North America will die in the first two hours, four million of them in Canada."[57]

CONCLUSION

In the Diefenbaker years, high-level decision makers such as George Pearkes, Charles Foulkes, Douglas Harkness, Arnold Heeney, Hugh Campbell, Frank Miller, and George Hees held beliefs which led them to advocate Canada's acquisition of nuclear weapons. Initially the Prime Minister was also convinced that Canada should acquire these weapons systems, but he eventually changed his mind and came to oppose their acquisition. Part of the explanation for Diefenbaker's changed position and outlook lies in the emergence early in the 1960s, at the centre of decision making in Ottawa, of people like Howard Green, Norman Robertson, and George Ignatieff who strongly opposed Canada's acquisition of nuclear weapons. These individuals, along with the peace movement and the growth of anti-American sentiment in Canadian society, clearly influenced the Prime Minister to rethink the nuclear issue.

Advocating nuclear weapons until late in 1960, Diefenbaker then began to harbour doubts about Canada's nuclear commitment, which he finally rejected in December 1962. Although he wanted Canada to remain a member of NATO, he eventually questioned the necessity of acquiring nuclear weapons as part of Canada's allied commitment. Despite pressure from US leaders, the Canadian media, and Canadian military officials, Diefenbaker became more inclined to take the view that Canada's acquisition of nuclear weapons would in fact contribute to international tensions and increase, not decrease, the likelihood of a global holocaust. His attitudes toward President Kennedy, the Cuban Missile Crisis, Kennedy's "sofa memo," and the US State Department's press release criticizing Canada's nuclear policy, all contributed to his growing fear of entrapment in the destabilizing and potentially destructive foreign ventures of the United States. Although Diefenbaker's changing convictions were not the only factor impelling his government to oppose nuclear weapons, they were of great importance.

It is interesting to consider that Canada was the only country during the early 1960s that rejected acquiring nuclear systems while it had the opportunity to possess them.[58] But this stance was short-lived, and Diefenbaker's successor as Prime Minister,

---

56   PCO, Cabinet Conclusions, 23 August 1961, p. 8, [SECRET].

57   DCC, Speech Series Collection, vol. 65, file 996, "Partial notes for an address at the Canadian Bar Association Dinner," Winnipeg, 1 September 1961, p. 11; Nash, *Kennedy and Diefenbaker*, 228.

58   At that time, three NATO nations (the United States, Britain and France) possessed their own nuclear weapons. Five other NATO countries (Belgium, the Netherlands, Italy, Greece and Turkey) entered into bilateral agreements with the United States under which they would acquire nuclear weapons systems. As a 1968 DND study for the Special Task Force on Europe added, these warheads were to be retained under American custody until their release was authorized by "joint decision."

Lester Pearson, acted quickly to embrace nuclear weapons. Yet, a few years later, Pearson would be succeeded as Prime Minister by Pierre Trudeau, who would in fact hold many of the same underlying beliefs and convictions as Green, Robertson, and Ignatieff.[59] Whereas the latter three were among the first influential Canadian policy makers to criticize and oppose nuclear weapons, John Diefenbaker's legacy with respect to Canadian defence policy was that he eventually allowed this questioning and criticism to take place, and became the first Prime Minister to countenance Canada taking an anti-nuclear stand.

Note

The assistance of the following people was invaluable during the research process. Elizabeth Diamond at the Diefenbaker Canada Centre; Isabelle Campbell at the Directorate of History in the Department of National Defence; Hector Mackenzie and Mary Halloran in the Historical Section of the Department of Foreign Affairs and International Trade; John Fletcher and Thelma Nicholson in the Privy Council Office; and Paul Marsden and Dick McClelland in the National Archives of Canada. Roger Hill at the former Canadian Institute for International Peace and Security (CIIPS) allowed me to cite from the CIIPS transcripts. Jack Granatstein, John Hilliker, Knowlton Nash, Basil Robinson, and Denis Smith were also sources of both invaluable information and insightful comments. I would also like to thank H. Peter Langille, Peyton Lyon, Cranford Pratt, Janice Stein, and David Welch for their valuable comments on earlier drafts. However, it should not be assumed these people share the perspective of this paper or agree with its conclusions. Neither are they to blame for any errors or omissions.

DND, DHist, DND for STAFEUR, "Canadian Military Interest in Europe," V 2390-1 (STAFEUR), 1 November 1968, p. 26, [SECRET].

59   See Simpson, "Canada's Contrasting NATO Commitments," ch. 4, 184-245.

THE PLANE TRUTH: THE AVRO CANADA CF-105 ARROW PROGRAM

Russell Isinger and Donald C. Story

In the chapter of his biography of John Diefenbaker that deals with the Avro Canada CF-105 Arrow,[1] Denis Smith observes:

> The saga of the Arrow from inspiration to demise has spawned an unusual mythology, sustained over forty years by an endless flow of newspaper and television features, a cult literature, and a play featuring an on-stage model of the aircraft. Thirty years after its destruction, tales were still told of phantom sightings of the doomed prototypes. The Arrow seems as deeply lodged in English Canadian memory as the Canadian Pacific Railway or the Calgary Stampede.[2]

The "cult literature" on the Avro Arrow tends to begin with the premise that technology such as the Arrow should be an end in itself, rather than the means to an end. To varying degrees, pro-Arrow enthusiasts have advanced a techno-nationalist argument that the benefits of the Arrow to Canada far outweighed the costs. These writers argue that the project should have been seen through, regardless of financial burden or operational requirement. The more egregious examples of these works focus obsessively on the Conservative Cabinet as the locus of decision making, and ignore, misinterpret, or manipulate the facts about the Arrow program to support the contention that Prime Minister John Diefenbaker made the wrong decision, likely in response to pressure from the United States. Thus, the Arrow's cancellation is portrayed as unjustifiable under any circumstances.[3]

---

1   The CF-105 was officially named Arrow in 1957; it will be referred to in this paper simply as the Arrow. The Arrow program should be understood to include the air frame, engine, air-to-air missile armament, and electronics system comprising radar fire control, communications, and flight control.

2   Denis Smith, *Rogue Tory: The Life and Legend of John G. Diefenbaker* (Toronto: McFarlane Walter and Ross, 1995), 634. To this list must now be added dozens of Internet sites and the highly fictionalized CBC docudrama, "The Arrow."

3   The popular literature varies widely in terms of the quality of the research and writing, but its enduring popularity is indicated by the number of second editions of books devoted to the Arrow.

The Arrow myth will endure regardless of what is written here. Melvin Conant's observation that "the Arrow affair has had far-reaching political repercussions and it will be a long time before the charges and countercharges about the soundness of the decision die down"[4] remains appropriate. But a serious challenge to the tenets of the myth that has captured the hearts and minds of Canadians for over forty years is long overdue. Our intention is to provide a concise and fresh account of what went wrong during the complex and controversial Arrow affair, based on declassified government documents and personal papers from the period.[5] What is clear from this evidence is that the decisions that led to the cancellation of the Arrow were made early on by the Liberal government of Prime Minister Louis St. Laurent, which had initiated the project and allowed it to accelerate and expand beyond recovery. We also outline a civil-military chain of command characterized by too much deference by the political authority, Liberal and Conservative alike, to the advice offered by the highest military decision-making body, the Chiefs of Staff Committee. This system of "bottom-up" decision making, coupled with the financial difficulties of a middle power procuring modern weapons systems at a time of transformation from the "bomber gap" to the "missile gap," doomed the Arrow almost from the beginning. The project's demise was thus the logical and probably inescapable consequence of three interrelated factors: a flawed weapons acquisition process driven by an overly ambitious Royal Canadian Air Force, harsh financial realities, and dramatic strategic shifts.[6]

In pursuing this study, we have gained much insight from the work of Lawrence Aronsen, who has examined the dynamics of the Canadian defence decision-making process in the postwar period. Aronsen uncovered a key feature of this process which goes a long way toward explaining why the Arrow program unfolded the way it did. He concluded that, rather than having a "military-industrial complex" such as is purported to exist in the United States, Canada had a "national security bureaucracy" composed of high-level officials in the military and in the bureaucratic, scientific, and corporate sectors of the government. Aronsen notes the observation made by Brooke Claxton, the Liberal Minister of National Defence who first backed the Arrow, that the important elements of the defence decision-making process were almost seamlessly integrated; notably, the service and research chiefs represented on the Chiefs of Staff Committee,[7] the Cabinet Defence Committee, and the Cabinet itself. In

---

See Palmiro Campagna, *Storms of Controversy: The Secret Avro Arrow Files Revealed*, 2nd ed. (Toronto: Stoddart Publishing, 1996); James Dow, *The Arrow*, 2nd ed. (Toronto: James Lorimer & Company, 1997); Murray Peden, *Fall of an Arrow* (Toronto: Stoddart Publishing, 1987); E.K. Shaw, *There Never Was an Arrow*, 2nd ed. (Ottawa: Steel Rail Educational Publishing, 1981); Greig Stewart, *Shutting Down the National Dream: A.V. Roe and the Tragedy of the Avro Arrow*, 2nd ed. (Toronto: McGraw-Hill Ryerson, 1997); and Les Wilkinson, Don Watson, Ron Page, and Richard Organ, *Avro Arrow: The Story of the Avro Arrow from Its Evolution to Its Extinction*, rev. ed. (Erin, ON: The Boston Mills Press, 1989).

4   Melvin Conant, *The Long Polar Watch: Canada and the Defence of North America* (New York: Harper Brothers, 1962).

5   These are largely held by the National Archives of Canada (NA), the Directorate of History and Heritage of the Department of National Defence (DHH/DND), and the Diefenbaker Canada Centre (DCC).

6   For an in-depth elaboration of this argument, see Russell Steven Paul Isinger, "The Avro Canada CF-105 Arrow Program: Decisions and Determinants" (MA thesis, University of Saskatchewan, 1997).

7   The Chiefs of Staff Committee made its decisions on the basis of consensus, and was comprised of five members of equal rank: the Chairman of the Chiefs of Staff Committee, the Chief of the Air Staff, the Chief of the Naval Staff, the Chief of the General Staff, and the Chairman of the Defence Research Board.

Aronsen's words, the Cabinet was extended right into the "labyrinth" of this national security bureaucracy, and because of this situation the latter wielded great influence on defence policy.[8]

Indeed, the defence decision-making process of this era vested pre-eminent power in the Cabinet Defence Committee, which was comprised of the Prime Minister, senior ministers and their respective deputies, and the service and research chiefs who were the indispensable source of advice on all defence-related matters. It was the Cabinet Defence Committee which effectively made all decisions on the Arrow, not Cabinet. Cabinet minutes show that near-perfunctory approval was given to the Cabinet Defence Committee's recommendations, which in turn had been largely determined by the recommendations of the Chiefs of Staff Committee.[9]

In this milieu, it was the Chiefs of Staff Committee that would prove to be both midwife and executioner of the Arrow. And within the Chiefs of Staff Committee, it was the Royal Canadian Air Force commanders — at first Air Marshal Roy Slemon, and later Air Marshal Hugh Campbell — who were the forces to be reckoned with. In pursuing their procurement wish lists, the RCAF also had influential allies in the Defence Research Board — Dr. Omond Solandt in particular — and the Department of Defence Production.[10] Thus, the arguments of the Chief of the Air Staff tended to carry the day with the other service chiefs. The ministers of defence and defence production, both Liberal and Conservative, in turn deferred rather uncritically to the advice of the Chiefs of Staff Committee on the Arrow's technological, tactical, and financial requirements. Adrian Preston has described this environment:

> Thus, in a curious reversal of British and American experience between 1945 and 1958, in which military power had been steadily eroded by political authority, the Canadian armed profession during roughly the same period exercised in terms of tasks, expertise, and political influence a virtually unbridled control of foreign and defence policy.[11]

By the early 1950s, Canada had embarked on the largest peacetime military buildup in its history to meet the perceived Communist threat, turning itself into what Reg Whitaker and Gary Marcuse have called "a national insecurity state."[12] In 1952, Claxton even remarked that "defence had become the single biggest industry in Canada."[13] The Arrow program was to be the centrepiece of Canada's continental

8   See Lawrence R. Aronsen, "Canada's Postwar Re-Armament: Another Look at American Theories of the Military-Industrial Complex," in *Historical Papers: A Selection from the Papers Presented at the Annual Meeting held in Halifax, 1981* (Halifax: Canadian Historical Association, 1981), 175-96.

9   On the formal structure of the civil-military decision-making process, see DHH/DND, General Charles A. Foulkes Papers (Foulkes Papers), file 14-2 Arrow, "The Story Of The CF-105 Avro 'Arrow,' 1952-1962," TD; and James Eayrs, *The Art of the Possible: Government and Foreign Policy in Canada* (Toronto: University of Toronto Press, 1961).

10   See D.G. Goodspeed, *A History Of The Defence Research Board of Canada* (Ottawa: Queen's Printer, 1958).

11   Adrian Preston, "The Profession of Arms In Postwar Canada, 1945-1970: Political Authority as a Military Problem," *World Politics: A Quarterly Journal of International Relations* 23, no. 2 (January 1971): 201.

12   Reg Whitaker and Gary Marcuse, *Cold War Canada: The Making of a National Security State, 1945-1957* (Toronto: University of Toronto Press, 1996), xi.

13   Canada, House of Commons, *Debates*, 27 November 1952, 136-37. On this period, see also David Jay Bercuson, *True Patriot: The Life of Brooke Claxton 1898-1960* (Toronto: University of Toronto Press, 1993).

air defence plan, but two errors made early in the life of the project all but sealed the Arrow's fate.

The first error occurred in December 1953, at the time when a Cabinet Defence Committee's recommendation was approved for a $27 million contract awarded to Avro Aircraft Limited to undertake development of two prototypes for a successor aircraft to the Royal Canadian Air Force's subsonic interceptor, the Avro Canada CF-100 Canuck.[14] It was envisaged that 500-600 Arrows, at a per-unit cost of $1.5-$2 million, would be required to re-equip nine regular and ten reserve squadrons by 1958-59. This was considered both a sufficient number to justify setting up a production line, and achievable within anticipated defence budgets. In this decision, however, lay the seeds of the Arrow's undoing, for neither the Cabinet Defence Committee nor the Chiefs of Staff Committee foresaw that the auxiliary squadrons would be incapable of operating such a sophisticated interceptor. The Chiefs of Staff Committee certainly knew at the time that the Arrow would be highly advanced, but the prestige of designing and building a tailor-made, state-of-the-art interceptor appears to have blinded them to the implications of its performance requirements.

By 1957 the government and the military would reap what they had sown: the auxiliary squadrons were disbanded, but the loss was not balanced by an increased number of regular squadrons. Thus, the original production run was cut by more than two-thirds. In order to achieve the economies of scale necessary for production, sales to or collaboration with the United States or Britain, which had previously been half-heartedly pursued, now became imperative. The possibility of American or British involvement was always unrealistic, however, and had, in fact, been dismissed early on by the Royal Canadian Air Force and the Defence Research Board as unnecessary. Both the United States and Britain had expressed encouragement and admiration for the Arrow from 1954 on, but at no time did they express any interest in participating in the project. Nor did the Cabinet Defence Committee have any illusions about the possibility of selling the aircraft, especially to the United States. "It seemed highly doubtful," the Cabinet Defence Committee had agreed in March 1955, "that the US would purchase any CF-105s produced in Canada."[15]

There were two reasons the United States would never purchase the Arrow. The first was made clear during a December 1955 Cabinet meeting when Ralph Campney, the Minister of National Defence, described a recent meeting he had had with Donald Quarles, the American Secretary of the Air Force: "Mr. Quarles and his advisors had a high opinion of the aircraft but felt it would be impossible for the US government to participate in developing it, or to commit themselves to buy it, because of the strong influence of the US aircraft industry in Washington."[16] Though the United States had been generous after the Second World War in its efforts to promote a Canadian high-technology aircraft industry and coordinate defence production, it had always maintained that the establishment of Canada as an alternative source of supply stopped short of the United States procuring front-line aircraft.[17] The Liberal

---

14   See Canada, House of Commons, *Sessional Papers* 837, 838, nos. 198, 198a-d (1959) for further contractual and financial information on the project.

15   DHH/DND, Records of the Chairman, Chiefs of Staff and Chief of Defence Staff, the Raymont Collection (CSC Papers), series three, 73/1233, Cabinet Defence Committee Minutes, Decisions, and Conclusions (CDC), file 1329, 3 March 1955, 3.

16   NA, RG2, Records of the Privy Council Office, Cabinet Conclusions (CC), vol. 2658, 7 December 1955, 12. In American military parlance, this is referred to as the "not-invented-here" syndrome.

17   See Lawrence R. Aronsen, "'A Leading Arsenal of Democracy': American Rearmament and the

government knew this had been the case with the Canuck, and would certainly be the case with the Arrow.

The second reason the United States would never have purchased the Arrow may be found in the RCAF's original desire to develop an aircraft perfectly matched to its operational requirements. The Arrow, after all, was designed around Canada's peculiar geographic needs. It was a two-seat, twin-engine, all-weather, supersonic interceptor. The second seat was intended for a navigator/radar operator on account of the lack of a sophisticated ground environment such as existed in the American air defence command. The second engine was a safety measure against the prospect of engine failure over the North, far from one of Canada's dispersed air bases. These all-Canadian features, rather than the America aircraft lobby, conspired to make the Arrow considerably more costly than its contemporaries, and unsuitable to American needs.[18] In examining the lack of foreign sales, Julius Lukasiewicz concluded that the lesson of the Arrow experience for Canada is obvious: "The key to effective participation in the aerospace enterprise is industrial collaboration on an international level. And, ideally, such collaboration should involve Canadian firms over the whole cycle of research, development, manufacturing, and worldwide marketing for a component or range of products."[19]

The second fatal error that sealed the Arrow's fate entailed the various decisions to accelerate and expand the program. Michael Brown, in analysing the politics of weapons acquisition programs in the United States, has stated:

> Acquisition programs run into trouble when they try to advance technology and employ concurrency at the same time. Powerful strategic and bureaucratic forces [have] led American military organizations to set their performance requirements far beyond the state of the art and to push their programs as fast as possible. The result, all too frequently, [has been] disastrous from an acquisition standpoint.[20]

Brown's assessment of the American experience could not be more pertinent to the Arrow case. The promoters of the Arrow within the national security bureaucracy all wanted the aircraft to be on the leading edge of aeronautical and technological design. And, because of the threat posed by Soviet atomic and hydrogen bomb developments and the so-called "bomber gap" between the East and the West, they wanted the Arrow deployed as soon as possible.

These twin imperatives led the Chiefs of Staff Committee to stress the need to accelerate the Arrow program. In March 1955, Cabinet authorized the adoption of a new American method of aircraft development known as Cook-Craigie. Cook-Craigie entailed the ordering and testing of forty development and pre-production Arrows delivered off an already established production line instead of the two hand-built prototypes. The Chiefs of Staff Committee estimated that the length of the project would be shortened and that overall costs would be reduced, even though

Continental Integration of the Canadian Aircraft Industry, 1948-1953," *The International History Review* 13, no. 3 (August 1991): 481-501.

18   Canada, House of Commons, *Special Committee on Defence Expenditures, Minutes of Proceedings and Evidence*, no. 5 (20 May 1960), 127.

19   Julius Lukasiewicz, "Canada's Encounter with High-Speed Aeronautics," *Technology and Culture: The International Quarterly Journal of the Society for the History of Technology* 27, no. 2 (April 1986): 257.

20   Michael E. Brown, *Flying Blind: The Politics Of The US Strategic Bomber Program* (Ithaca, NY: Cornell University Press, 1992), x.

initial costs would rise substantially. At the same time, Cabinet approval was also secured to include a Canadian-designed engine, the PS-13 Iroquois, designed by Orenda Engines Limited,[21] because Avro and the Royal Canadian Air Force were not satisfied with existing foreign engines. In the end, Cook-Craigie did little to accelerate deployment of the Arrow, and meanwhile it inflated costs. However, it was believed to be tantamount to a production commitment from the Liberal government, which was exactly what Avro and the RCAF most wanted from Cook-Craigie.

Thus, the Arrow program's costs had risen tenfold to $261 million in two years, and by September 1955 Avro was asking for an additional $59 million. Unnerved, the St. Laurent government ordered a thorough reappraisal of the Arrow program. Though cancellation was one of the options considered in the resultant report, in the end the Cabinet recommended continuing the project, albeit at a slower pace. In December 1955 Cabinet approved limiting the project to eleven initial Arrows, with a spending cap of $170 million over the next three years, which would delay deployment until 1960-61.[22] However, even though the government would thereafter attempt to monitor the expenditures on the project, costs would continue to escalate, in part because of subsequent decisions to develop the Arrow's electronics system and armaments.

In 1956, to arm both the Arrow and the Canuck, the RCAF joined the United States Navy in the Sparrow II missile program at an initial cost of $65 million, but when the Americans indicated in March 1956 that they had decided not to produce the Sparrow II, Canada in effect took over the entire project. Also in 1956, an initial $7 million contract for the ASTRA I electronics system was awarded to an inexperienced company because it alone was prepared to attempt to meet the RCAF's criteria. Cheaper, proven "off-the-shelf" missiles and electronic systems had been adamantly recommended by Avro, but these were considered not good enough for the Royal Canadian Air Force. The latter's successful insistence on, as Danford Middlemiss termed it, an "all-singing, all-dancing, gold-plated fighter"[23] had thus expanded the Arrow program from one to four advanced systems, and the costs of Sparrow II and especially ASTRA I would grow exponentially. The noted aviation historian Bill Gunston perhaps put it best when he wrote:

> Time and time again the history of military aircraft procurement has recorded a program that could have delivered 99% of the requirement within timescale and budget but which escalated away in a fruitless chase after the missing 1%.[24]

In February 1957, Cabinet approved cutting the eleven initial aircraft back to eight, with a spending cap of $217 million — higher than the previous limit — which would now delay deployment until 1961-62. Despite Cabinet's warning that the project could be halted or abandoned at appropriate stages if this was found to be

---

21   Avro and Orenda were divisions of A.V. Roe Canada Limited, their parent company.

22   A lengthy but extremely useful report. See NA, Records of the Department of National Defence, RG24, 83-84/226, vol. 20886, file CSC 10:9, pt. 4, Canada, Manufacture of Aircraft, 1948-1964, (Top Secret) 1948-1955," Report By The Working Group To The Ad Hoc Departmental Committee For The Reappraisal Of The CF105 Development Program, n.d.

23   Danford W. Middlemiss, "A Pattern of Cooperation: The Case of the Canadian-American Defence Production and Development Sharing Agreements, 1958-1963" (Ph.D. dissertation, University of Toronto, 1975), 188.

24   Bill Gunston, *Early Supersonic Fighters of the West* (Shepperton, UK: Ian Allen, 1976), 123.

expedient or necessary,[25] the project's costs were spiralling out of control. However, the St. Laurent government was unwilling to take the step that C.D. Howe, the Liberal Minister of Defence Production — who admitted back in 1955 to being given "the shudders"[26] by the magnitude of the Arrow program — would later acknowledge should have been taken: termination. Such a politically risky decision would have to be put off until the Liberals had won the 1957 federal election.

If the Liberals had been returned to government in 1957, there is little doubt that they would have cancelled the Arrow program and that an increasingly concerned Chiefs of Staff Committee would have acquiesced in the decision. But to everyone's surprise, the Liberals did not win, and Diefenbaker and Major-General George Pearkes, his Minister of National Defence, inherited the Arrow program along with a bedevilling host of other defence problems.[27] And the Arrow refused to die just yet, for, as James Stevenson has written:

> There are really only two phases to a big military program: too early to tell, and too late to stop. Program advocates like to keep bad news covered until they have spent so much money that they can advance the sunk-cost argument; that it's too late too cancel the program because we've spent too much already.[28]

The powerful Chairman of the Chiefs of Staff Committee, General Charles Foulkes, later complained that "The new Conservative Government, particularly the Prime Minister, was allergic to the procedures used by the previous administration."[29] Yet the Diefenbaker government continued to accept the advice proffered by the Chiefs of Staff Committee through the Cabinet Defence Committee in almost exactly the same manner the St. Laurent government had. It is true that Diefenbaker did not entirely trust the Chiefs of Staff Committee, lumping them in with other "Pearsonalities" who had served the previous government, but he trusted Pearkes, and Pearkes trusted Foulkes, and Foulkes and the other service chiefs were still persuaded by the RCAF's arguments.

Thus, in October 1957, Cabinet approved the Cabinet Defence Committee's recommendation to continue the Arrow program at a cost of an additional $173 million for twelve months, whereupon the project would be reviewed again after the Arrow's airworthiness had been proven in its first flight. With a minority government facing a budget deficit and the danger of a recession, this was an easy decision for the Chiefs of Staff Committee to obtain because it suited Cabinet politically. But, as H. Basil Robinson later wrote, Diefenbaker "carried the worry [about the Arrow] with him around the world — he always hoped that postponements might beget miracles — but the inevitable could not be stemmed."[30]

Unfortunately for the Arrow, in April 1957 Duncan Sandys, the British Minister

---

25   NA, CC, vol. 2657, 3 March 1955, 4.

26   Canada, House of Commons, *Debates*, 28 June 1955, 5380.

27   On this period see Reginald Roy, *For Most Conspicuous Bravery: A Biography of Major General George R. Pearkes, V.C., Through Two World Wars* (Vancouver: University of British Columbia Press, 1977).

28   James P. Stevenson, *The Pentagon Paradox. The Development of the F-18 Hornet* (Annapolis: Naval Institute Press, 1993), 305.

29   DHH/DND, Foulkes Papers, 16.

30   H. Basil Robinson, *Diefenbaker's World: A Populist in Foreign Affairs* (Toronto: University of Toronto Press, 1989), 85.

of Defence, released a highly influential White Paper which declared that the manned aircraft had been rendered obsolete by the guided missile.[31] As if to drive home Sandys's point, on the day in October 1957 that the first Arrow rolled out of its hanger in Malton, Ontario, the Soviet Union launched *Sputnik* into orbit, symbolically driving the Arrow from the headlines. Overnight, fears of a "bomber gap" between a stunned West and the East were replaced with fears of a "missile gap" as Western intelligence confirmed that the principal Soviet threat to North America would now come from intercontinental ballistic missiles. Accordingly, the strategic rationale behind Western defence began shifting from an emphasis on defence to deterrence.[32] The result was that "all over the capitalist world," as Robert Bothwell, Ian Drummond, and John English noted, "the smaller airframe makers and the 'national' airframe industries were in trouble"[33] as countries cancelled aircraft programs and those aircraft companies that were able to, shifted their resources into missiles.

Meanwhile, the fragile military consensus on the Arrow program had begun to break down in the face of the diminishing threat and decreasing defence budgets. One must keep in mind that at this time the Royal Canadian Air Force, the premier service, was allotted almost 50 percent of the defence budget,[34] and inter-service rivalry had been intensifying over the years as Foulkes and the navy and army chiefs realized that, if the Arrow program went ahead as planned, there would be little money to replace ageing frigates or to acquire new armoured vehicles and tactical nuclear missiles. As Lieutenant-General Howard Graham, then Chief of the General Staff, later wrote:

> Air Marshal Slemon, Air Force Chief from 1953 to 1957, and Air Marshal Campbell, who succeeded Slemon in 1957, as one might expect, continued to support the program even at prohibitive costs that consumed the greater part of any reasonable defence budget. The Navy and Army, through their chiefs — Admiral Mainguy (followed by DeWolf) and Lieutenant-General Guy Simonds (followed by Graham) — and the Chairman of the Chiefs of Staff Committee, General Foulkes, argued against it.[35]

Not only had inter-service differences surfaced but intra-service tensions within the ranks of the Royal Canadian Air Force. In addition to procuring a new interceptor, the Royal Canadian Air Force also had to re-equip the aircraft of its European-based squadrons for the new nuclear strike-reconnaissance role and procure nuclear-tipped surface-to-air missiles for continental defence. Campbell and Slemon, the latter now Deputy Commander of the North American Defence Command, were faced with the task of reconciling the equipment demands of two rival groups of

---

31   See *Defence: Outline of Future Policy*, Cmnd. 124 (April 1957). The United States and the Soviet Union were less enthusiastic than the British in their embrace of the missile, but they could afford to procure both kinds of weapons systems.

32   The American national intelligence estimates were largely based on U-2 spy plane over-flights of the Soviet Union. See Donald P. Steury (ed.), *Intentions And Capabilities: Estimates On Soviet Strategic Forces, 1950-1983* (Washington: Center For The Study Of Intelligence, Central Intelligence Agency, 1996).

33   Robert Bothwell, Ian Drummond, and John English, *Canada Since 1945: Power, Politics, and Provincialism* (Toronto: University of Toronto Press, 1981), 244.

34   See Jeff Rankin-Lowe, "A Decade of Air Power. Royal Canadian Air Force 1950-1959: Part I and II," *Wings Of Fame: The Journal Of Classic Combat Aircraft*, 2 and 3 (1996): 142-57.

35   Howard Graham, *Citizen And Soldier: The Memoirs of Lieutenant-General Howard Graham* (Toronto: McClelland and Stewart, 1987), 237.

officers, those committed to the North Atlantic Treaty Organization and those committed to the North American Air Defence Command.[36] It looked to be an impossible task within the existing defence budget.

As the end of the twelve-month extension approached, the Chiefs of Staff Committee debated alternative air defence plans which would see both the Arrow produced in some quantity — thirty-seven, sixty, or 169, with or without ASTRA I and Sparrow II, at a potential overall maximum cost of over $2.2 billion — and the other service requirements satisfied, but this proved a fruitless task. In August 1958, the Chiefs of Staff Committee and Pearkes recommended to the Cabinet Defence Committee that, owing to the exorbitant costs of the Arrow program, there was only one course of action left: cancel the project and buy from or cost-share with the United States the two Bomarc-B nuclear surface-to-air missile installations, their complementary ground environment, additional heavy and gap-filler radars, and approximately 100 comparable American-built interceptors. Foulkes later wrote:

> There would [have been] definite budgetary advantage in purchasing a United States aircraft, since USAF would meet all development charges, take all the risks, and sell to Canada at a reduced price made possible by keeping their production line going a bit longer to satisfy Canadian needs. There was a distinct advantage of being able to assess the cost of Canada's air defence commitment instead of having every few months to face the harassment of the A.V. Roe Company for more and more development funds.[37]

To a Conservative government elected on the promise of decreased expenditures and lower taxes, the Arrow figures were shocking. In response, the Cabinet Defence Committee ordered the Chiefs of Staff Committee to prepare a reappraisal report outlining all project decisions made from 1952 until 1958; essentially, they asked the Chiefs of Staff Committee to provide evidence that their expenditure projections were accurate. Although the Chiefs of Staff Committee had some qualms about the propriety of furnishing confidential information about a previous administration, the report was quickly put together and the bleak situation was confirmed.[38] The Cabinet Defence Committee recommended that Pearkes's and the Chiefs of Staff Committee's recommendation be approved, with one exception — the final decision on cancellation of the Arrow program was referred to Cabinet.

At no time during the lengthy discussions that occurred at six Cabinet meetings that followed in August and September 1958 did anyone seriously challenge the military and financial imperatives which had led to the Chief of Staff Committee's recommendation to cancel. However, Cabinet now became preoccupied with the ramifications such a decision would have on the economy, on national pride, and consequently on their own political fortunes. In September 1958 a decision was finally reached; Diefenbaker announced that the two Bomarc-B bases would be built, and eventually cost-shared on a one-third Canadian, two-thirds American basis. The ASTRA I and Sparrow II programs were also cancelled.[39]

---

36   Roy, *For Most Conspicuous Bravery*, 314-15, 321-22.

37   DHH/DND, Foulkes Papers, 8-9.

38   Another lengthy and extremely useful report. See DHH/DND, CSC Papers, series one, 73/1223, file 632, CF-105 Aircraft 01/30/58-08/19/58, "Report On The Development Of The CF105 Aircraft and Associated Weapon Systems, 1952-1958," (CSC Report), 19 August 1958.

39   Diefenbaker's 23 September 1958 statement is reproduced in Jon B. McLin, *Canada's Changing*

Even though the Diefenbaker government had secured the largest electoral mandate in Canadian history and had accepted the Cabinet Defence Committee's arguments about the need to cancel the Arrow program, political considerations were now paramount. The danger of a recession coupled with an unemployment problem in the Toronto area caused the government to defer a final decision for yet another six months. The Arrow was dead, but it was still on life support. Donald Fleming, the Minister of Finance, later wrote that "as an unemployment relief measure it must [have been] one of the most costly on record."[40] The delay of the inevitable may also have been owing in part to the lobbying efforts of three groups of Conservatives: the Toronto-area Members of Parliament, Ontario Premier Leslie Frost, and many of A.V. Roe's shareholders.[41] Cabinet hoped that the deferral would be a signal to Avro and Orenda to get their house in order in preparation for cancellation; instead, both saw what they wanted to see and concluded that the Arrow program had been granted a reprieve.

By 1959, five Arrows had flown and the sixth, fitted with the Iroquois engine, was being readied for its anticipated world speed record-breaking flight. Thanks to a redesign of the aircraft to accommodate a less expensive electronics system and missile, the overall per unit cost of the Arrow had fallen from over $12.6 million to $7.8 million. However, few in either the national security bureaucracy or the government appear to have taken seriously Avro's promise to deliver the aircraft at this lower cost. Furthermore, as Cabinet noted, "It would be better to cancel it now than to be confronted with no more work for Avro, and the other companies involved, after production of 100 aircraft was drawing to an end in 1961 or 1962. It was unwise to encourage the aircraft industry to continue to produce equipment that could quite well be obsolete by the time it was available."[42]

In the interim, Pearkes made an eleventh-hour attempt to sell the Arrow to the United States and Britain. James Eayrs later joked that, "had the Soviet Union itself come through with an offer, the Canadian government might have been tempted to accept."[43] The Americans and the British once again declined Canada's offer, but not before the latter caused Pearkes consternation when they tried to sell him instead their own ill-fated TSR-2 attack aircraft. The Americans were not unsympathetic to Canada's plight. At a January 1958 meeting, they had reiterated that they had no interest in purchasing the Arrow, as they were going ahead with their even more advanced F-108, the cost of which made the Arrow "look like something which might be picked up in a department store."[44] However, James Douglas, the American Secretary of the Air Force, then suggested that the United States could possibly

Defence Policy, 1957-1963: The Problems of a Middle Power in Alliance (Baltimore: The Johns Hopkins Press, 1967).

40   Donald M. Fleming, *So Very Near: The Political Memoirs of the Honourable Donald M. Fleming,* vol. 1 (Toronto: McClelland and Stewart Limited, 1985), 416.

41   See Roger Graham, *Old Man Ontario: Leslie H. Frost* (Toronto: University of Toronto Press, 1990).

42   NA, CC, vol. 1899, 3 September 1958, 3.

43   James Eayrs, "Canadian Defence Policies Since 1867," in Canada, House of Commons, *Special Studies Prepared for the Special Committee of The House of Commons on Matters Relating to Defence, Supplement 1964-1965,* 20.

44   DHH/DND, CSC Report, Appendix G, Annex I. The North American Aviation F-108 Rapier would be cancelled in September 1959 for much the same reasons as the Arrow. See also J.L. Granatstein, "The myth of the broken Arrow," *The Globe And Mail,* 11 January 1997, D2.

purchase several squadrons of Arrows and give them to the Royal Canadian Air Force. This offer was rejected by Norman Robertson, Canadian Ambassador in Washington, as being politically unacceptable to a country that had never accepted military aid. As J.L. Granatstein wrote, the truth was — and had always been — that "if Canada wanted to fly the Arrow, it would have to pay the shot."[45]

By February 1959, the six-month extension was nearing an end, and Avro was once again seeking permission to exceed the spending cap. Cabinet had met to discuss the Arrow program nine times in January and February 1959. Robert Bryce, the Clerk of the Privy Council and "almost the only mandarin Diefenbaker trusted,"[46] described these Cabinet debates as "frustrated, not heated, but not entirely calm."[47] Cabinet minutes clearly indicate that Diefenbaker and his ministers agonized over the effects such a decision would have on the economy, on the aircraft industry, on the perception of Canada's commitment to its alliances, and on the country's sense of achievement and sovereignty. But such nationalistic viewpoints were buried by the cold, hard financial and strategic facts coming from the Chiefs of Staff Committee.

On 20 February 1959 — "Black Friday" — Diefenbaker announced to the House of Commons that the Arrow and Iroquois programs were terminated.[48] Publicly, the Liberal Opposition, led by Defence Critic Paul Hellyer, attacked the government on how the decision was executed rather than the decision itself.[49] Privately, in a letter to Opposition Leader Lester Pearson a month before the cancellation, C.D. Howe admitted that the Liberals would have done likewise because, as he put it, "there is no doubt in my mind that the CF-105 should be terminated — costs are completely out of hand. … The proper line of attack should be directed to the government's temporizing and fumbling with this decision."[50] In the press, Toronto-area news-papers, not surprisingly, condemned the Diefenbaker government. Theirs was the story of the ruination of two companies on the cutting edge of aerospace technology, the dispersal of a team of highly skilled engineers and technicians, and the untimely end of a great national project. Outside of Toronto, however, editorial and public opinion was largely in favour of the cancellation, and applauded Diefenbaker for his political courage in finally killing the obsolete and costly boondoggle. The Arrow myth that would later enthral Canadians had not yet arisen. In 1959, its termination was a southern Ontario story, and of little concern to other Canadians.[51]

---

45 J.L. Granatstein, *Canada 1957-1967: The Years of Uncertainty and Innovation, the Canadian Centenary Series*, ed. Ramsey Cook, vol. 19 (Toronto: McClelland and Stewart Limited, 1986), 107.

46 J.L. Granatstein, *The Ottawa Men: The Civil Service Mandarins 1935-1957* (Toronto: Oxford University Press, 1982), 270.

47 R.B. Bryce, Ottawa, Ontario, to Russell Isinger, LS, 17 August 1991, 1. At one time an Arrow advocate, Bryce had changed his mind by 1958. See also DCC, John G. Diefenbaker Papers, MG01, VI, vol. 55, file 171, Arrow Conf., Defence Expenditures — Aircraft — Arrow — Confidential, 1958, 1960, R. B. Bryce, "Memorandum for the Prime Minister. Re: the 105 Problem," 5 September 1958.

48 Diefenbaker's 20 February 1959 statement is reproduced in McLin, *Canada's Changing Defence Policy*.

49 Ironically, this was the first debate in the House of Commons which had occurred on the Arrow program; it had only rarely been mentioned prior to cancellation. See Canada, House of Commons, *Debates*, 23 February 1959, Labour Crisis in the Aircraft Industry; 2 March 1959, Defence Policy, Planning, and Production; 3 March 1959, Defence Policy, Planning, and Production; and 2 July, 1959, Supply — National Defence.

50 NA, Clarence Decatur Howe Papers, MG 27, III, B20 vol. 109, file 75-7 Political — General, Mike Pearson to C.D. Howe, 21 January 1959.

51 A vocal press critic of the project was Blair Fraser of *Maclean's*. See Blair Fraser, "What led Canada

The Chiefs of Staff Committee were relieved that the decision had finally been made, but they were disturbed by the government's reliance on military rather than economic arguments to justify the cancellation. Jon McLin has concluded that this disingenuousness on Diefenbaker's part stemmed from his desire to associate the military with the decision.[52] In the RCAF's opinion, although the bomber threat had lessened, it still represented a threat which had to be met by interceptors as well as missiles. The Chiefs of Staff Committee doubted Diefenbaker's vague promise of replacement interceptors, and they were correct to have such doubts. Purchase of an American interceptor immediately after cancellation was politically unacceptable, and it would be 1961 before the service would receive sixty-six surplus American CF-101B Voodoos. In many ways this situation was the Royal Canadian Air Force's own fault: "devoted to its aeroplanes like cavalry to its horses,"[53] the force had chosen to fiercely support the dual procurement goals of obtaining both missiles and the world's finest interceptor, inopportunely at a time of financial, political and military uncertainty. This strategy had ultimately proven detrimental to their stated number one priority — obtaining an interceptor.[54] As James Eayrs lamented, "For a force for which the sky was the environment, rather than the limit, nothing [had] seemed impossible … pride led to hubris, hubris to the CF-105."[55]

John Porter later wrote: "The Arrow signified a coming of age of the Canadian aircraft industry. It proved to be an extraordinarily costly symbol."[56] This was certainly the case for Avro and Orenda which, much like the government, had done little to prepare for this contingency, although there was probably little the companies could have done at this point, precariously dependent as they were on a single government contract. Much of what they had done — including threatening a politically sensitive administration with massive layoffs, and hiring a Liberal advertising firm to conduct an intense public lobbying campaign — had been counterproductive. Essentially, the companies had operated as if they were crown corporations, a situation which Fred Smye, the President of Avro, later admitted to when he wrote, "Avro and Orenda were the industrial arm of the RCAF and servants of the government, as is any purely defence contractor. The companies had fulfilled this role solely from their inception and for a period of fifteen years."[57] Diefenbaker may have been correct when he later stated that "the company seemed horror-struck at ever having to compete in a normal marketplace situation."[58] Michael Bliss was even harsher in his judgement: "The

to junk the Arrow," *Maclean's*, 25 October 1958, 2, and Crawford Gordon, Jr.'s angry response, "We should and will go on building Arrows," *Maclean's*, 20 December 1958, 8.

52   McLin, *Canada's Changing Defence Policy*, 84.

53   "The Avro Nettle Patch," *The Economist*, 28 February 1959, 790.

54   Robert H. Clark, "Canadian Weapons Acquisition: A Case Study of the Bomarc Missile" (MA thesis, Royal Military College, 1983), 45.

55   James Eayrs, *In Defence of Canada: Peacemaking and Deterrence* (Toronto: University of Toronto Press, 1972), 123.

56   John Porter, *The Vertical Mosaic: An Analysis of Social Class and Power in Canada* (Toronto: University of Toronto Press, 1965), 551.

57   Fred Smye, *Canadian Aviation and the Avro Arrow* (Oakville, ON: Randy Smye, 1989), 83.

58   John G. Diefenbaker, *One Canada: Memoirs of the Right Honourable John G. Diefenbaker: The Tumultuous Years, 1962-1967*, vol. 3 (Toronto: Macmillan, 1977), 38.

evidence suggests that A.V. Roe was a classic promotional company ... built on wild optimism, taxpayers' money, media gullibility, and Canadians' naïve patriotism."[59]

While over 14,000 workers were laid off on "Black Friday," with many eventually leaving for jobs with other Canadian, British, or American companies or agencies, the diversified parent company, A.V. Roe, survived, and still operates under the name Hawker-Siddeley Canada Limited.[60] Neither did Canada's aerospace sector vanish with the Arrow's cancellation, largely owing to another Diefenbaker government initiative, the Defence Production Sharing Arrangement of 1959. In an arrangement analogous to the Canada-United States Auto Pact, Canada traded much of its domestic design capability for a large slice of a bigger American defence pie.[61] As Robert Bothwell has observed, "Canadian defence needs were satisfied with less costly American aircraft, and Canadian defence industrial needs were met by the conclusion of a defence production-sharing agreement with the United States, and by the stipulation that weapons bought by Canada involve some manufacturing in Canada."[62] Defence, like foreign policy, proved to be the art of the possible.

The existing Arrows were offered to several aeronautical agencies for use as research test beds, but they were rejected because it was simply too expensive to keep such a small number of aircraft flying. The six complete aircraft and the thirty-one other Arrows in various stages of completion were then stripped of classified and valuable material, and sawed and blow-torched into scrap metal — not because of Diefenbaker's vindictiveness, as has often been claimed, but simply, and sadly, owing to the standard operating procedures of the Department of Defence Production.

In conclusion, as John Holmes correctly summarized:

> When the Conservative party came to power in 1957 they proceeded without question to the culmination of continental defence association by hastily approving NORAD, and when they had buried the great nationalist Liberal adventure in aircraft building, the Arrow, they promptly sought in Washington a new agreement of defence production sharing. ... A Liberal government would almost certainly have done all the same things.[63]

Thus, the Avro Canada CF-105 Arrow passed into myth, where it will probably soldier on far longer than if it had actually entered service.

---

59 Michael Bliss, *Northern Enterprise: Five Centuries of Canadian Business* (Toronto: McClelland and Stewart, 1987), 475-76.

60 See Harry McDougall, "Black Friday: Five Years Later," *Saturday Night*, March 1964, 13-15.

61 See Danford W. Middlemiss, "Economic Defence Co-operation with the United States 1940-1963," in Kim Richard Nossal (ed.), *An Acceptance of Paradox: Essays on Canadian Diplomacy in Honour of John W. Holmes* (Toronto: Canadian Institute of International Affairs, 1982), 97; also in Norman Hillmer (ed.), *Partners Nevertheless: Canadian-American Relations in the Twentieth Century* (Toronto: Copp Clark Pitman, 1989), 167-93.

62 Robert Bothwell, "Defence and Industry in Canada, 1935-1970," in Benjamin Franklin Cooling (ed.), *War, Business, and World Military-Industrial Complexes* (Port Washington, NY: Kennikat Press, 1981), 117-18.

63 John W. Holmes, *The Shaping of Peace: Canada and the Search for World Order, 1943-1957*, vol. 2 (Toronto: University of Toronto Press, 1983), 284.

JOHN DIEFENBAKER AS PRIME MINISTER: THE RECORD RE-EXAMINED

Patrick Kyba and Wendy Green-Finlay

Some people labelled John Diefenbaker a failure as Prime Minister even before he completed his time in office, and this judgement continues to linger in the Canadian public's perception. Diefenbaker has been disparaged by journalists, historians, and political scientists alike for not achieving lasting success either in government or in politics — this despite his staggering electoral victory in 1958. Little mention is made of his "Vision for Canada," which not only helped produce that triumph but also inspired the New National Policy, the grain sales to the Communist bloc that rejuvenated the prairie economy and resuscitated the Progressive Conservative party in that region, or any of his successes in other realms of endeavour.

The intent of this paper is to examine the political leadership of John George Diefenbaker between 1957 and 1963 in an attempt to determine why this limited and often negative assessment of Diefenbaker as leader has come to dominate Canadian attitudes toward him. We will argue that the circumstances of his spectacular rise to and fall from power have overshadowed his accomplishments in office and, further, that the regional nature of much of his legacy has led to an unbalanced and unflattering portrayal of his prime ministerial career.

ACCENTUATING THE NEGATIVE

Few, if any, political figures have stirred more controversy than John Diefenbaker. Those who have written about him — and there have been many — have found it impossible to discuss the man and his career dispassionately. Until the publication of Denis Smith's *Rogue Tory: The Life and Legend of John G. Diefenbaker*, little effort had been expended in attempts to find a middle ground, and the balance has been tilted significantly toward the negative. Ungenerous judgements abound, the tone having been set by Peter Newman in *Renegade in Power*, published a scant six months after the Conservatives' electoral defeat in 1963. Newman depicted Diefenbaker as "promise unfulfilled" and his era as "a tragedy of missed opportunities."[1] According to

---

1   Peter C. Newman, *Renegade in Power* (Toronto: McClelland and Stewart, 1963), xi, 3.

Newman, "No other Canadian politician in this century could claim the emotional conquest of a generation; yet no Prime Minister ever disillusioned his disciples more. ... He gave the people a leadership cult, without leadership."[2]

The passage of time has not lessened the intensity of the negative sentiment felt about him. Michael Bliss, in *Right Honourable Men*, described Diefenbaker rather nastily as "a Nijinsky figure in the title role, a demagogue of dance, spinning and pointing and shaking,"[3] and Robert Fulford recently characterized him as "a dreadful politician and a detestable human being. I am ashamed that he was Prime Minister."[4] It would appear that these and other commentators, most of them from central Canada, tried to fit John Diefenbaker into their image of what a "successful" party leader and Prime Minister should be. When he did not satisfy the requirements of their model, they branded him a failure.

Diefenbaker's failure as a Prime Minister seems to have been viewed as an outgrowth of the type of personality and life experiences that he brought to the high office he occupied; his handling of particular issues; the expectations he created but did not satisfy; and his Saskatchewan/prairie mind set which placed him outside the traditional social, economic, political, and administrative mainstream. Let us look at each of these in turn.

Few would dispute the claim that John Diefenbaker was egocentric. He had a strong belief in his destiny, was deeply concerned with his place in history, and tended to view events through the filter of how they would affect his political standing. He loved the limelight, and was suspicious of anyone who appeared to threaten his position. The magnificent oratory which contributed so much to the electoral breakthroughs of 1957 and 1958 focussed attention on him and, after the massive victory in 1958, he became convinced of his unique understanding of the desires of the "common people." He came to personify the Progressive Conservative party — which did him no harm as long as he went from success to success in policy and administration. But he did little to create a team spirit among his Cabinet ministers, and when difficulties began to beset the government, he alone had to accept responsibility.

Diefenbaker's career as a criminal lawyer also proved something of a detriment. He was inclined to see people and issues in stark terms — for him or against him, guilty or innocent. This outlook coupled with his determination to win all battles, large or small, eventually cost him the party leadership, and to some extent his reputation as well. In this context, it must be remembered that Diefenbaker had virtually no managerial experience when he became Prime Minister. His attitude toward effective governance was that it "was as much a matter of inspiration as it was of administration."[5] He preferred consensus decision making, and was prepared to wait an inordinate length of time for consensus to emerge in Cabinet. When it did not, Diefenbaker too often had to act in less than propitious circumstances.[6] It is not

2   Ibid., ix.

3   Michael Bliss, *Right Honourable Men: the Descent of Canadian Politics from Macdonald to Mulroney* (Toronto: Harper Collins, 1994), 185.

4   Robert Fulford, *The Globe and Mail*, 31 July 1996.

5   John G. Diefenbaker, *One Canada: Memoirs of the Rt. Hon. John G. Diefenbaker*, vol. 2 (Toronto: Macmillan, 1976), 13.

6   For a fuller discussion of decision making in the Diefenbaker governments, see Patrick Kyba, *Alvin: A Biography of the Hon. Alvin Hamilton, P.C.* (Regina: Canadian Plains Research Center, 1989), 201-5.

surprising that, within three years of his taking office, the press began to characterize his government as one of indecision and drift.

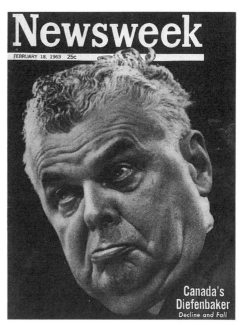

The major issues that caused opinion to turn against Diefenbaker were the cancellation of the Avro Arrow, the removal of James Coyne as Governor of the Bank of Canada, the devaluation of the dollar, and the refusal to equip the Canadian armed forces with nuclear weapons. These issues both created and fuelled a crisis of confidence in the Diefenbaker government, and led to a great deal of negative press. Of the four, only the decision not to proceed with the Arrow had a direct impact on the electorate, in that it cost a large number of people their jobs. Taken together, however, the government's decisions on these four issues earned it a reputation for indecisiveness and mismanagement which Diefenbaker never overcame. In the case of the Arrow, the government

Diefenbaker with "horns" as he appeared on the cover of Newsweek *in 1963 (courtesy the Diefenbaker Center Library).*

took the better part of two years to arrive at the same conclusion its Liberal predecessor had reached (but did not make public) before the 1957 election. With respect to the Coyne affair, Diefenbaker and his "expansionist" colleagues in Cabinet concluded early on that the Bank's tight credit policy stood in the way of their plans for economic growth, yet they waited months before firing this "unregenerate Grit"[7] — long past the time when such a step might have provided convincing evidence that the government would brook no opposition to its development policies. The Coyne affair, in turn, helped spark a run on the dollar which the government did not halt until the middle of the 1962 election campaign. This confirmed the suspicion that the government was not competent to manage the economy, and it damaged the party severely in a region of the country — urban Canada, especially southern Ontario — that was already uncomfortable with John Diefenbaker as Prime Minister.

The ground lost then could not be recaptured in the months prior to the 1963 election because of the Prime Minister's handling of the issue of nuclear arms for Canada. In general, his record in this area was one of making commitments, then refusing to accept the consequences. Specifically, the government failed to meet Canada's obligations to its allies, especially the United States, under the terms of the NATO and North American Air Defence agreements. The Prime Minister's refusal to honour these commitments not only antagonized the allies but also split the Cabinet. This, in turn, caused the defeat of the government in the House of Commons, provided the major issue which led to the Liberal victory in the 1963 election, and nearly brought his leadership of the Progressive Conservative party to an end. Unfortunately for John Diefenbaker, his failure over this and other issues came to overshadow his successes in other areas.

---

7   Diefenbaker, *One Canada*, vol. 2, 274.

Head and shoulders photo of Diefenbaker with "halo" (lights from chandelier in background, 3 November 1959 (courtesy the Diefenbaker Centre, MG01/XVII JGD 5684XB).

The defeat of the government in 1963 begs the question: why did Diefenbaker lose the support of so many of those who had given him the largest Parliamentary majority in Canadian politics to that time? The answer lies in the charismatic nature of his leadership, and the fact that he created expectations during the 1958 campaign that perhaps no one could have met. Diefenbaker's charisma (reflected in his ability to attract and hold people's allegiance) captivated the voting public in 1958. His magnetic personality and his oratorical skills enthralled those who heard him speak. He offered hope to a nation that was thirsting for innovative ideas for strengthening the economy, especially in the outlying regions of the country. But charisma alone is not sufficient to govern effectively. The "Vision for Canada" was a marvellous electoral weapon, and Diefenbaker used it with obvious effect. But it raised expectations across the nation — expectations that demanded gratification and which the long-term plans of the New National Policy could not satisfy.

The one exception was agriculture, and it was no coincidence that rural Canada was the only segment of the population that did not turn against Diefenbaker and his party. But the majority of Canadians no longer lived on farms, and urban Canada found several reasons to abandon the Progressive Conservatives because of the perceived deficiencies of the government. Nevertheless, it should be pointed out that the defeat in 1963 was not as dramatic as Diefenbaker's detractors would have us believe. The ninety-five seats the Conservatives won in that election compare favourably with the fifty-one seats George Drew had won ten years earlier when he was leader, and Diefenbaker's approval rating among Canadians never dropped below 34 percent. The other successful Conservative Prime Minister in the postwar era, Brian Mulroney, once hit a low of 13 percent.[8]

Another indictment of John Diefenbaker, and the final reason given for his fall from power, is that he came from outside the mainstream of Canada's political and economic élites. He was, as Donald Fleming described him — "a prairie man to the core."[9] His character had been shaped by his early life in Saskatchewan, his opinions influenced by that region's attitudes toward the issues he would face as Prime Minister, and his policies directed toward making the country's peripheries more central to national decision making. This undoubtedly helped him in 1958, but it also served to bring him down in 1962 and 1963, and later made it easier to discredit him.

---

8   Figures taken from Gallup Canada, "Leadership Appraisals 1941 to Present."

9   Donald Fleming, *So Very Near: The Summit Years* (Toronto: McClelland and Stewart, 1985), 713.

John Diefenbaker won his massive majority in 1958 in part because some regions of the country, especially the prairie provinces and Atlantic Canada, believed that they had not shared equally in the economic prosperity of the postwar period. The New National Policy, which Diefenbaker promised to implement as part of his Vision for Canada, pledged that agriculture would receive its fair share of the national income, and that the outlying regions of the country would receive as much attention and assistance from the federal government as the central provinces of Ontario and Quebec. In order to achieve these objectives, however, the state would have to be an active participant in the economy, and this deviated from the philosophy which had dominated both government and business in Canada for a generation. The notion of pan-Canadian economic development spurred by government action chal-

Diefenbaker holding his fists in the air like a boxer as he speaks from a podium during the 1957 campaign (courtesy the Diefenbaker Centre, MG01/XVII/JGD 1915).

lenged prevailing concepts of fiscal responsibility, especially within some circles in the Conservative party. As Newman wrote of the 1963 campaign, "Canada's financial, academic, bureaucratic, and journalistic élites were united in an obsessive dislike of John Diefenbaker and an unshakeable conviction that the only way to rescue the country from its political and economic chaos was to elect a sturdy Liberal majority."[10]

Diefenbaker and his Western "mafia"[11] did seem to threaten central Canadian dominance of the traditional centres of political and economic power. While this did not necessarily make their defeat inevitable, it certainly pushed them in that direction, and also coloured the accounts written of the period.

Additional evidence of Diefenbaker's Western perspective can be found in his attitude toward the role and place of Quebec in Canada. Here again, his commitment to equality came to the fore. While he accepted existing constitutional guarantees of language and religion, he would not countenance any actions which might confer special status on French Canadians in general and the province of Quebec in particular. He believed in "One Canada" — "a united nationality of equals"[12] — whether they be individuals or provinces. This is perhaps why Quebec's Quiet Revolution seemed to make so little impression on him. As Denis Smith wrote, Diefenbaker's "Western vision of the nation as a single community absorbing all its

---

10   Peter C. Newman, *The Distemper of Our Times* (Toronto: McClelland and Stewart, 1968), 3-4.

11   The architects of the New National Policy were Alvin Hamilton, Merril Menzies, Roy Faibish, Donald Johnston, Morris Miller, and Baldur Kristjanson — all born or raised in the West and most from Saskatchewan.

12   Denis Smith, *Rogue Tory: The Life and Legend of John G. Diefenbaker* (Toronto: MacFarlane Walter and Ross, 1995), 45.

subcommunities into a greater whole came into conflict with a revived French Canadian (or Québécois) nationalism."[13] Diefenbaker claimed, justifiably, that he was never anti-Quebec, but too often he left the impression that he neither understood nor appreciated that province and its aspirations. It was that perception, as much as any, that led to the disastrous decline in support for his party in Quebec in the elections of 1962 and 1963.

It has been observed as well that John Diefenbaker was an outsider even within his own party. It has been said that he was a loner, that he did little to create a team spirit within his Cabinet, and that his economic philosophy ran counter to conventional wisdom in the Conservative party at the time. To these characterizations one should add that he had a profound dislike of the "interests," especially those financial, media and political interests located primarily in central Canada, which he saw as obstacles to the achievement of his goals. Unhappily for him, many among these élites also happened to be traditional supporters of the Conservative party. Some, in fact, had opposed him from the day he announced his candidacy for the leadership, and organized a "Stop Diefenbaker" movement at the 1956 convention on the grounds that "he was totally unacceptable to Quebec and distrusted by the Toronto and Montreal financial circles."[14] Support for his candidacy was minimal in the Ontario-dominated caucus, and even after he seemed set to win the convention the prevailing sentiment among the old guard seemed to be that, "though he would be difficult, if not impossible, as leader, and a failure, after one election he would retire and the party could find a younger, abler man."[15] Thus, even though the unexpected victories of 1957 and 1958 quieted his detractors for a time, when support for the government began to slip, there were plenty in the party ready to drive the "renegade" from power, first as Prime Minister and then as leader. Their ranks were swelled by those who, for any number of reasons, had turned against Diefenbaker in office.

ACCOMPLISHMENTS OVERLOOKED

Political leadership in Canada has too often been judged solely in terms of electoral success. Other important achievements have been forgotten in the face of defeat at the ballot box. Government policies of long-term benefit to the nation seldom have been given equal prominence with those which have had a more direct and immediate impact. John Diefenbaker and his governments are among those who have suffered most from these biases.

The first of the Diefenbaker governments lasted from June 1957 to February 1958, and in these seven and a half months it passed an array of legislation and orders in council as impressive as any new government in Canadian history. When it faced the electorate in 1958, it could point to action in twenty areas, including increased assistance to the disadvantaged; home building loans and a nationwide program of construction projects to create jobs; increased financial assistance to the provinces; cash advances for farm-stored grain; legislation to stabilize farm prices; expanded markets for Canadian products; and projects to develop Canada's natural resources, especially in the area of power generation. To these, Conservative candidates could

---

13   Ibid., xiii.

14   John Meisel, *The Canadian General Election of 1957* (Toronto: University of Toronto Press, 1962), 27.

15   Anonymous party supporter quoted in Dalton Camp, *Gentlemen, Players and Politicians* (Toronto: McClelland and Stewart, 1970), 241.

add: the appointments of Royal Commissions on Energy, Price Spreads in Food Products, and the Distribution of Railway Boxcars for Prairie Grain Movement; the Atomic Energy Research and Development program which eventually produced the CANDU reactor; and amendments to the regulations governing oil and gas exploration on Crown land which directed more of the benefits from new reserves to the national treasury. And this was just an indication of what was yet to come.

The hiatus between elections had given Alvin Hamilton and Merril Menzies the time they needed to prepare the development portion of the election platform on which Diefenbaker would run in 1958. Northern development, within the context of national development, became the central theme of his campaign. From the beginning, he promised that his government would pursue ten objectives if returned to office:

> 1. A $100 million roads program in the Yukon and Northwest Territories to open up exploration of new oil and mineral areas;
>
> 2. A joint federal-provincial plan to build access roads to the north, tying in with the Territories roads at a cost of $75 million, and perhaps double that amount if all provinces joined the program;
>
> 3. Federal aid to "economically sound" rail lines to resources, including the proposed Pine Point railway from Northern Alberta to Great Slave Lake;
>
> 4. Exploration of the Arctic archipelago aimed at developing Arctic sea routes, with the further prospect of developing atomic icebreakers in the future;
>
> 5. A ten-year, $105-million scheme for thermal power plants in the Atlantic provinces, provided for in legislation in the previous session;
>
> 6. A $75-million development at Frobisher Bay on Baffin Island in the Arctic;
>
> 7. A possible second route via Saskatoon and Edmonton for the trans-Canada highway in Western Canada;
>
> 8. Federal sharing in Saskatchewan's power irrigation development of the South Saskatchewan River;
>
> 9. Hydro power development of British Columbia's Columbia River, and the signing of an agreement with the United States to share downstream power benefits;
>
> 10. A national conference to be called later in the year to map a national conservation policy.[16]

These initiatives captured the interest and imagination of the electorate, and, as R.M. Campbell has written, "The Conservatives won an overwhelming victory ... successfully pursuing the theme of a policy of 'vision' in economic development."[17]

With the Conservatives returned to power, Hamilton, as Minister of Northern Affairs and National Resources, began work at once to make the vision a reality, and in November of 1958 brought to Cabinet a document called "Action for a National Development Program" which outlined the major areas in which the government would have to act to meet its objectives. The long-range goal of the program was "an industrial nation of 50 to 100 million people, living in the northern half of the North American continent, processing its resources cheaper and better than its competitors.

---

16   National Archives of Canada (NA), Hamilton Papers, Speech files, Election address, 12 February 1958.

17   Robert M. Campbell, "The Diefenbaker Years Revisited," *Journal of Canadian Studies* (Summer 1983): 111.

Such a nation maintaining a high level of living would need the support of an intensively developed industrial and agricultural base."[18]

The agricultural base would be taken care of by the National Agricultural Program begun in 1957 and expanded throughout the Conservatives' period in office. The industrial base would require a pan-Canadian program of resource development founded on three essential propositions: economic nationalism, interventionist government, and partnership between public and private enterprise. First, Canadian resources would be used to benefit Canadians and to lessen foreign domination of the economy. Second, the government would intervene in the economy to provide the basic services essential to development, especially in northern Canada. Third, private enterprise would play a major role in future development, for the government did not see itself in competition with the private sector. It would proceed in three stages: first, to delineate the resources of the country; second, to encourage the creation of regional power grids which would have the eventual capability of forming an integrated national energy grid; and third, to advance keeping in mind the need for conservation of resources defined as the multiple use of resources, involving "intelligent utilization rather than passive preservation [or] irrational exploitation."[19]

By the time Hamilton left Northern Affairs and National Resources in October 1960, he was able to report progress on three fronts of direct concern to his department: a quickening of existing geological and hydrographic surveys in the Arctic; increased investment in transportation and communications facilities in the North; and new Territorial Oil and Gas Regulations which set the ground rules for future development of Canada's northern energy resources. During this period, Canadian representatives at the Law of the Seas Conference also lobbied successfully for a convention on the Continental Shelf, which gave littoral states control over natural land resources covered by water to a depth of two hundred metres, and which declared that territorial waters could be measured by drawing straight lines from headland to headland, thus adding greatly to the area subject to Canadian sovereignty. The conference also adopted a Russian amendment to a Canadian proposal which gave nations the right to resources found in deeper off-shore waters if they could exploit them. With these agreements in hand, this and future governments could proceed legally to develop Canadian resources off all three coasts.

Once exploration to determine the extent and location of the North's resources was under way, and a plan was in place as to how these resources could be best be utilized, construction of the development infrastructure could begin. Transportation would have to be an essential feature of the program, and the government, again of necessity, would play an important role in the provision of such facilities. A Territorial Roads Program was begun in 1958 to connect the southern parts of the Yukon and Northwest Territories with their valuable mineral, oil, and natural gas areas further north. At the same time, it made little sense to open these regions to development but leave them unconnected to the more settled parts of the country where the resources would be processed and distributed. Roads would have to be built through the northern areas of the western provinces to link up with those further north. These roads would also open up new regions for development within the provinces.

The access roads program might have been limited to the above had Diefenbaker

18   Privy Council Office (PCO), file C-20-9(1), Cabinet document DEV-1.

19   NA, Diefenbaker Papers, Speech files.

not decided to extend the offer of federal assistance to all provinces. He argued that every province should have the opportunity to develop whatever resources it possessed and, as a consequence, the "Roads to Resources" concept was expanded to include almost any proposal from the provinces.[20] Consequently, close to 4,000 miles of new roads were constructed, opening new areas to tourism, connecting fishing villages, and linking mining towns with the more populated south, as well as providing easier access to much of the north for geological surveys.

The second stage of the development plan laid down in the Action Program dealt with energy. If Canada's resources were to be used to industrialize to an extent capable of supporting a population of fifty to one hundred million people, the nation's energy sources had to be exploited to the fullest, and no source could be ignored. The government decided to proceed at first with schemes designed to increase the power supply in low-growth areas of the country. It began with the Atlantic Provinces Power Development Act, continued with its agreement to pay three-quarters of the cost of the South Saskatchewan River Dam, and ended by signing a treaty with the United States to develop the power potential of the Columbia River. If seen through to fruition, the result would have been "a national energy grid anchored at one end on the Hamilton River [Churchill Falls in Labrador] and at the other end on the Columbia and the Taku [in northwestern British Columbia]"[21] with power shunted from areas of surplus to those in deficit as required. The government also accepted the recommendations of the Borden Commission on Energy, which it had established early in its period in office. On 1 February 1961, it announced its National Oil Policy — to close the market east of the Ottawa River to Alberta oil, to reserve the Ontario market for Alberta crude, and to compensate western oil producers further for the loss of the Montreal-serviced market by permitting increased exports to the United States. This decision did not exactly square with the desire to use the nation's resources for the benefit of all, and it did cost Ontario residents an extra cent per gallon for gasoline, but it allowed western producers to expand their output and, in so doing, swelled western coffers for several years.

The third stage of the national development program dealt with conservation. The tangible result of the priority given to conservation was the Resources for Tomorrow Conference held in Montreal in late October 1961. The conference focussed on agriculture and land use, water, fisheries, forestry, wildlife, recreation, and regional development. At its conclusion, the delegates recommended that, in order to realize the possibilities engendered by the meetings, "The National Steering Committee be reconstituted, with a rotating chairmanship and with a secretariat responsible to all governments jointly."[22] The Canadian Council of Resource Ministers began operations on 5 February 1962, later changing its name to the Canadian Council of Resource and Environment Ministers, and ultimately to the Canadian Council of Environment Ministers in response to changing public concerns and the establishment of a federal and several provincial Departments of the Environment. Over the years, the council has proved to be the single most important body involved in federal-provincial environmental relations. It has provided a model of effective and cooperative federalism, and today has the responsibility for the harmonization of federal and provincial policies with respect to the environment.

---

20   Alvin Hamilton, interview with Patrick Kyba, 4 October 1982.

21   John G. Diefenbaker, *The Globe and Mail*, 10 September 1959.

22   Canada, *Proceedings of the Resources for Tomorrow Conference*, vol. 3 (Ottawa: Queen's Printer, 1962).

Just as agriculture headed the agenda of the Resources for Tomorrow Confer- ence, so it was high on the government's list of priorities. It became an integral part of the national development program. Increased exports of grain would solve the immediate problems of most Canadian farmers, especially those on the Prairies, but in the early 1960s one group continued to live a perilous existence — those whose land was marginal or whose holdings were too small ever to become prosperous. The Agricultural Rehabilitation and Development Act (ARDA) was intended to address this problem. The Act, introduced in January 1961, authorized the Minister of Agriculture to enter into agreements with the provinces to fund projects "for the alternative uses of lands that are marginal or of low productivity," "for the develop- ment of income and employment opportunities in rural agricultural areas," and "for the development and conservation of the soil and water resources of Canada."[23] Government action would be important to the success of the program, but self-help would also be emphasized in assisting marginal farmers to improve their lot. ARDA agreements with the provinces continued in some form until 1980 and, while assessments vary as to the overall difference they made to rural life in Canada, no one denies the utility of the many projects begun under its auspices.

ARDA represented a radical departure from traditional approaches to the prob- lems of rural underdevelopment. It attempted to break down the historical economic subordination of the hinterland to the metropolis through a strategy that integrated indigenous regional development and balanced regional growth, and which also involved the rural population itself in the planning process. The concept of self-help was new to rural planning, but eventually both the Vatican and the United Nations adopted the doctrine as the basis of their plans for rural development. Thus, despite "all its false starts, shortcomings and limitations, ARDA … made a constructive and promising beginning in a public attempt to come to grips with rural poverty and regional disparities."[24] At the same time, it provided concrete evidence to the farm population of central and eastern Canada that the government had an interest in their problems as well as those of the Prairies.

The efforts of the Diefenbaker government on behalf of agriculture warrant special attention because they probably did more to improve the fortunes of this sector of the economy than any other in Canadian history; yet these successes have been ignored for the most part by whose who have written on the period. Aside from the royal commissions it established to investigate two of the more vexing problems troubling the industry, it also legislated the Agricultural Stabilization and Prairie Grain Advance Payments Acts, designed to enable farmers to plan their production better and to tide them over until markets were found for the huge surpluses of grain which had accumulated over the previous decade. After 1958 the government announced its comprehensive National Agricultural Program, then in July 1959 it introduced the Crop Insurance and Farm Credit Acts. The former authorized the federal government to pay 20 percent of the premiums and 50 percent of the administrative costs of crop insurance schemes instituted by the provinces; the latter extended the existing Farm Loan Act and created the Farm Credit Corporation, with responsibility to administer a new system of long-term mortgage credit which made it easier for young people to begin farming and for established farmers to expand their operations. Six months later, Parliament passed the Prairie Grain Loans Act,

23   Canada, House of Commons, *Debates*, 25 January 1961.

24   J.N. McCrorie, *ARDA: An Experiment in Development Planning* (Ottawa: Queen's Printer, 1969).

which provided short-term credit to grain producers who could not harvest their crops, and the Prairie Grain Provisional Payments Act, which authorized the Wheat Board to make payments for the 1959-60 crop year in respect of future deliveries of unthreshed grain. The government offered other assistance as emergencies arose, and approved acreage payments as a short-term expedient to alleviate the plight of farmers whose income had declined markedly in recent years.

All these measures, however, did not solve the most important problem of the prairie farm community: it was producing more than the Wheat Board was selling. The difficulties would not be overcome until the government's plan to "accelerate sales abroad" proved successful. This did not occur until a fortuitous set of circumstances brought Alvin Hamilton to the Department of Agriculture in 1960 and an acute food shortage forced China to enter the international grain market as a buyer in bulk. The Chinese wanted a large quantity of Canadian grain, but had little cash to pay for it. They needed credit. If the deal were to be struck, the government would not only have to guarantee any bank loans made to the Wheat Board in order to finance the sales, but also agree to let the Chinese make their payments over time. Hamilton had no difficulty with these arrangements, but others in Cabinet, especially the Minister of Finance, did not like them at all. Eventually the Prime Minister had to intervene — and he did so, decisively, on Hamilton's side. This effectively ended the debate in Cabinet, the first sales went through, and more followed under similar terms which China honoured to the letter.

These sales to China brought much-needed growth to the economy of western Canada. The obvious success of the arrangements moved Hamilton to promise farmers that he would sell as much grain as they could grow. Such optimism had not been heard on the Prairies for generations, and it restored farmers' faith in their future. Canada's exports of wheat to China and the Soviet bloc during the 1961-62 crop year were the third highest in history and, for the same year, the Wheat Board made the highest average final payment to farmers to that time. In sum, the grain sales created legacies for both the Progressive Conservative party and the country as a whole. They restored the government's popularity with the prairie electorate and left a pool of support for the Conservatives in that region which lasted for thirty years. They also resurrected long-dormant provincial Conservative parties in all three prairie provinces. They probably did more to benefit the Canadian economy overall than any other single action taken by the Diefenbaker government. Finally, the grain sales opened a window to China which has remained open to this day. Canada continues to sell grain to China, Canadian politicians and businessmen travel there regularly searching for new markets for various products, and Chinese manufacturers come here for the same reason.

The New National Policy, which included the National Agricultural Program, was an effort on the part of Diefenbaker, Hamilton, and a small group of advisers to set the country on a new course after what they believed had been two decades of drift under the uninspired leadership of King and St. Laurent. They were motivated by Canadian nationalism, a commitment to social justice, and a conviction that government must create the conditions whereby private enterprise could develop the nation. They believed that Canada possessed a treasure-trove of wealth waiting to be tapped, and they were determined to see these resources used to achieve both economic and social goals, especially in the lower-income regions of the country.

Under the auspices of the New National Policy, most of the promises made during the 1957 and 1958 campaigns were kept. The Diefenbaker government concentrated first on natural resource development to spur the economy, create employment, and provide additional revenues for social programs. Later, it tried to link all aspects of governmental endeavour related to development, added an emphasis on human resources, and focussed on the relationship between productivity, investment, and foreign trade.

Of course, they did not succeed in everything they set out to do. Too many Cabinet ministers feared the political repercussions of this dramatic departure from traditional economic theory and practice. Officials in the Department of Finance found it easier to approve development proposals designed to assist specific sections of the population or regions of the country than those which would have given the federal government a powerful and permanent role in directing the economy.

Political defeat forced Diefenbaker from power. Nevertheless, and on balance, it can be said that much of both short- and long-term benefit occurred during his government's period in office, and the legends which have grown up around John Diefenbaker's fall from power should not blind one to the many accomplishments of his leadership.[25] Diefenbaker was a catalyst for change at a critical transition period in Canadian history. Perhaps his most significant legacy can be found in his government's attempts to diversify and strengthen the economy. Certainly, some success was achieved in the realm of regional development, and the building of infrastructure and the expansion of agricultural markets were welcomed by those who benefited most from these initiatives. And surely it is instructive that outside central Canada, even at the nadir of his national popularity, John Diefenbaker retained sufficient support to deny Lester Pearson's Liberals majorities in both 1963 and 1965.

CONCLUSION

A review of the literature on John Diefenbaker reveals that he has been judged more for his perceived inadequacies than for his real achievements. This perception has been perpetuated by journalists, politicians, and academics who, by and large, represent the views of central Canada. In fairness, it should be remembered that in order to be considered "successful," political leaders in Canada need to perform a variety of functions and to satisfy the needs and demands of a multitude of individuals and groups. They must state their goals clearly, and then persuade the electorate and the media of their ability to achieve them. They must implement policies which on some level will satisfy a majority of their followers and a substantial plurality of the public at large. In addition, their leadership, to be seen as effective, must be sustained actively over an extended period. This is not an easy task, especially in a nation such as Canada. Its vast geography, its cultural contrasts, and the differing economic needs of its various regions make effective national leadership complex and extremely difficult. This diversity also affects people's perceptions of their leaders. It gives rise to differing judgements as to relative success or failure based on personal expectations and regional differences. These judgements will vary over time as new circumstances arise.

Most of those who have written about John Diefenbaker have concluded that he was a failure as a leader, or that, while he may have had some successes, he never fully

---

25   A list of some of the other accomplishments of the Diefenbaker years would have to include the Bill of Rights; the creation of the National Capital Commission, the Board of Broadcast Governors, and the World Food Bank; preparatory work on what became Expo '67; establishment of the O'Leary, Glassco, and Hall commissions; the Prime Minister's stand against apartheid within the Commonwealth; and the extension of the franchise to aboriginal Canadians.

lived up to his promise and, therefore, must be considered a failure. On reflection, so damning a conclusion is not so obvious. Admittedly, his personality repelled some, he fumbled certain issues, he did not live up to everyone's expectations, and his priorities were not shared by the élites of central Canada. Nevertheless, it was his personal charisma that returned the Conservatives to power after a generation in opposition. It was his direct intervention that ensured that such ventures as the Roads to Resources Program and grain sales to China would proceed. And his priorities were shared by many, especially in the outlying regions of the country.

His initiatives continue to benefit Canadians today. John Diefenbaker appealed to those individuals and regions aggrieved that they had not participated equally in the prosperity of the postwar boom, and who felt marginalized by the central provinces' domination of the corridors of political and economic power. His principal goal was "a united nation of equals," and his policies were directed toward equalizing opportunities across the length and breadth of the land. It is perhaps not surprising that the people in those regions who had profited most under the status quo would be the first to turn against him. Likewise, one should not be astonished by the fact that those who stood to gain most from his policies stayed with him to the end.

As Denis Smith has written, "Diefenbaker broadened the Conservative party and restored it as a national movement representing all regions of the country. He offered Canadians, briefly, an expansive sense of collective possibilities. He established compassion, fairness and equal justice as principles of national policy."[26] A fitting eulogy when one takes his achievements as Prime Minister into account.

---

26   Smith, *Rogue Tory*, 577-78.

John Diefenbaker's One Canada and the Legacy of Unhyphenated Canadianism

Richard Sigurdson

This paper is about the political ideas of a former Prime Minister who was responsible for protecting individual rights and liberties under Canadian law, who was a world leader in the promotion of human rights, who championed multiculturalism, who introduced measures to ensure federal bilingualism while in office, who made a significant contribution to the establishment of equal political rights for Canada's First Nations, and who stood up against Quebec by insisting that there be no special status for that province. Were it not for the title of this book, one would be forgiven for thinking of another, sexier former Prime Minister. Mind you, this paper is about a *western* Canadian politician, a populist whose rhetoric praised the common sense of the average person, who promoted self-reliance and the ethos of free enterprise, and whose battle cry was aimed against the "big interests" in the Canadian establishment — Toronto socialites, media élites, university professors, intellectuals, and the like. Again, one may be forgiven if this brings to mind a certain contemporary Opposition leader who, however well-coifed and Hugo-Boss attired, cannot shake his image as a down-home, right-wing, prairie populist.

The subject of this article is, of course, John Diefenbaker, whose first election as Prime Minister forty years ago is commemorated with this volume. In this paper I will second a comment made by one of Canada's leading historians, Michael Bliss, who recently said of Diefenbaker that he "stood for a fascinating and still relevant combination of individualistic and egalitarian views," and who "anticipated leaders as diverse as Pierre Trudeau and Preston Manning."[1] Specifically, I will outline Diefenbaker's famous vision of "One Canada," and trace the legacy of his notion of an "unhyphenated" Canadianism. In Diefenbaker's words, this stood for "prejudice toward none and freedom for all. There were to be no second-class citizens."[2] One

---

1   Michael Bliss, *Right Honourable Men: The Descent of Canadian Politics from Macdonald to Mulroney* (Toronto: Harper Collins, 1994), 186.

2   John G. Diefenbaker, *One Canada: Memoirs of the Rt. Hon. John G. Diefenbaker*, vol. 2: *The Years of Achievement, 1957-1962* (Toronto: Macmillan, 1976), 33.

Canada, unhyphenated Canadianism: these catchy phrases were meant to counter not only the "two-nations" interpretation of Canada, but also the tendency among some ethno-cultural minorities to cling to their own ways and resist assimilation. As Diefenbaker put it: "We shall never build the nation which our potential resources make possible by dividing ourselves into anglophones, francophones, multicultural-phones, or whatever kind of phones you choose. I say: Canadians first, last, and always!"[3]

Diefenbaker espoused an essentially liberal-individualist ideal of society based on equal rights for all citizens regardless of race, religion, or language. These egalitarian sentiments are powerfully attractive in a liberal democratic society such as Canada. Thus, Diefenbaker's vision remains the ideal for many Canadians, especially in western Canada. Indeed, ideas like Diefenbaker's are currently championed by the Reform party, which similarly calls for an unhyphenated Canadianism and an equality of citizens and provinces. I wish to argue, however, that the notion of an unhyphenated Canadian citizenship, no matter how well intended, undermines the goal of an inclusive pan-Canadian political nationality. Still, such a notion or philosophy may well serve as a basis for a new form of *English*-Canadian nationalism — one with growing support among majority-group English Canadians but with little appeal to Quebeckers, First Nations Canadians, and new Canadians (especially those of non-European origin).

To many readers it may appear odd to find Diefenbaker described as a liberal and an individualist, and as someone whose legacy serves to frustrate rather than promote pan-Canadian nationalism. This is especially so since Diefenbaker is best known to students of Canadian political thought as the tragic hero of George Grant's unforgettable *Lament for a Nation*.[4] Here Diefenbaker is depicted as a valiant, though naïve, defender of what, according to Grant, had become indefensible in modern North America — an independent Canada. Diefenbaker's political defeat in 1963 symbolized for Grant the defeat of Canadian nationalism by the forces of modern liberalism. By thus dramatizing Diefenbaker's failure, Grant stimulated a new wave of nationalism among English-speaking Canadians. As a result, Diefenbaker's legacy came to include the inspiration his convictions gave to a generation of English-Canadian nationalists who, like him, believed in the dream of an independent Canada that would stand as a moral alternative to liberal, capitalist America. Yet this legacy owes more to Grant's influence than to Diefenbaker's actual ideas. Indeed, Grant was critical of Diefenbaker's invocation of a single, united Canada, and regarded Diefenbaker's interpretation of federalism as "basically American" (and coming from Grant, that was quite an insult). Like many of Diefenbaker's contemporaries, Grant realized that the One Canada idea was incapable of encompassing other peoples within Canada "who were concerned with being a nation."[5] Hence, we may applaud Diefenbaker's nationalist sentiments and his commitment to principle — as Grant did — without accepting the One Canada idea as an appropriate one for modern Canada.

---

3   Canada, House of Commons, *Debates*, 4 June 1973.

4   George Grant, *Lament for a Nation: The Defeat of Canadian Nationalism* (1965; Ottawa: Carleton University Press, 1982).

5   Ibid., 21.

"ONE CANADA":
EQUALITY, MULTICULTURALISM, RIGHTS, AND QUEBEC

What exactly is the substance of One Canada? The bedrock of John Diefenbaker's political philosophy is a strong belief in individual equality. This may not strike us today as particularly unique; indeed, it is an idea adhered to by virtually every proponent of contemporary liberal democracy. Still, Diefenbaker was one of the first and most articulate federal politicians in Canada to endorse unabashedly an egalitarian and individualistic ethos. Historically, the political culture in Canada had not placed equality ahead of other political values such as justice, authority, or stability. In fact, it was not until after the Second World War that egalitarianism started to become accepted and ingrained in our ways of life and thought. Up to this point, Canadian government policy reflected the opinion of the racial and ethnic majority that its values and institutions were superior to all others. Canada's depressing record of racism, displacement, exclusion, and forced assimilation of ethno-cultural minorities and Natives is now well known, as is the story of the government's racially based immigration and naturalization policies.

John Diefenbaker's sensitivity toward issues of equality reflects his western Canadian roots, as well as his personal experience as a Canadian from neither the English nor the French charter groups. As one biographer put it, Diefenbaker's vision of the country has deep roots in the prairie West:

> One Canada was born on the prairie trails; in the fire and comradeship of World War I; in the section shacks of the railroad among immigrants with unpronounceable names; in the dreams of a new world free of prejudice and discrimination. It was a Canada where every citizen possessed the same rights of citizenship; where the heritage of all was preserved, even that of the majority; where every citizen enjoyed the same chance to get ahead, regardless of what part of the country he lived in, what his name might be, or where his parents came from. It was a Canadianism respecting differences, not erecting them into impassable barriers.[6]

However colourful this prose, it captures the core regional values of the West, which Diefenbaker was so successfully able to articulate and to exploit for political gain.

As Roger Gibbins and Sonia Arrison explain, this general commitment to equality is the key element in western Canada's regional political culture.[7] Westerners, of course, have no exclusive purchase on the ideal of equality; but they are taken to expressing their views most forcefully, whether it be in pressing their right to equal treatment regardless of ethnic background or in espousing the principle of the equality of the provinces. This idea also comes out when westerners talk about "regional inequality" (which is not, strictly speaking, the same thing as the equality of the provinces), or when they voice their faith in populist majoritarianism (the idea that the will of the people can be established in a rough way by counting heads equally).

An important factor in the creation of this regional political culture was the pattern of immigrant settlement in the West, where successive waves of immigration brought to the Prairies new Canadians from a wide variety of nations and cultures.

---

6   Thomas Van Dusen, *Diefenbaker* (Toronto: McGraw-Hill, 1968), 69.

7   Roger Gibbons and Sonja Arrison, *Western Visions: Perspectives on the West in Canada* (Peterborough: Broadview Press, 1995), 46.

John and Olive Diefenbaker sitting at International Festival talking to three small girls in ethnic costume, Toronto, 1961 (courtesy the Diefenbaker Centre MG01/XVII/JGD 2938).

Although he was a fourth generation Canadian on his mother's side, and third generation on his father's, Diefenbaker was a member of a recognizably "ethnic" group — in his case, German Canadians. The importance of Diefenbaker's ethnicity is heightened by the fact that life was not easy for a person of German ancestry living in Canada during the years when the nation fought two horrible wars against the Germans. Hence, John Diefenbaker had personal experience of racial discrimination and distrust. This, he says, inspired his attack against hyphenated Canadianism:

> My whole purpose, from my university days, was to bring an end in this country to discrimination on a basis of race, creed, or colour. In the 1925 election, this emerged in a very practical way for me. I was labelled by some of the lower level workers of my opponent as a "Hun".... Matters were made a little better when I was simply called a German. I was not a German, not a German-Canadian, but a Canadian... . I suppose that those who have never experienced this sort of thing will never truly understand it. I have often wondered what the effect on my life would have been if my name had been my mother's, Campbell-Bannerman, rather than Diefenbaker.[8]

Like many westerners, Diefenbaker grew up among immigrants and Natives (he was fond of recalling, perhaps fancifully, his boyhood encounters with Gabriel Dumont[9]). And, like many of his neighbours, he adopted a version of multicultural-ism which was respectful of cultural and ethnic differences but which stressed *individual* equality rather than *collective* or group rights. To Diefenbaker, a Canadian was simply a Canadian, regardless of ethnic origin. In a speech in 1958, Diefenbaker

---

8   John G. Diefenbaker, *One Canada*, vol. 1: *The Crusading Years, 1895-1956*, 140-41.

9   Denis Smith, *Rogue Tory: The Life and Times of John G. Diefenbaker* (Toronto: Macfarlane Walter & Ross, 1995), 7.

stated: "Every one of us, throughout his life, has a particular project which he holds dear. Mine, because I was of mixed origins, was to obtain Canadian nationality."[10] By speaking this way, Diefenbaker promoted an attitude closer to the American "melting pot," or assimiliationist paradigm, than to what has come to be called the Canadian "cultural mosaic" model. Diefenbaker envisioned a political community in which individual differences in cultural heritage would be tolerated; but they would not become translated into differentiated group rights. Ethnic or racial differences were expected to be sublimated, over time, into the greater ethos of a collective "Canadian" community.

One means of forging this new political community, which met with Diefenbaker's strong approval, was the passage of citizenship legislation. Before 1947, Canada's Naturalization Acts conferred British subject status on all native-born Canadians and on immigrants naturalized in Canada. The Canadian Citizenship Act, the first legislation to define Canadians as something other than British subjects, came into effect on 1 January 1947. Speaking in favour of the Act in 1946, Diefenbaker voiced his desire to see the creation of "an unhyphenated nation.... Canada must develop, now that we achieve this citizenship, a unity out of diversity — a diversity based on non-homogeneous peoples of many religions, peoples of clashing economic differences based on difference, and jurisdictional differences as between federal and provincial authorities. The great challenge is to fuse these clashing differences." Signalling his own respect for the American melting pot tradition, Diefenbaker referred to his own words of 1944: "As I have said before, no one thinks of Mr. Roosevelt as a Dutch-American. No one thinks of General Eisenhower as a German-American. No one thinks of Mayor LaGuardia of New York as an Italian-American. They are great Americans."[11]

One can perceive this same line of thinking in Diefenbaker's continued attempts to eliminate the identification of ethnic origins in the Canadian census, and in his government's changes to the immigration system in 1962. He first spoke against the census taker's questions about ethnic origin in his maiden speech in the House of Commons in 1940.[12] He took some credit for the fact that this question was left out of the intermediate census of 1946, but was outraged when it re-appeared in 1951. As Prime Minister, Diefenbaker wanted to make sure that the 1961 decennial census asked, for the "first and last time," the simple question, "Are you a Canadian?"[13] This move was opposed by bureaucrats, demographers, academics, and especially French Canadians (who thought it would lead to an underestimation of their numbers across the country). Diefenbaker reluctantly backed down, but not before making his point. Another crucial issue for Diefenbaker was immigration. Under his prime ministership, immigration laws underwent a significant shift in emphasis as Canada became one of the first countries in the world to remove racial criteria from its immigration policies.

Diefenbaker saw no contradiction between his melting pot attitudes about multiculturalism and his commitment to the Crown, the Commonwealth, and British

---

10   Diefenbaker cited by André Laurendeau in "How to 'Weld' Us," 10 June 1958, in André Laurendeau, *Witness for Quebec: Essays Selected and Translated by Philip Stratford* (Toronto: Macmillan, 1973), 175.

11   Canada, House of Commons, *Debates*, 2 April 1946, pp. 510-11.

12   Ibid., 13 June 1940, pp. 748-51.

13   Diefenbaker, *One Canada*, vol. 2, 255.

parliamentary tradition. But in spite of his love of parliamentary tradition, he was willing to limit the powers of the Canadian Parliament by passing a Bill of Rights — the precursor to Pierre Trudeau's 1982 Charter of Rights and Freedoms. On the eve of introducing the bill, Diefenbaker addressed the nation, saying in part that his Bill of Rights "will make Parliament realize that rights are to be preserved. It will make Parliament more cautious in passing laws that would have the effect of interfering with freedom... . It will give to Canadians the realization that wherever a Canadian may live, whatever his race, his religion or his colour, the Parliament of Canada will be jealous of his rights and will not infringe upon those rights."[14] While Diefenbaker would have preferred to have entrenched these rights in the constitution instead of merely enacting a federal statute, such a task would have required provincial consent, and that was not possible at the time.

In federal-provincial relations, Diefenbaker's One Canada ideology led him to favour a centralized over a decentralized federalism. Like Trudeau, and unlike Manning, Diefenbaker believed that Canadians, as individuals, could claim benefits from the federal government as a matter of "right," regardless of their linguistic heritage or place of residence. His sense of regional equality also led him to support the notion that the poorer areas of the country — the Atlantic provinces and rural regions — had a right to equalization grants. Diefenbaker affirmed the equality of the provinces, but did not want them strengthened at the expense of federal authority. This put him at odds with the province-building premiers, but endeared him to nationalistic voters across the country. Diefenbaker defended the federal government's obligation to pass laws to preserve the constitutional freedoms of all Canadians, objecting that, if his provincial-rights opponents were correct, "then Canadian citizenship is a provincial variable. There will be nine kinds of Canadians in Canada whose freedoms will be based on the home address of each of us. If that contention is true, Canadian unity is a meaningless term."[15]

Finally, we must consider Diefenbaker's views on national unity and cultural duality. By far the most controversial aspect of the One Canada idea is its application to French-English relations. If, as Diefenbaker liked to say, there should be a single Canadian nationality which knows no hyphenated consideration, what does that say to French Canadians? For one thing, it equates French Canadianism with any other minority group experience. It implies that French Canadians are not much different from Ukrainian Canadians or Japanese Canadians. This approach, though popular with so-called "third-wave" immigrant Canadians, runs counter to the historical and constitutional identification of Canada as a nation of two founding peoples, French and English. Diefenbaker's One Canada vision is simply impossible to reconcile with any version of the "compact theory" of federalism, let alone with the "two nations" version. In fact, Diefenbaker's ideas conflict with all but the most benign visions of bilingualism and biculturalism.

For Diefenbaker, as a westerner, the creation of a national political identity naturally involved the assimilation of ethnic minorities into a composite rather than a bilingual and bicultural framework. That said, Diefenbaker respected the language rights of French Canadians as *individuals*. It was his government that introduced simultaneous translation in the House of Commons and began to issue bilingual pay

---

14   The Rt. Hon. John G. Diefenbaker, Address on "The Nation's Business" — 30 June 1960. Cited at http://www.rescol.ca/collections/discours/english/jgd/sp.1.htm.

15   Diefenbaker, *One Canada*, vol. 2, 254.

cheques. Diefenbaker was also the first non-French Prime Minister to address the Quebec electorate in their own language. Mind you, it was with mixed results. As one Diefenbaker biographer points out, "The reaction of French-Canadian audiences was compounded of horror at Diefenbaker's brand of French and awe that he was even attempting it. Diefenbaker seemed to share some of the horror as he struggled along; and eventually Quebec audiences accepted his French as a strange but impressive convulsion of nature, part of the national landscape, like Montmorency Falls."[16]

In spite of Diefenbaker's honest efforts to deny that he was anti-French or hostile to Quebec, the political symbolism of One Canada and unhyphenated Canadianism stood as an affront to the accepted idea among Quebeckers that Confederation was based on an accord between the French and the English. Diefenbaker would have nothing to do with this notion; nor would he tolerate the claim that Quebec is a province unlike the others. He did not believe that Quebec had any special require-ments because he did not believe in treating French Canadians as a distinct group of hyphenated Canadians. According to him, no group should have special treatment, special privileges, or distinct status. While this is consistent with his overall vision of Canada as a national community of rights-bearing individuals, it did not endear him to those who wanted to accommodate within Canada the legitimate desire of Quebeckers for greater degrees of self-determination.

THE LEGACY OF ONE CANADA
AND UNHYPHENATED CANADIANISM

The unfolding of Diefenbaker's One Canada ideology had profound conse-quences both for national politics and for the Progressive Conservative party. Diefen-baker opened up the prairie West to the Conservative Party and changed forever its image as a strictly WASP organization. Some measure of this transformation is found in electoral results. In federal elections held from 1900 to 1957 inclusive, the Liberals won 263 prairie seats to the Conservative's 141, for a margin of almost two to one. But from 1958 to 1988 inclusive, the Conservatives won 413 federal seats on the Prairies while the Liberals captured just 34 — a ratio of more than twelve to one in favour of the Conservatives. Indeed, until the rise of the Reform party in the 1993 election, the Conservatives were the party to beat throughout the West. Moreover, since Diefenbaker's day, Conservative MPs could be expected to have names like Mazankowski or Hnatyshyn as soon as Smith or Jones. The Conservatives had become a fixture on the Prairies, in part because they were now acceptable to ethnic Canadians — especially to second- and third-generation immigrant Canadians with continental European backgrounds.

Despite winning an unprecedented fifty of the seventy-five federal seats in Quebec in 1958, the Diefenbaker government squandered its opportunity to make a lasting breakthrough in that province. The Prime Minister turned his back on tradition by appointing few Quebeckers to Cabinet and rewarding none with a truly influential portfolio. Throughout the term of his majority mandate, moreover, he named seventeen royal commissions and put a French Canadian in charge of only one. Many suspected that he did not care about Quebec, and that he still clung to the Gordon Churchill theory that the party could win a majority government without support in Quebec. Whether for lack of interest or failure of vision, Diefenbaker proved

---

16   Van Dusen, *Diefenbaker*, 76.

incapable of comprehending the nature of the social and political changes occurring within Quebec. For these and other reasons, opinion leaders in Quebec, such as *Le Devoir* editor André Laurendeau, regularly took the Diefenbaker government to task for its blind spot on national unity. In what would, in retrospect, be his most prophetic editorial, Laurendeau called for the creation of a royal commission on bilingualism to investigate what Canadians thought about language issues and to suggest what should be done to make the country more truly bilingual.[17] Laurendeau and others campaigned hard for such a commission, and won over many sympathetic Conservatives. Ultimately, however, Diefenbaker could not accept a public debate that would so challenge his One Canada philosophy. On 18 January 1963, he put an end to any speculation by announcing officially that the plan had no place in his thinking. This decision greatly disappointed the small group of Diefenbaker loyalists in Quebec (such as the young Brian Mulroney), and convinced many in the party that Diefenbaker had to go if there was to be any chance of again capturing a significant number of Quebec seats.[18]

When the Liberals returned to power later in 1963, Lester Pearson established, almost immediately, a Royal Commission on Bilingualism and Biculturalism (soon known simply as the B & B Commission). Laurendeau was appointed co-chairman, along with Davidson Dunton, and served in that capacity until his sudden death in 1968. The first volume of the Commission's final report was issued at the end of 1967, introduced by Laurendeau's famous "blue pages" outlining his dualist vision for Canada: equality between the two founding peoples, official bilingualism, biculturalism, equal opportunity, and recognition of Quebec's distinctiveness within Canada. Of course, nothing could have been further from Diefenbaker's vision. So, from his seat on the Opposition front bench, Diefenbaker was the Commission's harshest critic. For good measure, he fought bitterly against the Pearson government's introduction of a new Canadian flag, one designed specifically to promote an inclusive Canadian identity free of overtly British symbolism. And later he was to lead the attack on official bilingualism and affirmative action for French-speakers within the federal bureaucracy. Not surprisingly, all this made him a hero of sorts among anti-francophones in English Canada, especially in the West.

Nevertheless, an essentially dualist approach to national unity issues was increasingly embraced, at least at the élite level, by all federal parties during the 1960s.[19] Even Progressive Conservatives flirted with the two-nations idea. At their Montmorency Falls "thinkers' meeting" in August 1967, party delegates agreed on the term *deux nations* as an appropriate expression of Canadian reality (although they took some liberty and translated it as "two founding peoples"[20]). To Diefenbaker, of course, this was a shameful abandonment of the non-French, non-English, "third-force" Canadians, and an unprincipled acquiescence to French-Canadian demands. His outrage motivated him to stage his ill-fated, rather pathetic, bid to retain the party leadership in 1967, ten months after he had been humiliated by Dalton Camp's

---

17   "A Proposal for an Inquiry into Bilingualism," 20 January 1962, in Laurendeau, *Witness for Quebec*, 187-89.

18   John Sawatsky, *Mulroney: The Politics of Ambition* (Toronto: Macfarlane Walter & Ross, 1991), 140.

19   Kenneth McRoberts, *Misconceiving Canada: The Struggle for National Unity* (Toronto: Oxford University Press, 1997), 30-54.

20   Dalton Camp, "Reflections on the Montmorency Conference," *Queen's Quarterly* 76 (Summer 1969): 185.

successful crusade to force a leadership convention. Clearly, Diefenbaker had no chance of winning the convention, but his emotional attacks on the two-nations idea did lead to the agreement by the convention co-chairperson to table the party's two-nation formula. However, Diefenbaker's assault on the idea (and on his opponents) did the party little good, especially in Quebec, and helped affirm many people's belief that only the Liberal Party could successfully accommodate across the cultural-linguistic divide.

Diefenbaker's successor, Robert Stanfield, was willing to accommodate many of Quebec's aspirations, but could not compete on the national unity issue with Pierre Trudeau, a Liberal who did not share Laurendeau's two-nations thinking but who did recognize the importance of the two linguistic communities in Canada. A large part of Trudeau's appeal to English Canadians was his perceived ability to deal firmly with the Quebec question. So even when his policies were not fully endorsed — as was the case with official bilingualism — there was some sympathy with his larger goal. Trudeau contrived to undercut the legitimacy of the government in Quebec as the sole reliable defender of the French language by enhancing the federal government's role as protector of language rights in all parts of the country. It is significant that when official bilingualism was instituted in 1969, there was no trace of Laurendeau's formula for an equal partnership between the two nations. In many ways, Trudeau was closer to Diefenbaker's views on unhyphenated Canadianism than he was to the thinking of most Quebec intellectuals: he did not accept the notion of special status for Quebec, he rejected the two-nations theory, and he regarded language rights as individual possessions rather than group entitlements. In addition, Trudeau demonstrated his affinity to Diefenbaker's understanding of the country in his promotion of such policies as official multiculturalism, an entrenched Charter of Rights, and a race-blind Indian policy.

In 1971 the Trudeau government unveiled a new policy of multiculturalism, one which extended equal cultural rights to all ethnic groups but with no recognition of Quebec's specificity. This reflected the attitudes of many "third-force" Canadians, especially in the West, and put an end to any discourse about biculturalism. As Trudeau explained in his address to the House of Commons, "although there are two official languages, there is no official culture, nor does any ethnic group take precedence over any other." A policy of multiculturalism, as Trudeau put it, "is basically the conscious support of individual freedom of choice."[21] The Trudeau government's policy of multiculturalism was a response to the dualistic thrust of the recommendations of the B & B Commission. In effect, the new policy substituted multiculturalism for biculturalism, thereby appeasing the representatives of third-force Canadians while drawing the ire of Quebec francophones. Whatever its consequences, the policy was designed to integrate non-British, non-French Canadians into Canadian society and provide a clearer basis for a distinctive Canadian identity — both goals that were in line with Diefenbaker's philosophy.

A similar rationale was evident in Trudeau's life-long dream of an entrenched Charter of Rights, which he saw become a reality in 1982. The primary goal of the Charter was the simple protection of rights and freedoms, but its secondary objective was the fostering of a new and inclusive national Canadian identity appropriate for all Canadian citizens, regardless of ethnic heritage. Trudeau's Charter was clearly indebted to Diefenbaker's Bill of Rights; many of its provisions were virtually identical

---

21   Canada, House of Commons, *Debates*, 8 October 1971, p. 8545.

to the earlier statute. Anti-discrimination — a key Diefenbaker value — was given even greater pride of place in the Charter than it had in the Bill of Rights. For ethno-cultural minorities, as well as for aboriginal peoples, the Charter's equality provisions were intended as an affirmation of the country's commitment to freedom and equality, regardless of race, colour, or creed.

Equal political rights for aboriginal Canadians was one of John Diefenbaker's proudest achievements. But he lived in an era when the battle for mere formal equality was the key aboriginal issue. By the 1980s there had been a shift beyond the goal of satisfying the requirements of the *equality of opportunity* to the objectives of an *equality of results*. By Trudeau's time, moreover, aboriginal leaders had become less concerned with winning equal individual rights than with securing some form of distinctive collective rights. Hence, the 1982 constitutional provisions included new aboriginal and treaty rights which went much further than Diefenbaker had envisioned in his time. Indeed, they marked a departure from the earlier attempts by the Trudeau government to desegregate aboriginal peoples through a policy of assimilation. In the aptly named "White Paper" of 1969, the Liberal government proposed legislation that would have terminated the existing relationship between the First Nations and the federal government, foreclosing future possibilities of special status for aboriginal peoples. Under this plan, Native Canadians would have been granted full citizenship rights — no more nor less than other citizens of Canada. As Trudeau said at the time, "We can go on treating the Indians as having a special status ... adding bricks of discrimination around the ghetto in which they live... . Or we can say you're at a crossroads — the time is now to decide whether the Indians will be a race apart in Canada or whether [they] will be Canadians of full status."[22] This is a fine expression of the individualist and egalitarian attitude Trudeau shared with Diefenbaker, but which could not be fully realized within the new context of collective rights and group entitlements. Still, many Canadians continue to interpret aboriginal issues according to this basically liberal-individualist point of view. For instance, Mel Smith, a prominent constitutional expert and former deputy minister in several British Columbia governments, has recently argued for a new aboriginal policy based on the two principles of Native self-reliance and equality under the law. In support of the latter, Smith writes, "It is contrary to all that Canada stands for to support a policy that extends special privileges based on race or ethnicity. This is a principle so fundamental to liberal democratic societies that it should not even be necessary to state it."[23] Similar rhetoric is employed by the Reform Party of Canada, as well as many provincial politicians.

The Trudeau years culminated in the successful patriation of the Constitution, but the Liberal party paid a heavy price, especially in Quebec. With the Liberals in disrepute, and the ideology of neo-conservatism on the rise in Canada and throughout the western world, Brian Mulroney won the leadership of the Progressive Conservative party and pledged to bring Quebec back into the Canadian family while putting the country's finances in order. In 1984 his government was elected, largely on the combined strength of the now-traditional Conservative support in western Canada and his popularity in Quebec. And he did not disappoint the party faithful (at least not immediately). After winning the largest majority since Diefenbaker's

---

22   Trudeau cited in Melvin H. Smith, *Our Home or Native Land? What Governments' Aboriginal Policy is doing to Canada* (Victoria: Crown Western, 1995), 1.

23   Smith, *Rogue Tory*, 263.

1958 triumph, he then proceeded to do what no Conservative had done since John A. Macdonald — win back-to-back majority governments.

Mulroney's party, however, was not a happy home for Conservatives who clung to Diefenbaker's vision of the country. Mulroney supported bilingualism and "distinct society" status for Quebec, and he brought into the party openly nationalistic Quebeckers such as Lucien Bouchard. Eventually, Mulroney's unsuccessful attempts to reconfigure the Canadian constitutional system, along with his unpopular economic policies, led to his departure from politics and to his party's spectacular downfall. The Meech Lake agreement, which was initiated in order to win Quebec's re-entry into the constitutional fold, raised serious problems for many English Canadians, many of whom thought that it gave too much power to Quebec. By the time its ratification deadline expired, a vast majority of English Canadians opposed the deal.[24] In turn, francophone Quebeckers interpreted this rejection of Meech as an insult, a humiliation, a cold refusal to recognize Quebec's distinctiveness. Lucien Bouchard left the Conservative Cabinet to establish his own federal party dedicated to Quebec separation, taking with him many of the Conservatives who had backed the party in Quebec since 1984. Mulroney's second attempt at constitutional renegotiation — one that would have accommodated Quebec but also reformed the Senate and recognized aboriginal self-government — was again rejected, both inside and outside Quebec. The only federal party in English Canada that had boldly challenged the Charlottetown Accord — the Reform party — reaped the benefits, as hordes of Conservative supporters, especially in western Canada, left their party in disgust and embraced Preston Manning's similarly conservative but unapologetically anti-Quebec vision of a "New Canada." Thus, having been elected in 1984 with a massive majority, including the vast bulk of the seats in both Quebec and the West, Mulroney's Conservatives left office nine years later, having created the two most serious political challenges to a unified country: the Bloc Québécois in Quebec, and the Reform party based in the West.

It is Preston Manning who has emerged as the key spokesperson for Diefenbaker-style ideas in the 1990s. Like Diefenbaker, the Reform leader calls for an unhyphenated Canadianism based on the equality of citizenship rights, a melting pot idea of multiculturalism, the equality of regions, the equality of provinces (though Manning is much more decentralist than Diefenbaker), and a One Canada view of Quebec's role within the federation. In many speeches, such as his address to the 1994 Reform party annual assembly, Manning might have been reading from an old Diefenbaker text: "I tell you, if we were rebuilding the national house, its foundations would be built on the bedrock of equality of provinces and equality of citizens, so that your standing with the government rests solely on your Canadian citizenship, not on your race, language, culture, gender, creed, or where you live in the country. We should all be treated as equals in our own house!"[25]

This approach is deeply entrenched in the western Canadian experience, and thus Reform has capitalized on its regional appeal and mobilized the former constituency of Diefenbaker Conservatives into a western-based party large enough to form the official opposition in the House of Commons. The Reform party ideology expands on the old Diefenbaker hostility toward special status, extending it to a

---

24   Robert M. Campbell and Leslie Pal, *The Real Worlds of Canadian Politics* (Peterborough: Broadview Press, 1991), 114.

25   Manning cited in Gibbins and Arrison, *Western Visions*, 49-50.

denunciation of collectivist aspirations expressed by Quebeckers, First Nations, and ethno-cultural minority groups.

Again in phrases that remind us of Diefenbaker, Manning explains his opposition to differentiated group rights:

> Reformers believe that going down the special status road has led to the creation of two full-blown separatist movements in Quebec and to the proposal of the Quebec Liberals to emasculate the federal government as the price of keeping Quebec in a non-confederation. It has led to desires and claims for "nation status" on the part of hundreds of aboriginal groups, claims which, if based on racial, linguistic, and cultural distinctiveness, are just as valid as those of the Québécois, if not more so. *It has led to a hyphenated Canadianism that emphasizes our differences and downplays our common ground, by labelling us as English-Canadians, French-Canadians, aboriginal-Canadians, or ethnic-Canadians — but never as Canadians, period.*[26] (emphasis added)

Such attitudes are at odds with many of Canada's official policies, but evidence suggests that the sentiments of many English Canadians run strongly against special rights for Quebeckers or for multicultural communities. Indeed, it seems that Canadians increasingly disagree with the idea of a cultural mosaic, in which each ethnic or racial group preserves its heritage with the help and sympathy of governments. Social scientists find that more and more Canadians would prefer to see Canada as a cultural melting pot like the United States.[27] Of key concern is the policy of official multiculturalism. This policy has been a target for heated criticism, often in the name of Canadian nationalism. Some prominent Canadians, including members of immigrant communities, say that the policy does little to encourage racial and ethnic harmony, but has the converse effect of hardening racial and ethnic prejudice by stressing the differences between groups rather than the shared ideals and values of all Canadians.[28] Indeed, there is concern that recent policies have undermined the traditions and symbols that are unique to Canada, leaving the nation without a clear identity cemented by unifying cultural institutions and customs. Some argue that the multiculturalism debates, along with the disputed meanings of nation and nationalism that are involved, have been tearing at the fabric of the country, forcing us apart rather than providing a source of cohesion and national pride. Again, these are concerns with which Diefenbaker would likely have had great sympathy. While Diefenbaker praised Canada's multicultural heritage, his was an earlier form of multiculturalism that recognized all individuals as having the same rights and duties regardless of their ethnic background. What he did not endorse was a form of multiculturalism that regards citizens as belonging to the country only via their membership in constituent ethnic subcommunities. It is this latter form of multiculturalism which has become the target for attacks from those who see official government policy undermining the principles of unhyphenated Canadianism.

---

26   Preston Manning, *The New Canada* (Toronto: Macmillan, 1992), 304-5.

27   For example, 72 percent of respondents in an October 1993 survey stated their agreement with the view that "the long-standing image of Canada as a nation of communities, each ethnic and racial group preserving its own identity with the help of government policy, must give way to the US style of cultural absorption." See Daiva Stasiulis, " 'Deep Diversity': Race and Ethnicity in Canadian Politics," in Michael S. Whittington and Glen Williams (eds.), *Canadian Politics in the 1990s* (Toronto: Nelson, 1995), 191-217, at 210. See also Reginald Bibby, *Mosaic Madness* (Toronto: Stoddart, 1990), chs. 1-2.

28   For example, Neil Bissoondath, *Selling Illusions: The Cult of Multiculturalism in Canada* (Toronto: Penguin, 1994).

THE IMPLICATIONS OF UNHYPHENATED CANADIANISM

The strongest connection between Diefenbaker's ideas and the current thinking in Reform camps is their shared perspective on the equality of citizens and provinces. Diefenbaker, as we have seen, promoted an essentially liberal-individualist notion of universalist citizenship. This view stresses the individual, including the individual's ability to transcend group or collective identity. In this scenario, the individual is free to choose his or her identity and is not defined by station in life, ethnic background, religious affiliation, and so on. On the face of it, this version of citizenship treats everyone equally — regardless of race, colour, or creed. Formal equality of right and equality before the law are the cornerstones of this approach. Rejected as undemocratic and unfair by Diefenbaker and his current disciples is any type of preferential treatment based on one's racial identity or ethno-cultural heritage. Such a practice, the argument runs, would "particularize" human beings, thus perpetuating exclusion and ghettoisation rather than inclusion and participation. Inequality and discrimination should be stamped out, of course, but that must be done by means of an active promotion of the *equality of opportunity* and not by the imposition of policies premised upon the *equality of results*. Thus, barriers to free and equal participation by minority groups should be torn down, but in a way that does not involve the privileging of minority individuals in societal competition. Likewise, individual francophone Quebeckers may be regarded as possessing a distinct cultural heritage, but their governments should not, according to this view, enjoy special powers to preserve and promote this distinctiveness. Hence, this individualist-universalist view of citizenship in no way denies to members of minority groups the rights to express their cultural differences. In fact, such free expressions of diversity are promoted and encouraged. Yet, as an *individual* and not a *collective* right, this right is qualified by the prohibition against impinging upon the rights of others (either outside the group or within it).

It is easy to see the attraction of such an egalitarian view of society. Indeed, it is difficult to think of a politician who would get far promoting the values of *inequality*. However, the ideas of absolute individual equality and the equality of the provinces conflict with other political values held dear in the Canadian political culture. In particular, individual equality runs up against the notion that communities have the right to self-determination. Thus, the notion of the equality of provinces frustrates the aspirations of Quebeckers. Similarly, the idea of an absolute equality of citizenship undermines First Nations persons' desires for greater degrees of cultural and political autonomy. And the majoritarian populism espoused by such politicians as Diefenbaker or Manning — the idea of counting heads equally — disadvantages cultural, racial, linguistic, and ethnic minorities.

As François Rocher and Miriam Smith point out, Diefenbaker's view of One Canada "ignored the very real problems faced by minorities in preserving their identity and the way that the level playing field and guarantees of individual rights would privilege the dominant group and prevent minorities from defining and defending themselves."[29] This is made most plain in the conflict between One Canada ideas and the attempt to recognize Quebec as a distinct society within Canada. There is simply no hope of reconciling the most minimal demands of recent Quebec governments with a One Canada nationalism based on the notion of provincial

---

29   François Rocher and Miriam Smith, "The New Boundaries of the Canadian Political Culture," delivered at the conference organized by the Centre for Canadian Studies, University of Edinburgh, UK, May 1996, (mimeo), p. 9.

equality. For Diefen941Obaker's ideal of a single, united Canada to flourish, Quebeckers would have to think of themselves primarily as Canadians rather than as Québécois. The reality, of course, is that a majority of Quebeckers define themselves as *Québécois d'abord* — Quebeckers first.[30] There appears to be little reason to believe that one can sell a One Canada concept of the nation to contemporary Québécois. This leaves few credible options for constructive change, none of which conforms to Diefenbaker's vision. For instance, some form of asymmetrical federalism might be sufficient to win Quebecker's approval for remaining in Canada while allowing the federal government to retain its authority in key jurisdictional fields in the other provinces. This would, however, clearly violate the One Canada principles laid down by Diefenbaker. Alternatively, one might imagine a decentralization of power to all provinces equally that would be dramatic enough to satisfy the Quebec government's requirements for control of the lion's share of responsibilities within the federation. The problem here, however, is that nothing would be done to address what Charles Taylor refers to as the "politics of recognition." That is, a lot of the battle in Canada's present constitutional crisis is over *recognition* — the acceptance by others of certain people in their identity. If the principle of the equality of individuals or provinces is taken to mean that the recognition of distinct societies is ruled out, then equality is being defined in such a way as to exclude the aspirations of Quebeckers or aboriginals for equality. According to Taylor, the prolonged refusal of recognition can erode the common understanding of equal participation on which a functioning democracy depends; and Canada is a "tragic case in point."[31]

If this is an accurate analysis, then Diefenbaker's vision of a single, united Canada — a political nationality that knows no hyphenated consideration — is an impediment to the resolution of the national unity issue. The Diefenbaker ideal might, however, form the basis for a new, specifically *English*-Canadian nationalism. For many observers, the time has come for us to start exploring the identity of English Canada and forging a specifically English-Canadian political nationality. For some, the issue is a matter of restoring a sense of national purpose and identity by repudiating most of the concessions made to minority groups in Canada. David Bercuson and Barry Cooper, for instance, insist that Canadians must re-establish a single national polity by decentralizing further the federal system (including ending the practice of equalization payments to the "have-less" provinces) and taking steps to get the Canadian financial house back in order by cutting taxes, eradicating the welfare state, privatizing state-run enterprises, and returning the nation to its *laissez-faire* roots.[32] This same attitude reverberates throughout the Reform party's platform, which similarly calls for an end to special status based on linguistic, racial, or cultural characteristics, and promotes a program of fiscal restraint. Party leader Preston Manning articulates a candidly "English-Canadian" conception of a New Canada. Among other things, he promotes the dismantling of official bilingualism and multiculturalism in the name of a common, unhyphenated Canadianism. Manning and his supporters advocate an alternative to the mainly leftist nationalism that was

---

30   Studies show that about 59 percent of Quebec francophones identify first and foremost with Quebec. See McRoberts, *Misconceiving Canada*, 246.

31   Charles Taylor, *Reconciling the Solitudes: Essays on Canadian Federalism and Nationalism* (Montreal and Kingston: McGill-Queen's University Press, 1993), 190.

32   David Bercuson and Barry Cooper, *Derailed: The Betrayal of the National Dream* (Toronto: Key Porter, 1994).

prominent in the 1960s and 1970s. This new nationalism resembles in some ways the patriotism found in the United States ("America, love it or leave it") and seeks to emulate the American sense of national unity and civic pride.

For many English Canadians, there is a strong appeal in this pitch for a greater emphasis on common characteristics and shared values. But although this is a popular model for Canadians outside Quebec to consider, there is no reason to believe that unhyphenated Canadianism can resolve the concerns of other key sub-national forces. Indeed, even if Quebec separates and what is left is a country without the need to protect a recognizable part of it as a homeland for francophones in North America, the aspirations of the First Nations and of ethno-cultural minorities may still be in need of resolution by means more sophisticated than the individualist notions of citizenship promoted by Diefenbaker and his descendants. Thus, an alternative conception of citizenship is required for a diverse society such as Canada, one that involves the cultural pluralist notion of differentiated citizenship. The theoretical underpinning of this viewpoint is a critique of liberal impartiality, or of the notion that we are all to be treated as equal citizens, regardless of sex, race, creed, cultural background, or class. While this type of abstract equality may appear to be an attractive ideal, cultural pluralists argue that equal treatment in practice merely perpetuates oppression and the exclusion of non-majority groups. True equality therefore demands some sort of institutionalized group representation. This politics of difference would replace the liberal priority of the abstract individual with an appreciation for one's cultural or ethnic group, since for many in Canada today it is the group which is the source of identity and meaning in an otherwise atomizing world. Solidarity and group cohesion must be preserved among those sharing a history, a language, a culture, a set of common aspirations, goals, or a way of life. A group's ability to confer identity upon those who are members is a primary good. This notion is still premised on the original liberal notion of universal equality, but it recognizes that beyond the protection of individual rights there must be a respect for persons as members of identity-conferring groups.

Of course, this cultural-pluralist notion of citizenship is in direct conflict with Diefenbaker-style individualistic liberalism. And it involves more than the issue of Quebec's place within the federation. In recent years, for instance, both First Nations and ethnic groups have been concerned with issues that go unresolved when confined to a strict individual equality model. Frustrated by the limitations of traditional models of equal citizenship, advocates for both First Peoples and new peoples argue that recognition and acceptance of difference are the crucial requirements of an inclusive citizenship.[33] From this perspective, equality means more than treating everyone in the same way, regardless of difference; it can mean treating different groups differently when the situation dictates. Such a way of thinking, needless to say, is not amenable to an unhyphenated understanding of citizenship. Indeed, those hyphens are crucial for the preservation of the constitutive elements of an individual's identity. For these reasons, the notion of unhyphenated Canadianism is not only an insufficient basis for an inclusive conception of citizenship for a Canada that includes Quebec, but is also an inappropriate model for a future Canada that may not include Quebec. As sweet as it may sound, the simple idea that all citizens should be treated equally does not satisfy the requirements for an inclusive citizenship, a meaningful sense of equality, or a respect for the deep diversity of a society

---

33   See Richard Sigurdson, "First Peoples, New Peoples and Citizenship in Canada," *The International Journal of Canadian Studies/Revue internationale d'étude canadiennes* 14 (Fall/Automne 1996): 53-76.

such as contemporary Canada. Indeed, to the extent that Diefenbaker's old rhetoric becomes new again (in part, owing to the rise of Preston Manning's Reform party), we seem to be assured only of continued strife and antagonism between the cultural majority and the various minorities which together constitute our country and define its identity.

FACTIONS, REVIEWS, AND REFORMERS: DIEFENBAKER'S LEGACY TO THE PROGRESSIVE CONSERVATIVE PARTY

David Stewart

John Diefenbaker occupies an important and controversial place in the history of the Conservative party in Canada. Of all the party's leaders, only the legendary John A. Macdonald led the party in more elections and won more elections. While Diefenbaker does not rival Macdonald in the affections of Conservatives, he, unlike most of his predecessors and successors, "left his party better off than when he found it"[1] in terms of electoral strength. In spite of this accomplishment, many, like Denis Smith, feel that "his political career ended in failure."[2]

Failure seems an apt word to describe Diefenbaker's political end, given the particular nature of his exit from the leadership. For while numerous Canadian party leaders have stepped down under internal pressure, Diefenbaker's leadership was effectively terminated by a majority of delegates to the party's convention. And no other leader has suffered the same humiliation that Diefenbaker experienced at that convention in 1967.

But failure or not, Diefenbaker's legacy is an important one. First of all, under his leadership the party secured a regional base in the electorate and emerged as the dominant party in English-speaking Canada. Second, the internal party (i.e., institutional) reforms brought in to drive Diefenbaker from the Conservative leadership continue to influence Canadian parties today. Third, the Diefenbaker faction that continued on within the party after his defeat, while causing much grief for his successors, Robert Stanfield and Joe Clark, managed to sustain itself and eventually contribute to the 1983 convention victory of Brian Mulroney, who would lead the Conservatives once again to power. Diefenbaker's final legacy was his demonstration of how to build support for a conservative party in western Canada.

IMPROVEMENT IN CONSERVATIVE FORTUNES

When Diefenbaker won the Conservative leadership in 1956, he took over a party that was notable for its failures. It had not won an election in a quarter of a century,

---

1   Richard Johnston et al., *Letting the People Decide* (Montreal: McGill-Queen's University Press, 1992), 59.

2   Denis Smith, *Rogue Tory* (Toronto: MacFarlane, Walter and Ross, 1995), 578.

and was not perceived as a serious contender for power. Indeed, in Quebec and on the Prairies, the party's electoral support was insufficient to send more than a handful of members to the House of Commons. Diefenbaker's leadership created a much stronger national party. Between 1930 and 1957, Conservatives held only 28 percent of the seats in the House of Commons; between 1958 and 1980, in contrast, they held 43 percent, and emerged as the dominant party outside Quebec. From 1958 to 1988, the Conservative party elected a plurality of MPs from provinces other than Quebec in every election save one (1968). Even in Diefenbaker's beleaguered final campaign as leader in 1965, he and his party out-polled Pearson and the Liberals outside Quebec. Liberal dominance in Quebec disguised the extent of the Conservative party's success in the rest of the country — success for which John Diefenbaker was largely responsible.

Under Diefenbaker the Conservatives secured a regional base that enhanced their competitive standing. With Diefenbaker, and after him, the Conservatives were the dominant party on the Prairies. In the five elections before Diefenbaker became leader, the party had won only 14 percent of the prairie seats. During and after his leadership (from 1958 to 1980) the party's winning percentage increased to a phenomenal 80 percent. These seats accounted for a third of the party's national total. The Prairies provided the core of the Conservative caucus, with MPs from this region often outnumbering the combined total from Ontario and Quebec.

Diefenbaker's leadership corresponds with the rise of a new party system in Canada in which the Conservative party was a force in most of the country and an overwhelming force on the Prairies.[3] The Prairies became the electoral base of the Conservative party, and an electoral wasteland for the Liberals. For this, too, Diefenbaker deserves much of the credit. In his assessment of the Diefenbaker legacy, Denis Smith concludes: "Diefenbaker broadened the Conservative Party and restored it as a national movement representing all regions of the country."[4] Related to this geographical broadening of the Conservatives was an increase in support from farmers, as well as a significant shift in the ethnic face of the party, from its primarily British nature.[5]

LEADERSHIP REVIEW

In 1919 and 1927, the Liberal and Conservative parties began using conventions to select their leaders. This change not only removed the power to choose leaders from the party's elected caucus, but concomitantly stripped the caucus's power to remove leaders. But this left nobody in the party with authority to remove the leader, since "there was no mechanism by which a convention could vote out a leader."[6] In

---

3   Johnston et al., *Letting the People Decide*, 61. The authors suggest that Diefenbaker's legacy was a broadening of the Conservative base, and note: "[that] the Conservatives could return a plurality in any province was a significant shift from the second party system."

4   Smith, *Rogue Tory*, 577.

5   See Johnston et al., *Letting the People Decide*, 56, 71; see also Richard Johnston et al., "The 1993 Canadian Election: Realignment, Dealignment or Something Else," a paper presented to the annual meeting of the Canadian Political Science Association, Brock University, 1996, p. 9. In "John Diefenbaker's One Canada and the Legacy of Unhypenated Canadianism" (published in this volume), Richard Sigurdson also notes how Diefenbaker made the Conservatives acceptable to "ethnic" Canadians.

6   Donald Blake, R.K. Carty, and Lynda Erickson, "Coming and Going: Leadership Selection and Removal in Canada," in A.B. Tanguay and Alain Gagnon (eds.), *Canadian Parties in Transition* (Scarborough, ON: Nelson, 1996), 220.

the Liberal and Conservative parties, leaders served, to a certain extent, at their own pleasure.

The Conservative party did have standing votes of confidence, but these were essentially empty formalities. In a cadre party such as the Conservatives, electoral success generally provides immunity from leadership challenge.[7] When electoral fortunes decline, this immunity is threatened. When Diefenbaker first lost the huge majority he had won in 1958, and then lost power altogether, elements in the Conservative party decided his time was up.

The 1965 election defeat spelled the end of Diefenbaker's leadership even as it confirmed his stature as one of the greatest campaigners the country has ever produced. The party was experiencing difficulty in raising funds, and its strength was concentrated in rural and hinterland areas — not the path to power in an increasingly urbanized country where most of the population resides in the centre.[8] His refusal to go quietly led to a change in party procedures that, in the end, helped modify its cadre-like nature.

The nature of Diefenbaker's hold on the leadership demonstrates an intriguing feature of Canadian political parties, namely, the ambiguous relationship between the parliamentary and extra-parliamentary wings. In cadre parties, the parliamentary wing is theoretically dominant, while the extra-parliamentary wing exists not to control elected members but to enhance their electoral chances.[9] The subservience of the extra-parliamentary wing rests on the assumption that the parliamentary wing places an emphasis on control of the government. It is possible, however, that the desire of individual parliamentarians for personal re-election may not coincide with the measures that the extra-parliamentary wing considers necessary to maximize the party's chances of forming a government. In essence, the elected Members of Parliament may feel their immediate interest in re-election to be compromised by the kind of campaign the extra-parliamentary wing decides it must wage in order to win. In this situation, there is likely to be conflict between the party's two wings. Such a situation clearly obtained in the Conservative party after 1965.

The response of those in the extra-parliamentary wing of the party who saw Diefenbaker and his caucus as a barrier to wider electoral success was to change the rules. Dalton Camp used his control of the extra-parliamentary wing to wage a campaign calling for the "democratization" of the party. As Denis Smith explains: "Camp suggested a procedural reform in the party to give its members a regular means of reassessing the leadership. The next annual meeting after an election in which the party had not gained power, he proposed, should face an automatic ballot on whether or not to hold a leadership convention."[10]

---

7   The description of the Conservative party as a "cadre" party refers to its organization and focus. Cadre parties have electoral success as their overarching goal, and place the achievement of power above the promotion of principle. A cadre party is dominated by its caucus and offers ordinary members only a limited voice. For the classic discussion of the cadre-mass distinction, see Maurice Duverger, *Political Parties* (1954; Cambridge: Methuen, 1978), 62-116.

8   For a discussion of these problems, see George Perlin, *The Tory Syndrome* (Montreal: McGill-Queen's University Press, 1980).

9   Dalton Camp endorsed this view when he was elected party president in 1964, declaring that the extra-parliamentary wing must be "in the service of the parliamentary party. Their policy must be our policy. And their leadership is ours." Quoted in Smith, *Rogue Tory*, 518.

10   Ibid., 543.

At the 1966 party convention, after Camp was re-elected as President, a motion of this sort was put to the delegates and approved by a substantial margin (563-186).[11] Shortly thereafter, the vast majority of Conservative MPs signed a pledge of support for Diefenbaker, placing the two wings of the party in conflict. There have been contending interpretations of the Members' support of Diefenbaker. Some, like Eddie Goodman, believe that "the pressure from Diefenbaker loyalists on the MPs to sign the pledge had been strong and few [in the extra-parliamentary party] took it seriously."[12] Blake, Carty, and Erickson, in contrast, suggest that the party "waited anxiously to see what Diefenbaker would do."[13] George Perlin elaborates: "The immediate fear of some members of the anti-Diefenbaker alliance was that Diefenbaker might use his caucus mandate to challenge the legitimacy of the decision to call a convention."[14]

In fact, the parliamentary wing was undecided about its options in light of the convention vote; some Diefenbaker supporters seriously considered the option of leaving the Conservatives to form a new party. Diefenbaker loyalist Robert Coates later stated: "It would have been an easy task to convince many, if not all of the western members who signed the oath of loyalty to John Diefenbaker to leave the party after the annual meeting."[15] Diefenbaker himself reported that "Forty [MPs] were prepared to form a breakaway party if I resigned."[16] But in the end, Diefenbaker took no such action, and, after time for reflection, "called for an immediate leadership convention to be made up entirely of democratically elected constituency delegates."[17]

Diefenbaker did contest the 1967 leadership convention, placing a distant fifth. His participation in the convention removed any questions regarding its legitimacy and, at its conclusion, he announced his support for the victorious Robert Stanfield. In so doing, "he accepted the party's right to decide to select a new leader and so legitimated a new process of 'leadership reviews' which effectively gave the party in convention the power to remove a leader."[18] These actions contributed to the "institutionalization" of the party, and moved it further away from a classic cadre form of organization.[19]

---

11   Camp's re-election was due in part to the voting of Ontario's at-large delegates. See Penny Bryden, "Federal/Ontario Relations in the Diefenbaker Era" (published in this volume) for a discussion of the troubled relations between Diefenbaker and the leadership of the Ontario Conservative party.

12   Eddie Goodman, *Life of the Party* (Toronto: Key Porter, 1988), 131-32.

13   Blake, Carty, and Erickson, "Coming and Going," 220.

14   Perlin, *The Tory Syndrome*, 85.

15   Robert Coates, *The Night of the Knives* (Fredericton, NB: Brunswick, 1969), 76.

16   John Diefenbaker, *One Canada: The Tumultuous Years, 1962 to 1967* (Scarborough, ON: Macmillan, 1977), 243.

17   Smith, *Rogue Tory*, 550. In calling for such a convention, Diefenbaker wished to eliminate the delegate-at-large positions appointed by those in control of the provincial associations. His call was unheeded.

18   Blake, Carty, and Erickson, "Coming and Going," 220.

19   Institutionalization "refers to the development of the party as an organization." See Peter Woolsten-croft, "The Progressive Conservative Party, 1984-1993," in Hugh Thorburn (ed.), *Party Politics in Canada* (Scarborough: Prentice Hall, 1996), 283. Among other things, institutionalization relates to the development of a powerful extra-parliamentary organization and a correspondence between the party's rules and its power structure. By accepting the actions of the party president and the party

THE DIEFENBAKER FACTION

Yet Diefenbaker's defeat and his words of support for Stanfield by no means ended the influence of the Diefenbaker faction within the Conservative party. Stanfield was faced with a caucus widely supportive of Diefenbaker, who proved unwilling to fade into the background. Stanfield's victory was seen as a victory for Dalton Camp and the anti-Diefenbaker faction, and Diefenbaker was angry that Stanfield in his victory speech indicated his determination "to get along with that fellow Camp."[20]

John Diefenbaker is one of only a few party leaders in Canada to contest an election after his/her leadership ended, and he remained a Member of Parliament until his death. As a member of caucus throughout the Stanfield era, Diefenbaker was, to say the least, less than supportive. Various accounts report his delight at Stanfield's defeat in 1968.[21] The 1968 election again left Stanfield with a caucus largely supportive of Diefenbaker, and Diefenbaker was prepared to cause difficulties — the most obvious being his stand on official bilingualism. Stanfield worked hard to reach out to Quebec, but his work was complicated by the actions of his caucus.

When the Official Languages Act was voted on in 1969, less than 60 percent of the Conservative caucus supported it. Indeed, seventeen MPs, including Diefenbaker, defied Stanfield and ensured that their opposition to the measure was recorded. These actions suggested a weakness in Stanfield's leadership and inhibited his ability to increase Conservative party support in Quebec.[22] Brown, Chodos, and Murphy suggest that "Diefenbaker as he danced in front of his new leader all the way from Toronto in 1967 to Ottawa in 1976, cover[ed] his path with banana peels instead of rose petals."[23] After losing three elections, Stanfield stepped down, and a convention was scheduled for 1976. According to George Perlin: "The source of the conflict which disrupted Stanfield's leadership was the persistence of factional cleavages from the earlier conflict over Diefenbaker's leadership."[24]

The 1976 leadership convention was not simply about the selection of a new leader; it was also a replay of the battles of 1966.[25] The candidates in 1976 could be easily assessed in terms of where they stood in 1966. On the side of Joe Clark, the eventual winner, stood most of the "Campites": Flora Macdonald, John Fraser, Heward Grafftey, and Sinclair Stevens. Remaining neutral, but with the bulk of his supporters voting ultimately for Clark, was another Camp supporter, Brian Mulroney. On the other side was Claude Wagner, who received the explicit endorsement of John Diefenbaker before the final ballot. Joining Wagner was long-time Diefenbaker loyalist Jack Horner, and Paul Hellyer, who in 1966 was a Liberal Cabinet minister.

---

convention, Diefenbaker clearly advanced the institutionalization of the Conservatives. His implicit acceptance of the notion that the party in convention trumps the party in Parliament is a significant event in the development of Canadian parties.

20 Geoffrey Stevens, *Stanfield* (Toronto: McClelland and Stewart, 1973), 195.

21 See, for instance, Goodman, *Life of the Party*, and Stevens, *Stanfield*.

22 George Perlin, "The Progressive Conservative Party: An Assessment of its Victories in the Elections of 1984 and 1988," in Thorburn, *Party Politics in Canada*, 300.

23 Patrick Brown, Robert Chodos and Rae Murphy, *Winners, Losers* (Toronto: James Lorimer, 1976), 47.

24 Perlin, *The Tory Syndrome*, 124.

25 Brown, Chodos and Murphy, *Winners, Losers*, 44: "because Diefenbaker never fully accepted the leadership of Robert Stanfield and because he has politically survived his successor, there is one aspect of the legend that is still germane. That is that Diefenbaker was betrayed by his own party."

As in 1966, the Diefenbaker forces were defeated, but were unwilling to accept defeat. Clark's leadership was challenged internally by Horner, who eventually crossed the floor of the House to join the Liberals. Another Diefenbaker loyalist, Stan Schumacher, dared Clark to challenge him for the nomination in the Alberta constituency containing Clark's home town. And long-time Diefenbaker supporter Robert Coates was elected as party president. Eventually "a number of strong anti-Clark partisans … had captured key posts in the national executive and were using that vantage to assail Clark."[26]

Clark proved unable to survive his party's electoral defeat in 1980. Ironically, it was the leadership review mechanism which he had supported in 1966 that terminated his leadership. The ouster of Clark represented a triumph for the remaining Diefenbaker loyalists, since "he was clearly identified with the old anti-Diefenbaker alliance and his victory … could be seen as a further demonstration of the ascendancy of this faction within the party."[27]

Ambiguity in the relationship between the parliamentary and extra-parliamentary wings of the party was again exhibited in the contest over Clark's leadership. Clark's caucus support was less than overwhelming, but that in itself was not sufficient to force the leader to resign; the 1966 reforms ensured that the decision rested with the party in convention.[28] Support by a simple majority of convention delegates, however, was insufficient to force the caucus to cooperate with its leader. In the end, although Clark received the support of 66.9 percent of those voting on the leadership review in 1983, the fact that "fully fifty percent of Clark's parliamentary colleagues voted for a leadership convention"[29] left him unable to continue. He announced his decision to call for a leadership convention in which he would be a candidate.[30] Clark's eventual defeat in that convention was a significant event in the Conservative party. Those who had supported Diefenbaker were finally on the winning side of an important decision after being "on the losing side in most of the conflicts in the party since the battle over John Diefenbaker's leadership in 1966-1967."[31]

Diefenbaker's death undoubtedly was a boon to the victorious Brian Mulroney, as Diefenbaker was not around to remind his loyalists of Mulroney's support for a leadership review in the 1960s. But Mulroney realized that, to secure the party leadership, he would have to gain the support of the Diefenbaker faction. He showed up uninvited at Diefenbaker's eightieth birthday party, and avoided direct association with the other Campites at the 1976 convention. "[W]hen Brian Mulroney constantly reminded delegates of his affection for and connections to 'The Chief,' and when he won the endorsements of such Diefenbaker loyalists as Alvin Hamilton and Robert Coates, he identified himself with those outsiders."[32] Moreover, he provided an

---

26   Patrick Martin, Allan Gregg and George Perlin, *Contenders: The Tory Quest for Power* (Scarborough, ON: Prentice Hall, 1983), 8.

27   Ibid, xiv.

28   The leader's independence from caucus spread to the Liberal party. When more than half his elected caucus pressed John Turner to resign prior to the 1988 election, he ignored them. His leadership had previously been confirmed by a leadership review vote held by the party in convention.

29   Ibid., 80.

30   Woolstencroft, "The Progressive Conservative Party," 286.

31   Martin, Gregg and Perlin, *Contenders*, 197.

32   Ibid., 198.

indication of his support for Diefenbaker's rejection of the notion of "two nations" by stating: "I do not believe in a theory of two nations … nor … in any concept that would give any one province an advantage over another."[33] Thus, his courting of the Diefenbaker faction was based both on symbolism and on the touchstone of "One Canada." As it turned out, the Conservative party came out of the 1983 convention relatively united, partly because time and Diefenbaker's death had dissipated some of the passions surrounding his ouster, partly because the Diefenbaker faction was finally on the winning side, and partly because Clark and his supporters accepted the outcome with good grace.[34]

In *The Tory Syndrome*, George Perlin argues convincingly that leadership divisions in the Conservative party were not based on policy. Nonetheless, it is impossible to understand Diefenbaker's legacy to the Conservative party without examining his populist approach and his positions on Quebec and the West.

DIEFENBAKER'S POPULISM

Part of Diefenbaker's appeal to Canadians lay in populism. Perlin suggests that "Diefenbaker was a populist [who] built his career on attacking the dominant élites in the country and asserting his identity with the 'average Canadian'."[35] This was a shift in emphasis for the Conservatives since, as Johnston et al. explain, "Before John Diefenbaker, populism and the Conservative Party were antithetical."[36]

Diefenbaker's populism was demonstrated more by his rhetoric and style than by any concrete policy measures. In 1942, in his first leadership campaign, he "cast himself in the role of populist tribune, a role he played to the hilt thereafter. He was particularly successful because he defined his attack on élites in such generalized form that any discontented group could attach itself to him."[37] While an ordinary Member of Parliament, he also often acted as if he were free of the bounds of party discipline, and later as party leader he tolerated independent stands taken by his parliamentary colleagues. He also described himself as being on the side of the people, who he contrasted with those who were all-powerful.

The most obvious manifestation of Diefenbaker's populism was the number and variety of supporters he brought to the Conservative party. Populism then, as now, had its greatest appeal in western Canada, and this helps explicate how Diefenbaker managed to make the Prairies the core of Conservative party support. Perlin discusses Diefenbaker's populism in terms of an "insider-outsider" dichotomy. The outsiders are those whose social characteristics differ from those of the dominant élite in the country, an élite that included central Canadians in urban centres, individuals with a professional or a corporate occupation, and those with a university education.[38]

Perlin notes that loyalty to Diefenbaker among members of his Cabinet and ordinary Members of Parliament was related to the number of establishment characteristics these individuals lacked. (During the Stanfield era, the opposition of Conservative MPs to the Official Languages Act was also related to this outsider

---

33   Brian Mulroney, *Where I Stand* (Toronto: McClelland and Stewart, 1983), 9.

34   Perlin, "The Progressive Conservative Party," 304.

35   Perlin, *The Tory Syndrome*, 127.

36   Johnston et al., *Letting the People Decide*, 65.

37   Perlin, *The Tory Syndrome*, 191.

38   Ibid., 82, 70.

dimension.) In essence, the fewer such characteristics, the higher the support for Diefenbaker and the position he favoured.[39] Diefenbaker attracted outsiders to the Conservative party and put them in positions of prominence within it. In Perlin's words: "Diefenbaker captured and gave expression to a latent populist sentiment which is an enduring basis of cleavage in the party."[40]

That the outsiders had come to play a prominent role in the party was demonstrated in the 1968 election when the Conservative party contracted to its core support. Less than half the Conservative MPs were from central Canada and, as Geoffrey Stevens explains, "Broadly speaking, the Conservative supporters in 1968 were older, rural, less affluent, and less well educated than Liberal supporters."[41]

Conservative support expanded again in the 1970s and 1980s, and the party clearly attracted increased support from "non-outsiders." But this contributed to a decline in the party's attraction for those who appreciated a more grassroots style. As a result, the Conservative party was somewhat vulnerable to attacks from the new, emerging Reform party, which celebrated "the common sense of the common people" and aggressively identified itself as populist. In the aftermath of the 1993 election, Diefenbaker-style outsiders dominated Reform's parliamentary benches.[42] Thus, Johnston et al. have suggested, "in a sense, Reform is the Diefenbaker Conservative Party, that is, the party that Diefenbaker's closest acolytes might have idealized had they not been forced to tolerate some of the coalitional baggage he inherited."[43]

DIEFENBAKER AND QUEBEC

Diefenbaker became Prime Minister in 1957 after a campaign which eschewed the traditional Conservative brokerage strategy of pursuing Quebec. Instead, following a strategy suggested by Gordon Churchill, the campaign focussed on English Canada and devoted fewer resources to Quebec.[44] The resulting perception that Diefenbaker cared little about, or was insensitive to, Quebec was reinforced when, in spite of the Conservatives' success in electing fifty Quebec MPs in 1958, he appointed few to his cabinet, and then only to minor portfolios. He was prepared, as Perlin notes, "to make some symbolic gestures toward the recognition of French Canadian concerns but they were not sufficient to satisfy the aspirations of a new, more liberal and assertive French Canadian nationalism."[45] Later, in opposition, Diefenbaker led the fight against the current Canadian flag, a fight opposed by the eight Conservative MPs from Quebec. Eventually, Leon Balcer, the man Diefenbaker had designated as his Quebec lieutenant, invited the Liberal government to invoke closure on the issue.[46] Finally, setting off the chain of events culminating in Diefenbaker's ouster,

---

39   Ibid., 70, 82.

40   Ibid., 182.

41   Stevens, *Stanfield*, 227.

42   An examination of the fifty-two Reform MPs elected in 1993 reveals that seventeen of them have no "insider" characteristics and a further twenty-one have only one. Given the party's weakness in central Canada, none of its 1993 MPs possessed all four establishment characteristics. Information on the MPs was taken from the *Canadian Parliamentary Guide* for 1994 and 1995.

43   Richard Johnston, Neil Nevitte, and Henry Brady, "Campaign Dynamics in 1993," a paper presented to the Annual Meeting of the Canadian Political Science Association, University of Calgary, 1994, p. 14.

44   Smith, *Rogue Tory*, 234-35.

45   Perlin, *The Tory Syndrome*, 63.

46   Diefenbaker, *The Tumultuous Years*, 193, 196.

Balcer in a letter to Dalton Camp charged Diefenbaker "with nourishing an anti-Quebec backlash" and recommended a change of leader.[47]

Diefenbaker's final leadership campaign in 1967 was premised on his opposition to special status for Quebec, a status he felt would inevitably follow from the Conservative party's flirtation with recognizing "the country's two founding peoples."[48] In his words: "I had advised my friends and supporters that I would not stand. 'Two Nations' eliminated all choice."[49] In his final speech as leader, he stated: "I am looking into the hearts of Canadians everywhere. I know what discrimination is. I know how much easier it would have been if my name had been my mother's name.... Let us be Canadians. Let us not deny equality to those whose surnames are not of the parent races."[50] This stance was consistent with the One Canada position Diefenbaker advocated throughout his career, and his "unhyphenated Canadianism" which, as David E. Smith has observed, was a general western Canadian view.[51] Diefenbaker's legacy to the party with respect to Quebec was a philosophy, rooted in the western Canadian political and cultural experience, that accorded Quebec no special position within the Canadian federation.

Yet Diefenbaker's opposition to special status for Quebec helped fashion a home in the Conservative party for "francophobes." The appeal of the party to this faction was strengthened by the opposition to the Official Languages Act displayed by Diefenbaker and some of his most prominent supporters. While Diefenbaker himself may not have been a "francophobe," his "ethnic appeal was quite subtle: as the bearer of a German surname he had personally experienced prejudice and so spoke with considerable moral authority when he insisted on an ethnically neutral definition of Canada; but that insistence could also serve as a cover for ethnically exclusive appeals, even if Mr. Diefenbaker himself did not intend as much."[52] For Canadians strongly opposed to special status for Quebec and/or bilingualism, the Conservative party provided a comfortable environment.[53]

The Conservative party as a home for Canadians who held such views would be rendered less habitable by Brian Mulroney. Mulroney's support for bilingualism and his government's negotiation of constitutional accords which explicitly recognized Quebec as a "distinct society" constituted a sharp challenge to those in the party, particularly westerners, who shared Diefenbaker's vision of the country. The Reform party's commitment to Canada as one nation of equal provinces, and its support for the repeal of the Official Languages Act,[54] would be much closer to Diefenbaker's conception of Canada than the Mulroney- and Charest-led Conservatives.

---

47   Ibid., p. 205.

48   Goodman, *Life of the Party*, 135.

49   Diefenbaker, *The Tumultuous Years*, 244.

50   Ibid., p. 247.

51   David Smith, *Regional Decline of a National Party* (Toronto: University of Toronto Press, 1981), 109.

52   Johnston et al., "Campaign Dynamics in 1993," 14. Denis Smith evokes a similar theme when he refers to "the darker prejudices Diefenbaker's words and silences called forth." See *Rogue Tory*, 554.

53   See, for example, George Perlin's discussion of the kinds of people attracted to the Conservative party. In Thorburn, *Party Politics in Canada*, 302.

54   Reform used the 1997 election campaign to make clear its opposition to the recognition of Quebec as a "distinct society." Its views towards this issue and official bilingualism are laid out in *The Blue Sheet*, Reform Party of Canada, 1995, 1, 5.

DIEFENBAKER AND THE WEST

As we have seen, the Conservative party under Diefenbaker emerged as the party of the West. After Diefenbaker, the Liberal party was unable to recover its support in the region, as has been chronicled by David E. Smith in *The Regional Decline of a National Party*. The West was won by Diefenbaker's appropriation of populist support and his One Canada platform, which had de-emphasised the dualist nature of the country.

But other Diefenbaker policies solidified his prairie support. With respect to agriculture, Diefenbaker undertook an aggressive campaign to export wheat, thus identifying his government "with the interests of the western grain farmer."[55] Moreover, Diefenbaker provided protection for energy producers, a measure which constituted the "first time Central Canadian consumers were forced to subsidize a western industry which seemed to have no realistic prospect of comparative advantage in the world market."[56] Hugh Thorburn has stated that Laurier fell from power in 1911 because "he broke the basic rule for success in Canadian politics, he gave priority to the outlying areas."[57] A case could be made that Diefenbaker made a similar error. Certainly, as David E. Smith has demonstrated, Diefenbaker headed a government which was much more sympathetic to western concerns than were the Liberal governments which succeeded him.[58]

The priorities of Diefenbaker's government secured the Prairies for the Conservative party. But Diefenbaker was overthrown as leader in part because many Conservatives felt the areas of support he won for the party were of diminishing political and electoral importance; the route to power lay in other directions. Nonetheless, as long as the Conservative party remained in opposition, westerners could believe that their alienation was basically the result of having a Liberal government in Ottawa. The election of the Conservatives in 1984 and 1988 shattered these illusions, but in 1993 the West repudiated the Conservative party. Reform out-polled the Conservatives in all four western provinces, and topped the polls in Alberta and British Columbia.

Western expectations were probably too great for the Mulroney government to satisfy. Moreover, one notable decision early on made it clear that the Mulroney Conservatives would not act as the party of the West — the CF-18 decision, in which the government awarded a maintenance contract to a company in Montreal, in spite of the fact that a western company submitted a technically superior and less costly bid. Thomas Flanagan identified this decision as a catalyst in the formation of the Reform party.[59]

CONCLUSION

The Diefenbaker legacy as initially outlined referred to the broadening of party support accompanying his tenure as leader. Unquestionably, the Conservative party was stronger after Diefenbaker than it was before, even with the internal divisions generated by his ouster.

---

55   Smith, *Regional Decline of a National Party*, 28.

56   Johnston et al., *Letting the People Decide*, 59.

57   Hugh Thorburn, "The Development of Party Politics in Canada," in Thorburn (ed.), *Party Politics in Canada*, 8.

58   Smith, *Regional Decline of a National Party*.

59   Thomas Flanagan, *Waiting for the Wave: The Reform Party and Preston Manning* (Don Mills, ON: Stoddart, 1995), 47.

The issues surrounding his departure provided three clear bequests to the party. The first was an institutional reform which made it easier for parties to rid themselves of leaders who were no longer wanted. Obviously, Diefenbaker did not initiate this reform himself. To his credit, though, he accepted the judgement of the extra-parliamentary party and stepped down. In his willingness to accept this judgement, Diefenbaker contributed to the democratization of his party; giving the party in convention the ability to change its leadership helped push the party away from a purely cadre form of organization.[60] The leadership review mechanisms pioneered in 1966 would have to be taken seriously by all subsequent Conservative and Liberal leaders.

The second bequest was that of an internal party faction unhappy with the 1966-67 party decisions. This faction, with which Diefenbaker was associated until his death, played a prominent role in the party under the leadership of Stanfield and Clark. It was an informal faction rarely seen in Canadian political parties, which exerted a clearly disruptive influence in intra-party politics. Its lingering resentment over the treatment of Diefenbaker in the mid-1960s undermined the leadership of both Stanfield and Clark and helped keep Liberal Prime Minister Pierre Trudeau in power. But it also helped to elect Prime Minister Brian Mulroney.

A third Diefenbaker legacy is the support he brought to the party. From Diefenbaker through to Mulroney, the Conservative party was the most successful Canadian party in electing members from outside the province of Quebec. Diefenbaker's success in this regard was related to his perspectives on Quebec and the West as well as his populist style. Many of Diefenbaker's opponents in the party felt, of course, that this disproportionately western and rural base was too narrow, and Stanfield, Clark, and Mulroney worked hard in subsequent years to transcend this core support.

These Conservative leaders realized that achieving and maintaining power meant getting support from Quebec, and Brian Mulroney led the Conservatives to successive parliamentary majorities by combining new support in Quebec with the western base secured by Diefenbaker. But this was a most vulnerable coalition. Diefenbaker's core support could not be taken for granted, and when it was, it was eventually lost to Reform, which was meanwhile following Diefenbaker's well-trodden path to western popularity. Reform presented an ambiguous approach to bilingualism that made the party acceptable to "francophobes," and a definition of Canada that appealed to western conceptions of the country by rejecting special status for Quebec, and by protesting the western region's relative exclusion from federal power. Reform appropriated the populism of Diefenbaker, talking of the common people and of the need to diminish the influence of "special interests." And it attracted the same kind of social outsiders that formed the core of Diefenbaker's support: support for Reform was strongest in western Canada and among voters of Northern or Eastern European origin.[61] Moreover, Reform's support, like Diefenbaker's, was relatively weak in major urban areas, but strong among farmers.[62] The legacy of support that Diefenbaker left to the Conservative party was lost during the Mulroney era. The problem facing Conservatives today is that they cannot be a viable party without it.

---

60   Diefenbaker also managed to highlight the undemocratic nature of delegate-at-large positions, positions appointed by provincial executives, and in calling for the selection of the party's leader solely by constituency delegates, he was well ahead of his time in terms of party democratization.

61   Johnston et al., "The 1993 Canadian Election," 18.

62   Flanagan, *Waiting for the Wave*, 157-59.

Diefenbaker, Parliamentary Democracy and the Canadian Bill of Rights

Robert M. Belliveau

Though more declaratory and symbolic than legally effective, John Diefenbaker's Bill of Rights was, as he often reminded Canadians, the achievement of which he was most proud.[1] Others agreed. Ellen Fairclough, Minister of Citizenship and Immigration in the Diefenbaker government (and the first woman to be appointed to Cabinet) referred to the Bill as a "personal success" for Diefenbaker. "It was the crowning of a life-long ambition by Mr. Diefenbaker," Paul Martineau, Diefenbaker's parliamentary secretary, has since remarked. Even Jack Pickersgill, no admirer of Diefenbaker, acknowledged that "apart from the Bill of Rights ... I could never see anything that Mr. Diefenbaker really wanted to do."[2]

That Diefenbaker was firmly committed to the principle of a bill of rights, and hence the protection of civil liberties, there can be no doubt. What has never been made clear, however, is his opposition to the idea of an entrenched bill of rights; that is, to a document that would have legally bound the democratically elected legislatures of Canada, thus placing rights and liberties beyond their reach. The purpose of this paper is to clarify Diefenbaker's position on an entrenched bill of rights. It does so by examining the manner and form in which the Canadian Bill of Rights evolved.

Hitherto, scholars have emphasized primarily the form the Bill eventually took — a parliamentary statute as opposed to a constitutionally entrenched amendment — and therefore have been inclined to analyse its evolution almost exclusively within the institutional framework of Canadian federalism. Because issues of civil liberties

---

1   Diefenbaker Canada Centre, John George Diefenbaker Papers (Diefenbaker Papers) MG 01, Speech Series, vol. 34, no. 794, Remarks to the Canadian Bar Association, 5 September 1959, Vancouver, British Columbia.

2   Peter Stursberg, *Diefenbaker: Leadership Gained, 1956-1962* (Toronto: University of Toronto Press, 1975), 218, 225.

often become absorbed by the complexities, vagaries, and frustrations of legislative competence, it is understandable that such a fixation on form has occurred. This article is more concerned with the manner of the Bill's evolution. Specifically, it purports to explain why the Bill assumed the form it did — by examining the convictions and characteristics of Diefenbaker's political thought.

Preoccupation with the form of the Bill of Rights is a natural consequence of the inevitable comparison that is made between it and the Charter of Rights and Freedoms enacted later by the Trudeau government. It is widely believed that the more effective way to protect civil liberties is to write them literally into the Constitution in the form of a constitutional amendment, thereby legally preventing governments from violating them. This begs the question: did the Diefenbaker government fail where the government of Pierre Trudeau succeeded?

While Trudeau consciously sought to subordinate Parliament to the determinations of the judiciary, Diefenbaker often equated the protection of civil liberties with the supremacy of Parliament. It is clear that both men were genuinely concerned about the capacity of legislators to override civil liberties; whereas Trudeau attempted to limit it, Diefenbaker advocated what might best be described as a policy of "legislative forbearance," a conscious but conditional withdrawal by Parliament from exercising its powers as they relate to civil liberties. In his recent biography of Diefenbaker, Denis Smith notes that Diefenbaker "genuinely rejected the belief that [decisions concerning civil liberties] should exist beyond Parliament's power."[3] Parliament, he believed, must always retain the capacity to affect or even suspend civil liberties, if required. For Diefenbaker, it was more accurate to conceive individual liberty as being derived not "from positive law or governmental action, but from an absence of positive law or governmental action."[4]

This paper is divided primarily into three parts. In the first section, I outline briefly the historical roots of the Canadian Bill of Rights, and Diefenbaker's early position on the need for such a Bill. Much of the impetus for a Bill of Rights was a direct result of the violations of civil liberties that had occurred at the hands of Canada's provincial governments, as well as the wartime encroachments by Parliament on liberty and freedom.

In the second section, I examine further the political thought of Diefenbaker as it related to the Bill of Rights and parliamentary democracy. In addition to his concern about flagrant violations of civil liberties, Diefenbaker worried about what he deemed a steady decline in the political rights of Canadians, made evident by the diminution in the powers of Parliament. Governments, he believed, had become too comfortable with orders in council, thus denying not only the rights of Parliament, but the rights of the Canadian people as well. Thus, for Diefenbaker, a Bill of Rights and the restoration in the supremacy of Parliament were virtually one in the same.

Finally, I turn to the drafting and implementation of the Bill, examining, in particular, the intentions and objectives of the Diefenbaker government. Here I draw on the Cabinet minutes and conclusions, the Department of Justice files, and the John G. Diefenbaker Papers. The Bill of Rights has received harsh criticism for being only declaratory in form and limited in scope. At the time of its passage through

---

3   Denis Smith, *Rogue Tory: The Life and Legend of John G. Diefenbaker* (Toronto: MacFarlane Walter and Ross, 1995), 347.

4   Peter W. Hogg, *Constitutional Law of Canada* (Toronto: Carswell, 1985), 258.

Parliament, a lawyer remarked sarcastically: "The Diefenbaker Bill of Rights provides protections to all Canadians, just so long as they don't live in any of the provinces."[5] I will argue, however, that in pursuing and eventually presenting a bill of rights for Canada, Diefenbaker never had any intention of *legally* binding Parliament, but rather sought to ensure that future parliaments would be *politically*, and perhaps *morally*, bound by civil liberties legislation.

PARLIAMENT, CIVIL LIBERTIES, AND THE EXIGENCIES OF WAR

Events both during and after World War II gave rise to a political climate in Canada in which efficiencies in government were often pursued at the expense of individual civil liberties. Wartime emergency powers and measures seemed necessary, but, given the requirements of freedom, democracy, and even those sentiments strengthened by the stated objectives of the war, it seemed almost inevitable that Canadians would come to question whether fundamental freedoms were in fact in jeopardy. Canada was, after all, a parliamentary democracy, and enjoyed all of the liberties guaranteed by the common law.

There was a growing concern about the erosion of civil liberties. Organizations such as the Toronto Civil Liberties League were making representations to the government as early as 1942.[6] Diefenbaker, too, shared in the concern. Initially, he was in agreement with the wartime measures taken by the government. "[N]ational safety is of paramount importance over private rights,"[7] he argued in his maiden speech before the House of Commons in 1940. As the war progressed, however, he consistently voiced his concern that the government, through executive orders-in-council and the delegating of legislative authority, was not allowing Parliament to debate its legislative program. He understood well enough the use of, and need for, executive orders, but he parted with accepted practices when such orders violated civil liberties. Spy investigations conducted by the government as well as the practice of internment raised serious questions about civil liberties. The many examples of the government's use of executive orders and encroachment on civil liberties have been documented elsewhere.[8] What is important here is that Diefenbaker's condoning of wartime measures and the suspension of civil liberties was grounded on his assumption that such was to be carried out by Parliament. In his view, only Parliament, and not the executive, had the right to legislate in a manner that violated civil liberties. In Great Britain, by contrast, he noted, the rights of Parliament as well as individuals were sometimes suspended, but "with the consent and under the control of Parliament."[9] This was not entirely correct,[10] but was nevertheless an early endorsement by Diefenbaker of the extraordinary, far-reaching powers given to Parliament.

---

5   Peter C. Newman, *Renegade In Power: The Diefenbaker Years* (Toronto: McClelland and Stewart, 1973), 230.

6   See J.W. Pickersgill, *The Mackenzie King Record*, vol. 1, *1939-1944* (Toronto: University of Toronto Press, 1960), 354-55.

7   Canada, House of Commons, *Debates*, 13 June 1940, pp. 748-51.

8   R. MacGregor Dawson, *The Government of Canada*, 5th ed., revised by Norman Ward (Toronto: University of Toronto Press, 1981), 268-75.

9   Canada, House of Commons, *Debates*, 25 March 1942, p. 1622.

10   See, for instance, Sir Alfred Denning, *Freedom Under the Law* (London: Stevens and Sons Ltd., 1954), 10-13.

By 1946, Diefenbaker was making reference to a clear and direct relationship between freedom and parliamentary government: the quality of freedom was directly proportional to the efficacy of parliamentary institutions. "Freedom under law and the maintenance of our Parliamentary Institutions" and "Restore the Flag of Freedom to Parliament Hill" were two potentially stirring appeals made by the Conservatives at this time.

It was in the spring of 1946 that Diefenbaker first proposed that Parliament adopt a bill of rights. During a debate on the government's Canadian Citizenship Bill, he moved an amendment, proposing a bill of rights which, he argued, would signify "what citizenship stands for."[11] "Such a measure," commented the *Globe and Mail*, "would be ... as important as the Citizenship Bill itself."[12] Diefenbaker's proposed amendment provoked a great deal of discussion, most of which centred on two points: the necessity of a bill of rights, and the authority of Parliament. Discussion regarding the latter did not at that time focus on the authority of Parliament *vis-à-vis* the provincial legislatures but in relation to the executive. In moving the amendment, Diefenbaker reiterated that he was "unalterably opposed to any alteration or diminution of the rights of Canadian citizens *by Order in Council independently of Parliament*"[13] (emphasis added). Again, he was not "unalterably opposed" to the diminution of rights, *per se*, but to their denial by the executive through order-in-council in the absence of Parliament.

FEDERALISM AND CIVIL LIBERTIES

In addition to the questions of wartime measures and executive control of Parliament, there was also the unavoidable question of who had legislative jurisdiction over civil liberties — i.e., the federal question. Canada was at that time a peculiar federation with a division of powers that was, at best, vague on the question of civil liberties. In 1947, the King government had struck a special joint committee of the Senate and House of Commons to examine the question of human rights and fundamental freedoms. Though the committee's terms of reference were explicit with regard to any international obligations Canada might have in relation to human rights and freedoms, it was not long before it focussed its sights on domestic jurisdictional concerns with regard to a bill of rights. Diefenbaker's membership on the committee was largely responsible for this shift in focus.

The history of civil liberties court cases from the *Alberta Press Case* to the Quebec Appeals involving the Witnesses of Jehovah and the freedom of religion, have been well documented elsewhere.[14] The *Alberta Press Case* of 1939 is well known and remembered for Sir Lyman Duff's doctrine — or, as one scholar has termed it, "judicial invention"[15] — of an implied bill of rights. Without going into the details of the case, Chief Justice Duff of the Supreme Court of Canada, in striking down an Alberta statute affecting speech, affirmed that Canada had inherited "a constitution

---

11   Canada, House of Commons, *Debates*, 7 May 1946, p. 1300.

12   *Globe and Mail* editorial, 20 May 1946, cited by Diefenbaker in "Bill of Rights" (Radio Broadcast), 23 May 1946, Diefenbaker Papers, Speech Series, vol. 5, no. 185.

13   Canada, House of Commons, *Debates*, 7 May 1946, p. 1301.

14   See Peter H. Russell, Rainer Knopff and F.L. Morton, *Federalism and the Charter: Leading Constitutional Decisions* (Ottawa: Carlton University Press, 1989).

15   Hogg, *Constitutional Law of Canada*, 636-38.

similar in principle to that of the United Kingdom," whose parliamentary system required free public discussion and debate; this freedom could not be curtailed by provincial legislation. What was significant was Duff's non-statement on Parliament's right of speech curtailment, the possible implication being that such freedoms lay beyond even Parliament's reach. In a separate, more straightforward opinion, Justice J. Cannon found the Alberta statute curtailing freedom of the press ultra vires precisely because it related to the criminal law jurisdiction of Parliament. According to Cannon: "The federal Parliament is the sole authority to curtail, if deemed expedient and in the public interest, the freedom of the press in discussing public affairs and the equal rights in that respect of all citizens throughout the Dominion... ."[16]

Alberta Press was delivered in 1939. Perhaps significantly, in all the years that followed, particularly those during which Diefenbaker was focussed on his Bill of Rights, he made little if any reference to Duff's doctrine of an implied bill of rights. However, when asked of the constitutionality of a bill of rights, he did cite the judgement of Justice Cannon, arguing that "it was never intended that any provincial authority should be allowed to derogate from those freedoms which are the inherent right and heritage of every Canadian and British subject."[17] Diefenbaker seemed unprepared to embrace Duff's implied notion that civil liberties stood beyond even Parliament. What appealed to Diefenbaker's sense of reason was not only Cannon's defence of parliamentary institutions, but his insistence that only Parliament, and not the provinces, could legislate in relation to civil liberties.

Early in his pursuit of a bill of rights, Diefenbaker took a strong position on the matter of Parliament's legislative competence — strong enough that he publicly advocated the use by Parliament of the extraordinary powers of disallowance and reservation. In the case of the Padlock Law, which was in effect a miniature War Measures Act in its own right passed by the Duplessis government, Diefenbaker expressed concern over the King government's failure to use disallowance.[18] In fact, when he was a member of the special joint committee of Parliament on human rights and fundamental freedoms, he argued that the government "forgot" to do its duty when considering the controversial piece of legislation. Like Eugene Forsey, Diefenbaker believed that the powers of disallowance and reservation could be used to keep provincial legislatures in check, particularly where civil liberties were concerned.[19] When proposing his amendment to the Citizenship Act, he argued that one of the principal benefits of a bill of rights would be to "strengthen the hand of the Minister of Justice in the matter of the disallowance of any statute which would deny freedom anywhere in our country."[20]

As much as Diefenbaker may have been convinced of Cannon's position, he would later alter his own position with respect to the constitutionality of a bill of rights. It is a truism that the politics of Canadian federalism rarely affords our politicians an environment in which they can maintain consistent positions on policy. In the case

---

16   Reference Re: Alberta Statutes [1938] 2 S.C.R. 100, in Russell, Knopff and Morton, *Federalism and the Charter*, 293-94.

17   Canada, House of Commons, *Debates*, 16 May 1947, pp. 3157-58.

18   Government of Canada, *Joint Committee of the House of Commons and Senate on Human Rights and Fundamental Freedoms* (Ottawa: King's Printer, 1947-48), 120.

19   Ibid.

20   Canada, House of Commons, *Debates*, 16 May 1947, p. 3158.

of Diefenbaker, a man who had a penchant for wavering, this was doubly a problem, one which would later cause analysts to spend days, months, even years distinguishing rhetoric from true intentions. The position that Diefenbaker came to take was that, in the matter of rights, the constitutional powers of the provinces would have to be respected. No doubt he arrived at this position in part because his party, in many respects out of its reaction to the centralizing policies of the Liberal government, had assumed the stance of defender of provincial rights.

THE SUPREMACY OF PARLIAMENT AND THE BILL OF RIGHTS

What distinguished John Diefenbaker from most parliamentarians of his time was his reverence for Parliament and its institutions. "Parliament is more than a procedure," he stated in 1949, "it is the custodian of the nation's freedom."[21] If there was one common strain in his views concerning parliamentary institutions, it was the connection which he drew between them and freedom: in short, the efficacy of parliamentary institutions determined the degree of political, and thus civil, liberty.

Of all institutions, the one which best expressed this relationship between civil liberty and parliamentary government was Her (His) Majesty's Loyal Opposition. The institutionalized opposition was what Walter Bagehot referred to as one of the efficient elements of parliamentary government, a consequence of Cabinet government which enabled Members of Parliament to be critical of the Crown's representatives and yet remain loyal to the Crown.[22] For Diefenbaker, an important measure of a successful democracy was the extent to which the Opposition was capable of performing its role. In a speech before the Empire Club of Canada, he elaborated:

> The Opposition that fulfils its functions makes as important a contribution to the preservation of the parliamentary system as does the government of the day. ... [T]he Opposition must fearlessly perform its functions. When it properly discharges them, the preservation of our freedom is assured... . The Opposition upholds and maintains the rights of minorities against majorities. It must be vigilant against oppression and unjust invasions by the Cabinet of the rights of the people... . It finds fault; it suggests amendments... . It must ... prevent the shortcuts through democratic procedure ... for Governments tend to prefer rule by Order-in-Council to Parliament... . Parliament will only remain the guardian of freedom and our free institutions so long as His Majesty's Loyal Opposition is fully responsible and effective in the discharge of its functions.[23]

The initial jurisdictional issue emanating from discussions concerning a bill of rights involved not so much the federal principle as it did the authority of Parliament in relation to the executive. This issue was particularly relevant in the context of wartime measures. It would rise again, however, notably during the 1956 Pipeline Debate as the Conservatives in opposition fought the St. Laurent government's use of closure to cut off parliamentary debate. For Diefenbaker, the Pipeline Debate represented a conscious — indeed, an arrogant — violation of parliamentary procedure and, by extension, of the liberties and freedoms guaranteed through it. In the national election that followed in 1957, Diefenbaker in fact turned the Liberal government's disregard for Parliament into a central campaign issue.

---

21   Ibid., 22 September 1949, p. 146.

22   Walter Bagehot, *The English Constitution* (London: Collins Clear-Type Press, 1963), 61-69.

23   Diefenbaker Papers, Speech Series, vol. 8, no. 318, October 1949.

It was during the election of 1957 that Diefenbaker began with regularity to incorporate his Bill of Rights message into his pledge to restore the supremacy of Parliament. Others in the party, while agreeing in principle with the platform and the issue of parliamentary supremacy, were not sure if the electorate would easily grasp, or even care about, the intricacies of parliamentary government. But Diefenbaker was confident that if he could convince the voters that, under a Liberal government, their freedom and the integrity of their institutions were jeopardized, he could win the election. When he charged that the Liberals "trampled on the rights of Parliament … tore up the Constitution, [and] trampled on the rights … of free men," he quite deliberately equated the rights of Parliament with those of "free men."[24]

A BILL OF RIGHTS FOR CANADA

Although the Speech from the Throne opening the twenty-third Parliament on 14 October 1957 made no mention of a bill of rights for Canada, Davie Fulton, the Minister of Justice, had assured the press the previous summer that a proposal was under review by his department.[25] As Fulton later recalled, he had merely raised the idea of a bill at an initial staff meeting, and to his surprise was immediately presented with a draft by Elmer Driedger, the Associate Deputy Minister.[26] Driedger and the Deputy Minister, Wilbur Jackett, were veterans of the Department of Justice, and were doubtless aware of Diefenbaker's public advocacy of a bill of rights.

The decision to proceed unilaterally with a parliamentary statute was made "fairly quickly," to use Fulton's words.[27] Shortly before Christmas 1957, Fulton met with Jackett and other departmental officials. Having exhausted all possibilities of the form that the Bill might take, including entrenchment by constitutional amendment, Justice had decided on a statute confined to Parliament. At the suggestion of Jackett, there was much enthusiasm shown for a declaration of "broad principles [in the form] of an interpretation act."[28] The memoranda from Justice at the time indicate that the Bill was intended to be interpreted later in a way that would prevent "unintentional or unconscious encroachments or restrictions on human rights and fundamental freedoms." Nor should it be interpreted in a manner that would authorize an encroachment.[29] This, it was argued, would go a long way toward addressing fears over an increasingly powerful, and potentially intrusive, government and bureaucracy.

The approach taken by the Department of Justice, and Jackett in particular, toward the Bill of Rights bore an uncanny resemblance to Diefenbaker's. Sharing Diefenbaker's concerns, Justice officials repeated in several memoranda that the purpose of the Bill was to mitigate the consequences to individual freedom posed by

---

24 Television Broadcast, 5 June 1957, cited in John Meisel, *The Canadian General Election of 1957* (Toronto: University of Toronto Press, 1962), 59-60.

25 "Rights Bill Under Study, Fulton Says," *The Winnipeg Free Press*, 14 August 1957.

26 Mr. Justice E. Davie Fulton, His Memoirs with Peter Stursberg, transcript of interview, 2 December 1980, a joint oral history project of the Parliamentary Library and the Public Archives of Canada (now National Archives of Canada [NA]).

27 Ibid.

28 NA, Justice, RG 13, file 180667, "Canadian Bill of Rights," 1957, "Memorandum for the File," 17 December 1957.

29 Ibid., "Memorandum Re: Bill of Rights," 19 March 1958.

John Diefenbaker and delegate holding copy #10 of the Bill of Rights, at the Progressive Conservative annual general meeting, Ottawa, 16-18 March 1961 (courtesy the Diefenbaker Centre MG01/XVII/JGD 3299).

the growing complexities of governing a modern social and economic system. Though it was agreed that "Canadians today enjoy the human rights and fundamental freedoms that would be the subject matter of a Bill of Rights," Jackett believed that the case for a Bill "might be based on the fact that our modern social and economic system requires such a volume of complex statutory rules and regulations and such a vast administrative organization that there is an inherent danger that the 'rights' and 'freedoms' of the individual have been in the past, and will be in the future, sacrificed in favour of administrative or other advantages."[30]

One of Diefenbaker's concerns was the delegation of authority by Parliament to a growing number of regulatory and administrative bodies through orders-in-council. This had an adverse effect on the principles of responsibility and accountability. One method through which those principles could be restored, Diefenbaker recommended, was to establish a parliamentary committee to look into violations of civil liberties. This way, Parliament would be made aware of, and ultimately responsible for correcting, such violations. Diefenbaker wanted a Bill of Rights that would stem from and be protected by Parliament. He wanted it compatible with the parliamentary principle.

Fulton has recalled that there was no disagreement over the form the Bill was to

---

30   Diefenbaker Papers, Prime Minister's Office Series, vol. 365, file 413.1, pp. 285122-27, "Memorandum for the Prime Minister," 29 April 1958.

assume.[31] If Diefenbaker had any reservations about a Bill in statutory form, he certainly would have made them known; after all, this was his Bill of Rights. When Fulton formally presented the proposal for a Bill of Rights to Cabinet in May 1958, the discussion focussed on two points. The first was almost exclusively political, and dealt with the viability of selling to the public a Bill of Rights that opened with the affirmation that the following rights and freedoms "have always prevailed." The necessity of the Bill would naturally be questioned. Second, there were concerns about the desirability, if not the legality, of the Bill's applicability to laws "enacted before or after the commencement of this Act." Cabinet nevertheless approved the Minister's proposal. It is interesting to note that there was no mention of the possibility of a constitutional amendment.[32]

Fulton immediately raised Cabinet's concerns with his department. Driedger assured him that the Bill did "not purport to bind future Parliaments." The clause in question was "merely a rule of interpretation and not legislation ... directed to the judiciary" and was consistent with the form of similar provisions within the Interpretation Act, R.S., 1952, an act which reserved to Parliament the power to repeal or amend any legislation.[33] Departmental officials, Fulton, and Cabinet as a whole were all firmly committed to the principle of parliamentary supremacy.

When the Bill came up again for discussion in Cabinet two weeks later, it discussed ways to save the War Measures Act — which, if enacted, would likely conflict with the Bill's provisions. The Cabinet documents report that there was "a great deal to be said for including a saving clause ... [for war measures were] clearly required in times of emergency."[34] Fulton presented two ways to proceed. The first was simple: exempt the Act from the Bill. The second was more creative: provide for the Act's amendment by the Bill. As he explained it, the Act would come into force, but override the Bill only through a proclamation by the Governor General in Council. Parliament would thereinafter be afforded an opportunity not only to debate the proclamation, but to revoke it. In opposition, Fulton, Diefenbaker, and others had resented Parliament's powerlessness to influence emergency executive actions which affected human rights and freedoms. Fulton's proposal was put forth with the assurance that Parliament, and not the executive, would ultimately determine the quality of civil liberties.

Robert B. Bryce, Clerk of the Privy Council and Secretary to the Cabinet, had entered the debate with a third alternative. Such a foray was not uncommon for the country's chief public servant, who frequently offered advice and assistance of every kind. Though Diefenbaker was initially suspicious of him, Bryce became "almost the only mandarin Diefenbaker trusted."[35] Two days before Cabinet met to discuss Fulton's options, Bryce wrote Diefenbaker outlining his thoughts on the matter. He

---

31   Fulton, His Memoirs with Peter Stursberg.

32   NA, Records of the Privy Council Office, RG 2, series A5a, Cabinet Minutes and Conclusions, vol. 1898, 10 May 1958; the two memoranda are filed as Cabinet Document no. 111/58, but are also found in Diefenbaker Papers, Prime Minister's Office Series, vol. 365, file 413.1, pp. 285122-27, "Memorandum for the Prime Minister," 29 April 1958.

33   "Memorandum for the Minister of Justice," 12 May 1958, Justice, file 180667-1, "The Canadian Bill of Rights," 1957.

34   NA, Records of the Privy Council, RG2, series A5a, Cabinet Minutes and Conclusions, vol. 1898, 27 May 1958.

35   J.L. Granatstein, *The Ottawa Men: The Civil Service Mandarins, 1935-1957* (Toronto: Oxford University Press, 1982), 270.

referred to the "sweeping simplicity" of Fulton's first option, the one which merely exempted the War Measures Act from the application of the Bill. He thought, if slightly amended, it could be defended. While Fulton's second option "preserves the rights of Parliament," Bryce argued, it quite possibly could bring about the defeat of the government if the so-called proclamation was defeated. Moreover, he questioned whether it would be feasible to gather together enough ministers (four) to issue a proclamation in a "war situation we now contemplate." The threat of a nuclear war was real. As an alternative, Bryce suggested a "more significant and selective role for Parliament" in time of war: "In essence this role would be that Parliament must take positive action in order to continue in effect for more than ninety days any measures taken under the War Measures Act which in fact infringe upon the rights and freedoms recognized in the Bill of Rights."[36] This, he believed, would put the government to some trouble to explain and justify a continuance of war measures before Parliament. Bryce's proposal, although passed over for Fulton's, was in principle similar to Fulton's inasmuch as they both purported to check the executive in one way or another.

Before being introduced in the House for first reading in the fall of 1958, the proposed Bill was put to another test of parliamentary supremacy, this time from parliamentary counsel. In a memorandum addressed to Bryce, counsel raised the concern that the section of the Bill giving the Minister of Justice the authority to review all future legislation that might come into conflict with the Bill, in effect gave the Minister "judicial powers." The memo concluded on a note of irony: "While the Bill purports to declare the rights, it deprives them of their greatest and all powerful remedy — the supremacy of the Parliament of Canada."[37] When Diefenbaker became aware of this claim, he cautioned Cabinet that he was "not entirely satisfied with the draft Bill" and made it clear that he was against "the derogation of existing rights of Parliament."[38] In the end, Fulton suggested a minor wording change that alleviated Diefenbaker's concerns and was accepted by Cabinet.

There was a consistent focus by the government on ensuring that Parliament's role and the efficacy of its institutions were neither compromised nor diminished in any way. Indeed, there was a conscious intent to enhance where possible the role of Parliament in matters related to civil liberties. The section of the Bill outlining the duties and review powers of the Justice Minister stemmed from previous calls for a "watchdog" on human rights and freedoms. The clause amounted to a "notwithstanding clause" which would allow the Minister to give approval to future legislation notwithstanding the Bill. Diefenbaker would again raise this issue in Cabinet over a year after it was initially discussed.[39] What was discussed both in Cabinet and later through correspondence indicates that, in the government's view, the clause would in fact strengthen the role of Parliament but, while preserving the principle of parliamentary supremacy, would also have the effect of imposing political constraints on future Parliaments. As Fulton put it: since "*no Parliament can bind a future Parliament,*

---

36   Diefenbaker Papers, vol. 17 of Restricted Sub Series, file 413.1 Conf., pp. 286526-28, Bryce to Diefenbaker, 4 June 1958.

37   Diefenbaker Papers, Reference Series, vol. 68, "Memorandum Re: Bill of Rights," 7 August 1958, pp. 39821-25.

38   NA, Records of the Privy Council Office, RG2, series A5a, Cabinet Minutes and Conclusions, vol. 1899, 26 August 1958.

39   Ibid., vol. 2745, 5 July 1960.

we [the Department of Justice] *could only provide that, in order for future statutes to override the Bill of Rights* such statutes must expressly so provide" (emphasis original). This, he believed, would still enable Parliament, if required in "the national interest," to deny fundamental rights and freedoms.[40] The principle of parliamentary supremacy remained legally intact, but had been altered inasmuch as the Bill was clearly designed to impose political constraints on future Parliaments.

The Bill of Rights was given first reading in the fall of 1958, and then died on the order paper. It was reintroduced into Parliament in 1960 and was, according to Cabinet, to be passed "without fail." Between parliamentary sessions, many criticisms were made of the Bill, several of which put forward the idea of a constitutionally entrenched Bill of Rights that would legally bind the provinces as well as Parliament. This prompted Diefenbaker in the fall of 1959 to consider whether or not the provinces should be consulted. The Opposition continuously asked whether the government would approach the provinces, and if not, why not? Unwilling either to consult the provinces, assuming that they would not consent, or to let his unwillingness to do so be known, he took no action. Cabinet concluded that it was "preferable to avoid a constitutional fight," and essentially stay the course.[41] The Bill received Royal Assent on 10 August 1960, having received only minor changes from the initial draft of 1957.

CONCLUSION

This paper began with the assertion that an examination of the manner in which Diefenbaker conceived his Bill of Rights would yield a greater understanding of the form it eventually assumed. In the existing literature on the Bill, there has been a preoccupation with its relationship to federalism, while little attention has been given to its relationship to the institutional and theoretical underpinnings of parliamentary democracy. Although federalism is by no means irrelevant to the evolution of the Bill, the official record of the period clearly demonstrates that parliamentary democracy is of greater significance. Throughout his career, Diefenbaker championed the representative principle of parliamentary government as the cornerstone of self-government, representation being the most fundamental of political rights. The maintenance of this principle, Diefenbaker contended, was contingent on the "solemn pledge" of representatives to uphold and protect the fundamental civil liberties of their constituents. Any limits on the representatives' authority, whether through institutional reform or the abuse of power, was repugnant to Diefenbaker, who repeatedly asserted that the quality of civil liberties was directly related to that of parliamentary institutions.

Diefenbaker agreed that a bill of rights would impress on parliamentarians, especially those in government, the central importance of civil liberties. If curtailment of such was necessary and warranted, it should occur in a formal, deliberate, and visible manner, preferably through an Act of Parliament. Following his election to Parliament in 1940, Diefenbaker was consistently critical of executive encroachments on civil liberties, or, more generally, the rise of executive power at the expense

---

40   Diefenbaker Papers, vol. 17 of Restricted Sub Series, file 413.1 Official, Fulton to Diefenbaker, 5 July 1960, pp. 286538-41.

41   NA, Records of the Privy Council Office, RG2, series A5a, Cabinet Minutes and Conclusions, vol. 2745, 8 October 1959.

of Parliament. This growing trend, manifested through orders-in-council and legislative delegation, represented a derogation of the rights of Parliament and, consequently, a decline in the quality of civil liberties. As Progressive Conservative leader, he pledged in 1957 to restore the rights and supremacy of Parliament by limiting executive power, and thereby restoring the "rights of free man." The intent of this pledge was to force the executive to govern through Parliament. There is no evidence to suggest that he acknowledged a contradiction between this pledge and his proposed Bill of Rights. In his mind, there was none. When it was argued by parliamentary counsel that his Bill would in fact limit the rights of Parliament, he quickly moved to assure Cabinet that such was neither his intention nor his desire. As far as entrenchment of the Bill was concerned, Diefenbaker believed that such a move would have to be considered in light of the parliamentary principle. In other words, it was the parliamentary context that facilitated the manner in which the Bill of Rights was first conceived, and which then dictated the form it eventually assumed.

Note

This paper taken from "Mr. Diefenbaker, Parliamentary Democracy, and the Canadian Bill of Rights" (MA thesis, University of Saskatchewan, 1992).

THE DIEFENBAKER BILL OF RIGHTS AND THE QUESTION OF A CONSTITUTIONALLY ENTRENCHED CHARTER, 1960-1971

Christopher MacLennan

For John Diefenbaker, the 1960 Canadian Bill of Rights was undoubtedly the crowning achievement of his troubled government. From his days as a criminal lawyer in Saskatchewan through his many years in Parliament, Diefenbaker forcefully defended the rights of the individual against intrusions by the state. Even closer to his heart were his efforts to secure equality for those Canadians who, like himself, were not solely of British or French ancestry. As he wrote years later, "My advocacy of a Bill of Rights was to assure Canadians, whatever their racial origins or surnames, the right to full citizenship and an end to discrimination. This was basic to my philosophy of 'One Canada, One Nation'."[1]

While Diefenbaker clearly advocated a Canadian bill of rights, it was less clear what form the bill should take. At times in the 1940s, he seemed to indicate that only through constitutional entrenchment would the measure truly achieve its purposes. More often, he stressed the importance of parliamentary supremacy, and thus gave tacit support to a statutory bill. While sitting in opposition, Diefenbaker had the luxury of remaining ambiguous. He avoided detailed explanations of his designs in favour of listing the civil liberties abuses of the Mackenzie King government. For Diefenbaker, the goal was the bill itself; the form could be determined later.[2]

---

1   John G. Diefenbaker, *One Canada: The Memoirs of the Right Honourable John G. Diefenbaker*, vol. 2: *The Years of Achievement, 1957-1962* (Toronto: Macmillan, 1976), 255.

2   On human rights in Canada in the postwar period, John Diefenbaker and bills of rights, see Ramsey Cook, "Canadian Liberalism in Wartime: A Study of the Defence of Canada Regulations and Some Attitudes to Civil Liberties in Wartime, 1939-1945" (MA thesis, Queen's University, 1955); D.A. Schmeiser, *Civil Liberties in Canada* (Toronto: Oxford University Press, 1964); Mark MacGuigan, "The Development of Civil Liberties in Canada," *Queen's Quarterly* 72 (Summer 1965): 270-88; Walter S. Tarnopolsky, *The Canadian Bill of Rights* (Toronto: McClelland and Stewart, 1975); R. Romanow, J. Whyte, and H. Leeson, *Canada... Notwithstanding: The Making of the Constitution, 1976-1982* (Toronto: Carswell-Methuen Publications, 1984); John Bagnall, "The Ontario Conservatives and the

Once he was Prime Minister, the realities of federal-provincial relations seem to have convinced him to choose the statute option. Throughout the drafting process, the newly elected Conservative government firmly held that a statutory bill of rights limited strictly to federal jurisdiction was the better course. Diefenbaker staunchly defended this choice by stating that accommodation with the provinces was unlikely. Yet he could not bring himself to discard completely the possibility of a constitutional amendment. As late as July 1960, Diefenbaker indicated that if an agreement could be reached with the provinces, he was willing to entrench a bill of rights and thus limit the powers of Parliament. Hence, Diefenbaker managed to open the door to a constitutional bill and exhort the virtues of his statute at the same time. Clearly, he remained unsure, even with a draft Bill in his hands.

Despite the fanfare given the enactment of the Canadian Bill of Rights in 1960, many voices challenged its worth. By 1960, the Bill's advocates had reached a loose consensus that a significant shift in the system of rights protection was necessary. Most believed that only a constitutionally entrenched rights guarantee would achieve this kind of shift. As a statute, Diefenbaker's legislation did not fit the bill. This paper will study the course of the Bill of Rights throughout the 1960s and early 1970s and its effect on the entrenchment debate. Through an examination of the Bill's origins and its subsequent reception in the courts and law journals, I intend to show that the perceived failure of the 1960 statute laid the foundation for Pierre Elliott Trudeau's suggestions in 1968 and 1971 for a constitutional amendment. While Bora Laskin may have been correct in his assessment that "we would be as well off without a Bill of Rights as to have one so limited in its reach, so limited in its effect," Diefenbaker's Bill helped pave the way for an entrenched rights guarantee, the very type of change Laskin himself advocated.

Between 1929 and 1960, the efforts to secure protection for human rights in Canada passed through three distinct stages. During the Great Depression and World War II, civil libertarians concentrated on a series of easily identified legislative measures which both levels of government used to curtail individual rights. Political activists such as F.R. Scott, F.H. Underhill, and J.S. Woodsworth mounted a relentless attack on Section 98, Duplessis's Padlock Law, and the use of deportation to rid the country of the foreign unemployed. Through a public campaign in Parliament and the press, and through the creation of the Canadian Civil Liberties Union and the League for Social Reconstruction, civil libertarians attempted to convince Ottawa and Quebec of the dangers to individual rights which these acts posed. With the outbreak of World War II and the subsequent introduction of the Defence of Canada Regulations, these same individuals intensified their efforts, while new voices joined the chorus. Throughout these decades, the goals of civil libertarians remained the same: they sought the repeal of the offending legislation. The system which protected rights was not challenged.

This situation had changed radically by the end of the war. Despite the wartime efforts of civil libertarians, King's Liberal government had continued its curtailment of civil liberties. The web of wartime economic and social controls had grown steadily,

---

Development of Anti-Discrimination Policy: 1944-1962" (Ph.D. dissertation, Queen's University, 1984); Michael Mandel, *The Charter of Rights and the Legalization of Politics in Canada* (Toronto: Thompson Educational Publishing, 1989); William Kaplan, *State and Salvation: The Jehovah's Witnesses and Their Fight for Civil Rights* (Toronto: University of Toronto Press, 1989); Denis Smith, *Rogue Tory: The Life and Legend of John G. Diefenbaker* (Toronto: MacFarlane, Walter, and Ross, 1995).

raising concerns that Ottawa intended to maintain them in the postwar period. More significantly, the planned deportation of Japanese Canadians and the extraordinary infringements on basic civil liberties apparent in the Gouzenko affair convinced many Canadians that human rights were truly under attack, and that simply lobbying the government to restrain itself was no longer adequate.[3]

To heighten the growing concern for civil liberties, Canadians watched the American civil rights movement unfold throughout the 1940s and 1950s. After World War II, American blacks increased their efforts to achieve recognition of their rights to equality. During the 1950s, Canadian newspapers, and especially the new medium of television, reported the sometimes violent clashes between Southern whites and black activists intent on securing their rights to vote and to integrated public education, particularly after the 1954 United States Supreme Court decision in *Brown v. Board of Education.*[4] Racial confrontations such as that at Little Rock, Arkansas in 1955, were widely reported and commented upon in the Canadian press. Although it is difficult to assess the precise impact of these events on Canadians, the civil rights movement focussed a sharp light on the problem of racism in American society, and this scrutiny served to highlight similar issues in Canada. While Canadian human rights advocates noted the differences between the two countries, they nonetheless looked south for possible solutions to the problems they saw at home. Together, the popular movement by blacks in the United States and the various measures adopted by American legislators to fight racism had a clear influence on many Canadians.

As civil libertarians watched the American civil rights movement and searched for a response to the distressing curtailments of human rights in Canada, they found a shining example in the United Nations. The UN's attempts in the late 1940s to enshrine universal human rights in the organization's Charter and in numerous conventions vindicated the concerns of Canadian civil libertarians. More important, the UN's attempt to codify human rights into an International Bill of Rights provided Canadian activists with a model for their own efforts. With this example, civil libertarians now demanded positive restraints on governmental power in Canada.[5]

Between 1946 and 1957, Canadians lobbied for measures to better protect individual rights in Canada. Distrusting the federal government and the provinces, civil libertarians argued that only through a constitutional limitation on all legislative power in Canada would individual rights truly be secure. Those concerned with human rights not only proposed numerous pieces of legislation to curtail racial,

---

3   For an examination of the criticisms levelled at the Mackenzie King government by civil libertarians, see Reginald Whitaker and Gary Marcuse, *Cold War Canada: The Making of a National Insecurity State, 1945-1957* (Toronto: University of Toronto Press, 1995), and Christopher MacLennan "Towards the Charter: Canadians and the Demand for a National Bill of Rights, 1929-1960" (Ph.D. dissertation, University of Western Ontario, 1996).

4   In 1954, the United States Supreme Court declared in *Brown v. Board of Education* that the Fourteenth Amendment to the constitution required equal admission, regardless of colour, to public schools. In response, groups of southern whites initiated an often violent resistance to the Supreme Court's orders. For a general survey of the American civil rights movement and its wider implications, see William H. Chafe, *The Unfinished Journey: America since World War II* (New York: Oxford University Press, 1991), 86-91, 148-68.

5   On the UN's human rights activities, see James Frederick Green, *The United Nations and Human Rights* (Washington: The Brookings Institute, 1956). For Canada's part in these efforts, see Cathal J. Nolan, "Reluctant Liberal: Canada, Human Rights and the United Nations, 1944-65," *Diplomacy and Statecraft* 2 (November 1991): 281-305.

religious, and sexual discrimination; they now demanded an overarching bill of rights as a means of protecting civil rights in Canada. If they recognized the extraordinary circumstances that the war and the spy scandal presented, they also witnessed how quickly the government's respect for traditional civil liberties broke down. By advocating a national bill of rights, civil libertarians sought not only to restore Parliament's respect for individual rights and freedoms, but to establish a new system of human rights protection in Canada, one which would not allow a repeat of the World War II experience.

The appeal of this goal became readily apparent. From 1944 to 1957 there was incredible growth in the number of organizations and individuals concerned with the better protection of human rights. While Jehovah's Witnesses battled Quebec in the courts, labour congresses pressured both Ontario and Ottawa for fair practices legislation. Influenced by the United Nations, organized labour, ethnic associations, and women's groups joined the human rights lobby, and their involvement greatly expanded both the range of the debate and the ideas on how to secure better rights protection. New civil liberties organizations emerged, and old ones reappeared. By the 1950s the few voices which had spoken in defence of civil liberties in the Depression had grown to a chorus.

In Parliament, John Diefenbaker, Alistair Stewart, and Arthur Roebuck challenged the Liberal government's record on civil liberties, and agitated for a response to suggestions of a rights guarantee. In 1946, Diefenbaker charged that the government's handling of the Gouzenko spy scandal had created a new "liberty-conscious" public, and that it was now necessary "to declare once and for all the rights that are incident to citizenship in this country." He attacked the government's suspension of *habeas corpus* by order-in-council, and warned that the press had given almost universal support to the need for such a bill of rights. Diefenbaker also suggested that the creation of a committee of the House of Commons was necessary to determine the status of human rights in Canada and to discuss the question of a national bill of rights.[6]

Diefenbaker's proposed bill drew directly upon the criticism he and others had levelled at the Mackenzie King government's suspension of civil liberties during the war and its aftermath. In 1946 he had proposed an amendment to the government's Citizenship Bill which contained three clauses: the first guaranteed freedom of speech, religion, and the right to peaceable assembly; the second held that *habeas corpus* could only be suspended by act of Parliament; and the third insured the right to legal counsel when giving evidence. Limited in scope, this amendment revealed the prairie lawyer's thinking on the subject at the time.[7] To him, a bill of rights should

---

6   Canada, House of Commons, *Debates*, 7 May 1946, 1300-1303. On *habeas corpus*, Diefenbaker argued that "Parliament should determine once and for all that never again will that right, without which there can be no freedom or liberty under law, be denied except in cases of emergency and by Parliament itself." Ibid., 1302.

7   Diefenbaker wrote in his memoirs that he first began to draft a Canadian bill of rights during his practice in Wakaw (*One Canada: Memoirs of the Right Honourable John G. Diefenbaker*, vol 1: *The Crusading Years, 1895-1956* [Toronto: MacMillan of Canada, 1975], 252); however, there is no evidence to support this claim. More likely, the events of the previous few years introduced Diefenbaker, as well as others during that time, to the idea that a bill of rights was necessary. To support this contention, immediately after the defeat of his amendment and the subsequent attention given to him in the press, Diefenbaker requested information on human rights and bills of rights from various institutes in the United States. See letters from Diefenbaker to International Conciliation, the Carnegie

protect those traditional civil liberties developed over the centuries of British juris-prudence. Most important, the bill should reaffirm the pre-eminence of Parliament in the protection of individual freedoms. The rights of all Canadians were vested in Parliament. Therefore, only Parliament could suspend them.

The combined efforts of the civil libertarians of the Depression and World War II and the human rights advocates inspired by the United Nations forced the federal government to deal with their demands for a national bill of rights. Despite three parliamentary committees, numerous delegations, and countless written submis-sions, however, the Liberal governments of Mackenzie King and Louis St. Laurent refused to support the calls for a rights guarantee. The Liberals, who repeatedly pleaded respect for human rights, maintained that problems of constitutional juris-diction and the interests of the provinces blocked the government's ability to implement the proposal.

Quebec was perhaps the most important factor in the federal government's inaction. Throughout the entire period in which advocates were demanding a national bill of rights, the Union Nationale government of Maurice Duplessis served as a brake on any discussions of an entrenched rights guarantee. Beginning in the 1930s, Duplessis made known his position that civil rights were a provincial matter, including the power to abridge those same rights. For the Quebec premier, the protection of Quebec against communism and the religious proselytizing of Jeho-vah's Witnesses necessitated the curtailment of certain rights, and this was the prerogative of the province. In an address before the Canadian Bar Association in 1948, Duplessis defended the Padlock Law and, at the same time, delivered a warning to anyone who wanted to interfere: "In the province of Quebec you will find law-abiding citizens. We may have some legislation which you do not like. We respect your opinion, but we like the legislation we have… . A law such as this may not suit some of the other provinces; that is a matter for the provinces themselves to decide."[8] Obviously, Duplessis had moved little since the 1937 enactment of the Padlock Act. He maintained his stand that civil liberties were under provincial jurisdiction, and he would use his political power to ensure this primacy.

On the issue of a national bill of rights, Duplessis's stance offered little room for negotiation. According to the premier, bills of rights were "meaningless big words." In any case, human rights were outlined already in the Bible, and there "will never be another charter that is as perfect."[9] Sentiments such as these appear to have mirrored the general attitude in Quebec. Throughout the 1940s and 1950s, there was a notable absence of francophone Quebeckers among those who demanded the better protec-tion of human rights. With a few exceptions, such as Claude Jodoin and Pierre Trudeau, Canadian activists demanding a national bill of rights were anglophones. With little or no evidence of popular support among francophone Quebeckers, and

---

Endowment for Internal Peace, International Safeguard of Human Rights, and Americans United for International Organization, 20 May 1946, Diefenbaker Papers, 1940-1956 Series, Vol. 2, Microfilm Reel M-7414, 001220-001222.

8   Address by Maurice Duplessis, 31 August 1948, *The 1948 Yearbook of the Canadian Bar Association and the Minutes and Proceedings of the Thirtieth Annual Meeting*, 19-20.

9   Ontario Jewish Archives, Records of the Joint Community Relations Committee, Box 72, File "1950," Report on meeting between Maurice Duplessis and the Canadian Congress of Labour, 2 February 1950, Joint Advisory Committee on Labour Relations, "Report of Activities on Improved Human Relations in the Labour Field," January 1950.

with a provincial government openly hostile to any limitations on its power to deal with civil rights, policy makers in Ottawa had few options concerning constitutional safeguards. Quebec's determined struggle against the Jehovah's Witnesses in the courts throughout the 1940s and 1950s, and the failure of the Dominion-Provincial Conference in 1950, provided the Liberal government in Ottawa with clear evidence that if it wanted to meet the demands of civil libertarians, it would surely lead to confrontation with Quebec City.

In any event, Ottawa firmly believed that demands for a national bill of rights were unwarranted. Liberal governments argued that Canadians could rely on English common law, with its long tradition of safeguarding civil liberties, including the Magna Carta, the Bill of Rights, and the accepted principles of the rule of law. Even if these failed, Ottawa held that the supremacy of Parliament offered a better guarantee to Canadians than any constitutional list of rights. As Jack Pickersgill stated, good government was the best answer to those demanding a bill of rights.

In response to its critics, the Liberal government had also developed a well-rehearsed answer as to why the Canadian Constitution was better left as it was. According to Stuart Garson, the Minister of Justice in the St. Laurent government, the crux of the matter rested on the simple determination of what was the best manner to protect the human rights of Canadians: "With me it is a purely pragmatic question, which method works better to achieve the closer approximation to the objectives which we are seeking?"[10] In his analysis, the answer was clear: parliamentary sovereignty. Garson held that the adoption of a bill of rights represented a fundamental departure from Canada's constitutional traditions. But he took this argument a step further. He believed that, in itself, parliamentary sovereignty provided the best guarantee of protection to Canadians' rights. He argued that a simple comparison with the United States provided clear proof of his position. He pointed to the lynchings in the southern states and the "wholesale denial" of the franchise to American blacks in these same jurisdictions, despite the protections found in the US Bill of Rights. In response, he wondered, "How, in the face of these happenings ... it can be argued that constitutional guarantees in the United States or in any other country have been a greater guarantee of freedom than the sovereignty of Parliament in Canada ... is something that I do not understand."[11] For the Justice Minister, then, one system worked, the other did not.

Clearly, the Liberal governments of the 1940s and 1950s believed that the desire for positive change to the Canadian system of rights protection had garnered limited public support. Despite the parade of delegations, written demands, and two petitions containing hundreds of thousands of signatures, King's government refused to accept that Canadians no longer trusted Parliament and now wanted a constitutional bill of rights. As J.L. Ilsley concluded at the 1948 parliamentary committee, he saw no evidence of a "firm public opinion" in favour of a bill of rights.

In fairness, the views of Canadians were difficult to assess. Activists such as Irving

---

10   Queen's University Archives (QUA), Arthur Reginald Marsden Lower Papers, Box 7, File A-120, Stuart Garson to A.R.M. Lower, 12 November 1949.

11   QUA, Lower Papers, Box 7, File A-120, Garson to Lower, 31 October 1949. In one letter, Garson argued that the agitation for a Canadian bill of rights stemmed from the Progressive Conservatives' inability to mount an effective opposition in Parliament. He believed that once the Conservatives regained their strength, "the main reason for a Bill of Rights will, in my judgement, disappear." See ibid., Garson to Lower, 23 February 1950.

Himel, Glen How, and Claude Jodoin argued that these petitions and the number and size of the organizations that had endorsed a constitutional bill of rights were obvious proof of widespread support for their cause.[12] Nevertheless, the Liberal governments of Mackenzie King and St. Laurent pointed to three straight election victories in 1945, 1949, and 1953 where, despite the contentions of civil libertarians, their records on human rights played no part. Thus, although many Canadians questioned the safety of individual rights in Canada, and while many supported calls for a constitutional guarantee, after 1946 these concerns rarely held the political centre stage. By the beginning of the 1950s, while the movement itself expanded, the issues which gave rise to the calls for a national bill of rights slowly faded from public memory and appeared to vindicate the Liberal position that broad support simply did not exist.

Between 1957 and 1960, however, the Conservative government led by John Diefenbaker altered this situation significantly. Diefenbaker, the "apostle of civil liberties," proudly announced his intention to enact a national bill of rights, and within a year of taking office introduced a draft of the promised legislation. For those who had championed the cause since the 1940s, this heralded a new stage in the movement. After nearly fifteen years of trying to convince Ottawa of the need for a rights guarantee, from 1958 to 1960 civil libertarians and human rights advocates focussed their efforts on analyzing Diefenbaker's proposed legislation.

At the centre of the discussion was the issue of entrenchment in the Constitution. In the search for measures which would substantially transform the Canadian system of rights protection, most advocates agreed that only through constitutional amendment would a bill of rights truly be effective. Since the Gouzenko affair, civil libertarians and human rights advocates had demanded not only better respect for Canadians' individual rights but also a significant shift in the system of protecting them. While those who pushed for a bill of rights encouraged the development of other protective measures, early in the debate a loose consensus held that only an entrenched bill of rights would achieve the kind of institutional change they desired. Indeed, the 1950s marked some of the most important advancements in human rights protection in Canada. With Ontario's lead, various provinces and the federal government took their first steps in the field of fair practices legislation. At the same time, the Supreme Court handed down decisions on a series of civil liberties cases which added greatly to the protection of human rights in Canada. Nevertheless, this did not satisfy those who demanded a national bill of rights. Each of these developments, while helping to secure individual rights, had little effect on the *method* of human rights protection. For bill of rights advocates, success could only be achieved through a constitutionally entrenched limitation on all legislative powers in the country.

With the passage of the 1960 Act for the Recognition and Protection of Human Rights and Fundamental Freedoms, the long postwar campaign for a national bill of rights ended in partial success. After over thirty years of agitation on civil liberties

---

12   Among the groups that lobbied the federal government for better rights protection were the Canadian Labour Congress (Claude Jodoin, president), the Canadian Jewish Congress, the Canadian Federation of University Women, the National Committee of Women of Canada, the Japanese Canadian Citizens' Association, the Jehovah's Witnesses (represented by Glen How) and various organizations devoted strictly to rights issues, such as the Association for Civil Liberties (Irving Himel, president).

issues, and fifteen years of direct lobbying, civil libertarians and human rights advocates scored a pyrrhic victory; they had achieved a major piece of legislation on human rights, but one which did not contain some of the basic tenets of their argument. Worse, the existence of the new measures undermined any continued efforts to secure these ignored demands. Bora Laskin succinctly concluded: "we would be as well off without a Bill of Rights as to have one so limited in its reach, so limited in its effect."[13] By 1960 the campaign for a national bill of rights, although hardly sharply focussed, had reached the conclusion that any rights guarantee must extend to all legislative jurisdictions in Canada, and must be made part of the Constitution to be truly effective. John Diefenbaker's Bill of Rights accomplished neither.

Despite Diefenbaker's exhortations on the statute's importance, various facets of the Canadian legal community questioned its significance.[14] The Canadian Bar Association (CBA), which had remained remarkably quiet during the debate in the 1940s and 1950s, grumbled that perhaps the "deficiencies" in the Diefenbaker Bill of Rights made a constitutional amendment necessary. In 1966, the CBA held a panel discussion to answer the question, "Had the Bill of Rights proven its effectiveness?" The answer returned was "not yet." In response, the British Columbia Branch proposed that the CBA take the initiative to "prepare a draft Bill of Rights designed as a constitutional amendment to the British North America Act to be effective in relation to the matters coming within both federal and provincial jurisdiction."[15]

By the late 1960s, then, the CBA clearly had begun to move in the direction of a constitutional solution to the question of human rights protection in Canada as a reaction to the Diefenbaker statute. This position became evident during the debates concerning the October Crisis of 1970. The response of the federal government and the ramifications for civil liberties were harshly criticized by the CBA. The use of the War Measures Act, despite the existence of the Canadian Bill of Rights, was seen by many as proof that the statute was meaningless against a real threat to human rights. Others in the association disagreed, arguing that the government needed such power. As a result, the association adopted a weak resolution that demanded that all rights and freedoms contained in the Canadian Bill of Rights should "continue in force" during periods of emergency. Nevertheless, the CBA moved increasingly toward an alternative method to protect Canadians' civil liberties.[16]

More important, however, the courts chose to ignore the Bill of Rights. Although the statute clearly instructed Canadian courts to "construe and apply" all federal laws

---

13   National Archives of Canada, MG 28 V75, Records of the Jewish Labour Committee of Canada, Vol. 22, File 2, 2, Bora Laskin, "The Proposed Bill of Rights," Speech given to the National Human Rights Conference, 10 December 1958.

14   On the Bill of Rights in the courts and for legal scholars' opinions, see E.A. Tollefson, "Canadian Bill of Rights and the Canadian Courts," *Saskatchewan Bar Review* 26 (1961): 106-11; Bora Laskin, "Canada's Bill of Rights: A Dilemma for the Courts?" *International and Comparative Law Quarterly* 11 (April 1962): 519-36; E. McWhinney, "A New Base for Civil Liberties," *Canadian Bar Journal* 8 (February 1965): 28-36, 43; and W.S. Tarnopolsky, "The Canadian Bill of Rights From Diefenbaker to Drybones," *McGill Law Journal* 17 (1971): 437-75.

15   *The 1966 Yearbook of the Canadian Bar Association and the Minutes and Proceedings of the Forty-Eighth Annual Meeting,* 164.

16   *The 1971 Yearbook of the Canadian Bar Association and the Minutes and Proceedings of the Fifty-Third Annual Meeting,* 53.

in accordance with the rights listed therein, judges proved reluctant to take so bold a step as to render inoperative legislation that contravened the Bill of Rights. Instead, in a series of human rights cases, including *Louis Yuet Sun v. The Queen* and *Robertson and Rosetanni v. The Queen*, the Supreme Court avoided the issue by concentrating on other points of law. In one of the few instances where the Bill of Rights was discussed at length, Justice Davey of the British Columbia Court of Appeal noted the problems presented by the act: "The difficulty in interpreting and applying the very general language of the Canadian Bill of Rights has not been exaggerated. It is, in my opinion, impossible at this early date, to fully grasp all the implications of the Act, or to determine its application in circumstances that cannot be foreseen."[17] Obviously, the courts stepped lightly in their interpretation of the Bill.

Not until the 1970 Drybones case did the Supreme Court offer a comprehensive decision on the Bill's power to suspend offending legislation. On 8 April 1967, Yellowknife police charged Joseph Drybones, a member of the Dogrib nation, under Section 94 of the Indian Act for being intoxicated off an Indian reserve. Drybones appealed his conviction to the Supreme Court on the grounds that the Indian Act imposed harsher penalties for public intoxication than did liquor laws for non-natives. This, he argued, infringed upon the "equality before the law" provisions of the Canadian Bill of Rights. In a majority decision, the Court held that Section 94 of the Indian Act contravened the Bill of Rights, which rendered the section inoperative.[18] Diefenbaker argued in his memoirs that this judgement finally vindicated his belief in the statute's importance, and quieted those who claimed it was little more than a "pious and ineffectual declaration."[19] Indeed, the Drybones case led to renewed discussion of the Canadian Bill of Rights and its legal implications for the protection of human rights in Canada. By 1970, however, political events already had conspired to shift the focus of the human rights dialogue away from the controversial rights statute and threatened eventually to make Diefenbaker's beloved Bill redundant.

On 4 September 1967 the new federal justice minister, Pierre Elliott Trudeau, appeared before the Canadian Bar Association's annual meeting and announced the Liberal government's intention to draft a new bill of rights to be entrenched in the Constitution. According to Trudeau, "the adoption of a constitutional Bill of Rights is intimately related to the whole question of constitutional reform. Essentially we will be testing — and hopefully establishing — the unity of Canada. If we reach agreement on the fundamental rights of the citizen, on their definition and protection in all parts of Canada, we shall have taken a major first step toward basic constitutional reform." Like the host of critics who chastised Diefenbaker's proposals in 1958-1960, Trudeau argued that the Canadian Bill of Rights was too narrow in scope and offered little protection against parliamentary supremacy. With this speech, and in his *A Canadian Charter of Human Rights*, published six months later,

---

17   *R. v. Gonzales* (1962), 32 D. L. R. (2d) 290. Cited in Tarnopolsky, "The Canadian Bill of Rights," 446. See also *Louis Yuet Sun v. The Queen* [1961], S.C.R. 70 and *Robertson and Rosetanni v. The Queen* [1963] S.C.R. 651.

18   *R. v. Drybones* (1970) S.C.R. 282. For a discussion on the significance of the case, see Tarnopolsky, "The Canadian Bill of Rights," 443-57; J.G. Sinclair, "The Queen v. Drybones: The Supreme Court of Canada and the Canadian Bill of Rights," *Osgoode Hall Law Journal* 8 (December 1970): 599-619; P. Cavalluzzo, "Judicial Review and the Bill of Rights: Drybones and its Aftermath," *Osgoode Hall Law Journal* 9 (December 1971): 511-51; and Peter Hogg, *Constitutional Law of Canada* (Scarborough: Thomson Publishers, 1992), 781-91.

19   Diefenbaker, *Years of Achievement*, 264-65.

the new Justice Minister dismissed Diefenbaker's cherished statute as "useful work" from the past.[20]

If the Drybones case had vindicated Diefenbaker's opinion of his 1960 Bill of Rights, then Trudeau's pronouncements confirmed the arguments of those activists who had been calling for a constitutional amendment since the mid-1940s. In the 1940s and 1950s, opponents of those who demanded a national bill of rights argued that the Constitution was an impediment to achieving an entrenched rights guarantee. Even Diefenbaker, who claimed on occasion to support the suggestion of entrenchment, held that the jurisdictional jealousies of the provinces precluded any agreement on the matter. Trudeau turned these arguments on their head. Instead of seeing an entrenched bill of rights strictly as a goal, he saw it as a tool to solve Canada's constitutional impasse and establish a new national unity. With these proposals firmly in hand and his election as Prime Minister in 1968, Trudeau set the country on the road to the 1982 Charter of Rights and Freedoms, a road that originated in the human rights debates of the previous forty years.

Trudeau's Charter of Rights was the type of substantial, institutional change which bill of rights advocates had demanded since the 1940s. Enshrined in the Constitution, the Charter placed human rights beyond the normal reach of Parliament and provincial legislatures. More significantly, the subsequent rash of Supreme Court decisions based on the Charter has revealed a marked shift in the *method* of rights protection in Canada. These types of changes did not occur under the Diefenbaker Bill of Rights. By the late 1960s, the negative response of the courts to the Bill had confirmed the arguments of civil libertarians that a statutory bill was inadequate. Many critics pointed to this development and concluded that only through entrenchment in the Constitution would human rights truly be protected. Simply correcting the errors of the past or adding to the existing machinery was not enough.

Despite the shortcomings which critics saw in the Diefenbaker statute, the true importance of the bill of rights movement lies not in the eventual act of 1960. It rests, rather, in the awareness of human rights issues that it generated in Canada. In a pioneer analysis, Ramsay Cook concluded that the drastic curtailment of civil liberties during World War II under the Defence of Canada Regulations "was made possible by indifference or lack of faith and understanding of liberal institutions on the part of the majority of the Canadian people. ... the roots of liberalism have not grown deep in the arid soil of Canada's heterogeneous community."[21] In postwar Canada, a genuine concern for the safety of individual rights and fundamental freedoms produced a dynamic exchange of ideas across the country. In part, this represented a remarkable thread of continuity, as many key civil libertarians from the 1930s renewed their efforts to safeguard human rights within a number of emerging organizations such as trade unions, women's groups, and ethnic associations. These advocates focussed on a number of problems, on both the federal and the provincial front, and through their efforts raised the issue of human rights protection in Canada to new heights. At the core of many of the arguments for better measures was the demand for a national bill of rights. Activists in Canada sought to enshrine the

---

20   Pierre Elliott Trudeau, "A Constitutional Declaration of Rights," in *Federalism and the French Canadians* (Toronto: Macmillan, 1968), 54-55; and *A Canadian Charter of Human Rights* (Ottawa: Queen's Printer, 1968). For background on Trudeau, see Stephen Clarkson and Christina McCall, *Trudeau and Our Times*, 2 vols. (Toronto: McClelland and Stewart, 1990-1994).

21   Cook, "Canadian Liberalism in Wartime," 277-78.

Canadian meaning of liberty as a symbol of the nation's respect for human rights. As a result, the enactment of the 1960 Bill of Rights coupled with the arguments developed by human rights advocates throughout 1929 to 1960 provided fertile ground for the ideas of Pierre Elliott Trudeau. For good or ill, this ground eventually bore the 1982 Charter of Rights and Freedoms.

MONEY AND POLITICS:
RELATIONS BETWEEN ONTARIO AND
OTTAWA IN THE DIEFENBAKER YEARS

P.E. Bryden

In order to understand federal-provincial relations in Canada, most scholars have turned their attention to episodes of vitriolic debate and hard bargaining, demonstrating a far greater interest in the dysfunctional relationship than in the functional. This is certainly true for Ontario's relations with Ottawa, as witnessed by the number of studies investigating the years prior to World War II when Ontario led the charge for an expansion of provincial rights.[1] My interest, however, is in understanding the more peaceful intergovernmental relationship that developed between Ontario and Ottawa in the years after 1945. Not only was Ontario generally accepting of federal incursions into social security — clearly a matter of provincial jurisdiction — and federal attempts at constitutional re-negotiation, but the province also came to articulate and defend "the national interest" in virtually all areas of federal-provincial relations. This represents a remarkable change from the prewar atmosphere. Why had Ontario become so agreeable? What returns did the province expect? How deep did the commitment to functional federalism run? An investigation into one unique period in the relationship between the two levels of government, a rare period when the same party was in power in both Toronto and Ottawa, provides some clues about the extent of the cooperation and the reasons for Ontario's position.

For Ontario, the opportunity to forge a close working relationship with a national government of the same partisan stripe had been a long time in coming. The last time Ottawa and Toronto had been governed by the same party was during the final gasps of Harry Nixon's Liberal régime in Ontario during the war, but that was only the final chapter of Mitch Hepburn's dominance, and Hepburn's acrimonious

---

1   See Christopher Armstrong, *The Politics of Federalism: Ontario's Relations with the Federal Government, 1867 to 1942* (Toronto: University of Toronto Press, 1982); Garth Stevenson, *Ex Uno Plures: Federal-Provincial Relations in Canada, 1867-1896* (Montreal and Kingston: McGill-Queen's University Press, 1993); Paul Romney, *Mr. Attorney* (Toronto: Osgoode Society, 1986); "From Constitutionalism to Legalism: Trial by Jury, Responsible Government, and the Rule of Law in the Canadian Political Culture," *Law and History Review* 7 (1989); and Robert Vipond, *Liberty and Community: Canadian Federalism and the Failure of the Constitution* (Albany: State University of New York Press, 1991).

battles with Prime Minister Mackenzie King had soured federal-provincial relations, it seemed, virtually beyond redemption.[2] With the election of George Drew as Premier of Ontario, the new provincial treasurer, Leslie Frost, began to smooth the way for more amicable intergovernmental relations, at least in terms of fiscal federalism. Yet despite this new harmony, provincial Conservatives held out little hope for significant progress in their relations with Liberals in Ottawa. Even the prospect of Drew becoming Prime Minister, after he had become national party leader, had held little promise for improved federal-provincial relations; as national leader, Drew was constantly at odds with the Ontario Conservatives, whom he seems to have promptly forgotten once he vacated the Premier's chair.[3]

Premier Leslie Frost's relations with Liberal Prime Minister Louis St. Laurent were reasonably good, at least when seen relative to the Hepburn-King rivalry. Frost's initiation of discussions on hospital insurance in 1955 was a sign that Ontario was prepared to play a leadership role in the development of national social policies, supporting Ottawa's move into provincial jurisdiction as a necessary step in establishing national standards.[4] On the question of extending the wartime tax rental agreements, however, Frost was less accommodating. Ontario refused to rent all its direct tax fields to the federal government in 1947 and 1952, and continued to demand greater tax flexibility in order to raise the revenues required to finance the development of the Ontario infrastructure. Thus, while Ontario's postwar relationship with Ottawa was reasonably positive, it was not free of problems.

It was clear that the Ontario Conservatives viewed John Diefenbaker differently than any of the previous Prime Ministers or leaders of the federal party. In 1956, Frost threw his support behind Diefenbaker's candidacy for the leadership, and followed up with valuable assistance during the 1957 election. In addition to campaigning for Diefenbaker, Frost loaned Allister Grosart to the federal organization to oversee election strategy. The relationship between Frost and Diefenbaker was an uncommon alliance of the provincial and federal Conservative parties, and one that announced the beginning of a new period of closer relations.[5] While Frost had at first "a good deal of doubt as to the wisdom or practicability"[6] of centring the federal election campaign around a statement of Conservative principles, Diefenbaker's new National Policy included a number of points that were of particular interest to Ontario. Most important was the promise that a Conservative administration would respect the constitutional rights of the provinces, particularly in the implementation of a more

2   See John T. Saywell, *"Just call me Mitch": The Life of Mitchell F. Hepburn* (Toronto: University of Toronto Press, 1991). Much of the book is devoted to an analysis of the long and vitriolic fights between Hepburn and Mackenzie King.

3   Denis Smith, *Rogue Tory: The Life and Legend of John G. Diefenbaker* (Toronto: Macfarlane Walter and Ross, 1995), 200; Archives of Ontario (AO), Hugh Latimer Papers, MU 4543, minute books of the Executive Committee of the Ontario Progressive Conservative Association.

4   P.E. Bryden, *Planners and Politicians: Liberal Politics and Social Policy, 1957-1968* (Montreal and Kingston: McGill-Queen's University Press, 1997), 6-15.

5   See Smith, *Rogue Tory*, 203-4; Rand Dyck, "Links Between Federal and Provincial Parties and the Party System," in Herman Bakvis (ed.), *Representation, Integration and Political Parties*, vol. 14 of the research studies, Royal Commission on Electoral Reform and Party Financing (Toronto: Dundurn Press, 1991), 148.

6   Diefenbaker Canada Centre (DCC), Diefenbaker Papers, reel M-5555, vol. 18, file 391, January-May 1957, Frost to Alvin Hamilton, 7 January 1957.

equitable division of tax revenues between the two levels of government. This was especially important to Frost who, in introducing the "next Prime Minister of Canada" to a Toronto audience, noted:

> the direct tax fields belong equally to the provinces and the federal government, the latter having complete control of the indirect tax field as well. It is not a matter of the federal government giving Ontario or the provinces anything. That is the patronizing attitude in Ottawa. All that we ask is a reasonable part of our own. A part which is reasonably commensurate with the size of the job we have to do, and upon the accomplishment of which task much of Canada's future depends.... We are not even asking the half which is ours, but we are asking what is reasonable.[7]

Frost expected that Diefenbaker would agree to such a reasonable division of resources, and while Conservative national policy did not go quite so far as to recognize provincial autonomy, as some Ontario politicians wanted, there was ample evidence that the new Conservative government would loosen the federal stranglehold on the provinces.[8]

Once in office, Diefenbaker moved fairly quickly on the issues of federal-provincial relations, calling a conference with the Premiers late in November 1957. It was to be a series of information-gathering discussions centring on "Dominion-Provincial fiscal relations but should afford an opportunity to discuss other current issues which have an important bearing on our fiscal relations." Specific proposals arising out of this first meeting would be considered at a later date.[9]

There were a few early signs that the Prime Minister's approach to provincial matters did not correspond with Frost's. In the wake of the election, Diefenbaker's advisors insisted that the Conservatives design policies that "concentrate on the rural areas in all the provinces," and the leader himself flirted with the inclusion of representatives of the municipalities at the federal-provincial conference. This would have given a clear advantage to depressed rural areas, but was a move that Frost warned would be "chaotic," and constitute interference with the "business of the Provincial Government."[10] Diefenbaker heeded Frost, whom he had "watched with admiration" and regarded as an important political ally. But it was clear that the Prime Minister would not forsake his agrarian populist roots, despite suggestions to Ontario that he would oversee a more equitable division of Canadian resources.[11]

With only a minority victory, and uncertain of how to handle the reins of government, Diefenbaker's Conservatives moved warily toward their first meeting

---

7   Ibid., "Notes on Remarks by the Hon. Leslie M. Frost, QC, at Massey Hall," 25 April 1957; *Globe and Mail*, 26 April 1957.

8   DCC, Diefenbaker Papers, reel M-5777, vol. 22, file 391.8, M.W. Menzies to Diefenbaker, 10 April 1957.

9   Ibid., reel 7834, file 306.1 B government B federal-provincial relations B federal-provincial fiscal arrangements, 1957, Diefenbaker to Frost, 31 October 1957.

10   National Archives of Canada (NA), Gordon Churchill Papers, MG 32 B9, vol. 38, Duff Roblin file, Churchill to Roblin, 27 August 1957; DCC, Diefenbaker Papers, reel M-7834, file 306.1 B government B federal-provincial relations B federal-provincial fiscal arrangements, 1957, Frost to Diefenbaker, 25 September 1957.

11   Ibid., reel M-7943, file 391.52 Ont. Political parties B PC Party B PC Associations and Clubs B Provincial PC Associations B Ontario 1957-63, notes for Diefenbaker's speech to the Ontario PC Association, 5 November 1957.

Dominion-provincial conference, 1957 (courtesy the Diefenbaker Centre, MG01/XVII/JGD 2998).

with the provincial Premiers. Ontario had major reservations about the existing 1957 tax arrangements: the method of calculating equalization grants was "defective," as it equalized provinces virtually to the Ontario level and it "failed to provide adequate recognition of the increasing demand for services in a rapidly growing industrial economy." While the province had reluctantly agreed to let the federal government rent the income tax field, it had re-entered the corporate tax field in order to obtain the additional revenue it deemed necessary.[12]

The first federal-provincial conference with Diefenbaker at the helm seemed nonetheless "destined to meet in a spirit of confidence and hope and mutual understanding.... The feeling of the Ontario delegation is that Mr Diefenbaker will show more appreciation of the financial responsibilities and needs of the provinces and their municipalities."[13] Aware of Ontario's position, federal Finance Minister Donald Fleming told the conference that the new government regarded the 1957 tax rental agreement as a failure, in that it did not "provide adequate access to revenue consistent with the responsibilities of provinces." That Ontario and Quebec had refused to enter into the agreement with the federal government showed that the plan "must be faulty in some important respects."[14] Fleming's clarification of federal

---

12   AO, Department of Finance, Policy Division Subject Files, RG 6-44, box UF 34, file: Federal-Provincial Relations with Particular Reference to Ontario's Position, 1947-1963, "Federal-Provincial Relations with Particular Reference to Ontario's Position, 1947-1963," p. 23.

13   *Globe and Mail*, 25 November 1957.

14   DCC, Diefenbaker Papers, reel M-7834, file 306.1 B government B federal-provincial relations B

responsibilities in fiscal affairs, however, was weak. He simply noted that "the Federal position differs from that of the provinces in that it not only has its own large responsibilities within its broad constitutional fields, but it must also in the national interest be prepared to coordinate and consolidate varying and sometimes conflicting interests."[15] The conference would turn out to be exploratory in nature; the lack of preparation by the federal government, while by no means surprising, precluded any serious agreements being reached. What had not been anticipated, at least by the provinces, was Fleming's weak defence of the national interest.

Premier Frost's opening address to the conference was characteristic. As was his habit, he stressed the cost of managing a flourishing economy, a concern that led Newfoundland Premier Joey Smallwood some years later to reflect:

> I remember [Frost] saying when he was in office as the Premier of this great province at a Dominion-provincial conference, saying something like this. He said, "You have all read that we have had three thousand new industries come to Ontario since the war." This was about ten years after the war. They already had three thousand new industries. He said, "You think this is wonderful, don't you?" — looking around at the nine of us, the other Premiers. "You think this is wonderful. You don't realize the other side of it, all the new schools we have to build and all of the housing and all of the hospitals and all the new roads and paving and everything else." I said, "Stop, you're breaking my heart."[16]

Despite the reaction of the other Premiers, Frost never wavered from his insistence that Ontario needed more tax room in order to finance growth. He reminded the conference that, "if we are to have a healthy industry capable of offering expanded opportunities of employment to our growing labour force, the provinces and the municipalities must be placed in a financial position to enable them to play their essential part. Our paramount requisite is that of increased revenues."[17] His proposals followed a well-worn track in asking for a greater provincial share of the tax abatement — up to 15 percent of the corporate and income tax fields, and fifty percent of the succession tax field. Just as characteristically, his proposals were disregarded. The federal government could not meet both Ontario's demands for greater tax manoeuvrability and the demands of have-not provinces for higher equalization payments. It made no difference to Diefenbaker that Frost had supported him in the leadership and national election campaigns, or that Frost had supported Diefenbaker's proposal of an Atlantic Adjustment Grant to "permit provinces and regions to broaden and diversify their economies on their own account [and create] an inevitable strengthening of our regional economy."[18] These political debts would not be repaid by an offer of greater provincial tax access.

On other issues of federal-provincial relations, Diefenbaker was prepared to heed Frost. While the agreement on a joint federal-provincial hospital insurance program

---

federal- provincial fiscal arrangements, 1957, Suggestions for Notes for a Speech to be Delivered by the Minister of Finance at the Closed Session of the Dominion-Provincial Conference.

15 Ibid.

16 Morning session of the Confederation of Tomorrow Conference, 27 November 1967. Quoted in Thomas J. Courchene, *What Does Ontario Want?* (Toronto: Robarts Centre for Canadian Studies, York University, 1989), frontispiece.

17 *Proceedings of the Dominion-Provincial Conference*, 1957, Ottawa, 25-26 November 1957, p. 15.

18 Ibid., 38; Interview, Dalton Camp, 19 February 1997.

had actually been achieved in the dying days of the St. Laurent administration, Diefenbaker became determined to put his mark on the program, and would later use its implementation as an example of his party's commitment to the extension of social security. It was most likely as a result of pressure from Ontario[19] that the federal Conservatives agreed now to eliminate the requirement, set by the previous Liberal government, that six provinces commit to participating before any federal funds would be made available. However, the Diefenbaker government refused to implement any of the other changes Ontario envisaged. These included a sharing of administrative costs between the two levels of government, an increase of the total federal cost share from approximately 50 percent to at least 60 percent, and the inclusion of home care, and mental, tubercular, convalescent, and chronic care hospitals under the system.[20]

Because Diefenbaker had been in power for such a short time, and because the Conservative party had been out of power for such a long time, it is not surprising that the initial First Ministers' Conference would produce "no general overhaul, [and] no specific new approach to the tax rental formula."[21] What did come as a surprise, however, was the universal silence on defining the national interest. As tax analyst R.M. Burns has pointed out:

> The objectives which had inspired the development of the agreement approach in the first place seemed almost forgotten at both levels of government and in their place was an over-riding interest in the political opportunities based on a philosophy of "What is there in it for me?" Perhaps this was an inevitable consequence of the growth of provincial responsibilities and the accompanying reassertion of provincial rights which had been eroded by the depression, the war, and the reconstruction period. The provinces were primarily concerned with their own limited problems, and perhaps to some extent taken with the opportunity of influencing the first federal minority government in many years. The Government of Canada may have confused the national interest with its own central preoccupation. But in terms of a national perspective, this experience offered little encouragement to those who had hoped to see a broader outlook as the nation matured.[22]

This weak focus on the national interest was not overlooked at the conference. Manitoba Premier Douglas Campbell led an assault on Ottawa, condemning the national government for demanding agreement on a financial adjustment for the Atlantic provinces without first dealing with more general fiscal arrangements, the supposed topic of the meeting.[23] Ontario's chief economist, George Gathercole, writing to Frost, agreed with the notion of establishing the general terms of the tax-sharing arrangements first, although he did not agree with Campbell's position

---

19   See R.M. Burns, *The Acceptable Mean: The Tax Rental Agreements, 1941-1962* (Toronto: The Canadian Tax Foundation, 1980), 169.

20   NA, Donald Fleming Papers, MG 32 B39, vol. 64, file Hospital Insurance Plan B 1957, Ottawa, Research Department, "Comparison of the Federal Government's Hospital Insurance Legislation with the Plan Proposed by the Government of Ontario," 5 July 1957; ibid., H.D. Clark to K.W. Taylor, 9 July 1957.

21   *Globe and Mail*, 26 November 1957.

22   Burns, *The Acceptable Mean*, 169-70.

23   AO, Department of Finance Papers, federal-provincial correspondence, RG 6-115, vol. 10, file: federal-provincial memoranda, etc., 1958, Campbell to Diefenbaker, 18 December 1957.

in its entirety. In Gathercole's writings we see the beginning of an attempt on Ontario's part, for the first time, to understand and interpret the national interest in federal-provincial negotiations. Gathercole, who was not merely Frost's economic advisor but a trusted friend and right-hand man in matters far beyond economic policy,[24] suggested that Ottawa's approach was not entirely misguided. While he noted that the "general tax-sharing arrangements should provide non-Atlantic provinces with adequate revenue in normal times," he stressed that "the Federal proposal of special adjustments to the Maritime Provinces recognizes a special and continuing financial imbalance that dates from Confederation days — a point which Mr. Campbell apparently fails to appreciate."[25] Another Conservative party insider would also later recall that Frost's support for the Atlantic Adjustment

John Diefenbaker and Leslie Frost, 1958 (courtesy the Diefenbaker Centre, MG01/XVII/JGD 562).

Grant at the conference marked him as the only "giver" present at the conference. Yet, he added, it also opened the door for increasingly insistent future calls for specialized regional programs from other Premiers.[26]

Despite not being rewarded with higher tax rental fees, Ontario's relations with Ottawa remained harmonious. Diefenbaker knew very well the importance of the support he had received from the Frost government in Ontario. Frost, too, understood the importance of federal-provincial harmony. In his frequent correspondence with the Prime Minister, the Premier's tone was always friendly, if slightly paternalistic. With almost a decade of government experience, Frost was, after all, the more successful politician. He had advice for the Prime Minister on budgets and deficits — "having constructed a dozen budgets myself, I have some little experience"[27] — and meanwhile he continued to press Diefenbaker on the question of the tax-sharing agreements. Claiming that Ontario had supported Diefenbaker in the 1957 election because the people wanted a bigger cut of federal tax revenues, Frost reminded Diefenbaker that a 15-15-50 (percent of income tax, corporate tax, and succession duties) revenue abatement to the provinces was in "the considered opinion of Ontario ... the minimum to meet the [revenue] requirements."[28] He did admit, on

---

24   Interview, Donald Stevenson, 17 July 1996.

25   AO, Department of Finance Papers, federal-provincial correspondence, RG 6-115, vol. 10, file: federal-provincial memoranda, etc., 1958, Gathercole to Frost, "Note on Hon. Douglas Campbell's letter of December 18, 1957 to Rt. Hon. J. G. Diefenbaker," 1 February 1958.

26   Interview, Dalton Camp, 19 February 1997.

27   AO, Department of Finance Papers, federal-provincial correspondence, RG 6-115, vol. 10, file: federal-provincial memoranda, etc., 1958, "Excerpts B letter from Hon. Leslie M. Frost, Prime Minister of Ontario, to Rt. Hon. John G. Diefenbaker, Prime Minister of Canada," n.d.

one occasion, that "this may be beyond the financial capacity of the Federal Govern-ment to achieve all in one year."[29] Frost meanwhile enlisted the support of the editor of the influential *Globe and Mail*, Oakley Dalgleish, who privately proposed to the Prime Minister that "interim steps could be taken" toward the ultimate goal of achieving Ontario's proposed division of tax revenue.[30] When Diefenbaker an-nounced toward the end of January that the provinces would have access to 13 (up from 9) percent of the income taxes collected by Ottawa, it seemed that Frost's advice had been somewhat persuasive.

Diefenbaker went to the electorate again in 1958. His sweeping election victory, the largest yet seen in Canadian political history, seemed a blanket endorsement of federal Conservative policies. But there were differing views on the mandate that the Conservatives had been given. According to one view, Ontario had handed Diefen-baker another election victory and thus deserved to be rewarded. Diefenbaker, however, believed he had won on his own terms by appealing to the Canadian electorate with national development projects and visions of "One Canada." There was some truth in both views, but the two could not co-exist comfortably. While differences between Toronto and Ottawa were not yet apparent to the public, as Frost and Diefenbaker were always willing to share a stage, private relations between the two levels of government were beginning to show signs of strain. Premier Frost, always avuncular, became increasingly assertive in his demands for the recognition of the costs incurred by Ontario's unique position in Confederation. Diefenbaker, for his part, became enamoured with his landslide election victory, which, combined with constant praise from his federal confidants, seemed to distract him from providing a national vision for a nation of growing regions. Into the void slipped Leslie Frost to articulate in measured tones some semblance of a national policy.

Initially, Frost restricted his vexation about the course of intergovernmental fiscal relations to private correspondence with the Prime Minister. "I have been greatly disturbed about the terminal recalculation of our adjusted payments" under the 1957 agreement, he complained. Revised calculations had not been used in determining the extent of Ontario's "fee" for the rental of the corporation and income tax fields, at a loss to the province of $41.1 million. Because of this "matter of very serious importance," Frost threatened that "Ontario should make no further repayments for succession duty credits."[31] But Ontario's version of which provincial statistics should be used in determining the value of the rented taxes was never accepted.

Diefenbaker's consistent refusal to meet Ontario's demands in the fiscal field, which at the very least suggested to Ontario Conservatives that he was not suitably impressed with their support for him in the 1958 election, led the Ontario govern-ment to take an increasingly hard line on the division of tax revenue. The minor upward readjustment of the provincial abatement of the income tax field from 9 percent to 13 percent in 1958 was not the first of a series of incremental readjustments,

28   Ibid.

29   Ibid., vol. 11, file: federal-provincial correspondence, 1958, draft, Frost to Diefenbaker, n.d.

30   Ibid., vol. 10, file: federal-provincial memoranda, etc., 1958, "Excerpts B letter from Hon. Leslie M. Frost, Prime Minister of Ontario, to Rt. Hon. John G. Diefenbaker, Prime Minister of Canada," n.d.

31   AO, Department of Finance Papers, federal-provincial correspondence, RG 6-115, vol. 7, file: General Correspondence, Frost to Diefenbaker, 17 February 1959; ibid., Frost to Fleming, 3 February 1959.

as Frost had expected and had been willing to accept, but the last of the proposed alterations. Frost changed his approach. He no longer set his goal as achieving a 15-15-50 arrangement. Instead, he argued that "the present conception of federal-provincial tax sharing was a failure," and that, as the federal and provincial governments both occupied the direct tax fields equally, they should share the proceeds equally.[32] The new goal was a 50-50-50 division of revenues from the three direct-tax sources.[33] Without a recognition of equality, Ontario would be forced to find money to cover its increasing expenses elsewhere. The only reasonable alternative lay in the collection of a retail sales tax which, while technically a direct tax, could "have the aspect of indirect taxes by reason of the requirement that retailers shall act as agents."[34] Diefenbaker had provoked the Ontario government into adopting a more aggressive stance.

In addressing the public, Frost was still saying that relations between the governments in Ottawa and Toronto "are incomparably the greatest in our history."[35] Yet those relations were not nearly as harmonious, nor as beneficial to Ontario, as had been expected in 1957. Nor was Diefenbaker providing the leadership anticipated in other areas. Behind closed doors, Ontario's approach both to federal-provincial relations and to fiscal policies moved in new directions. Weary of the incessant bickering over the formula used to determine the level to which provinces would be equalized, and irritated that Ottawa was refusing to accept a more fundamental shift away from equalization and toward a more equitable division of tax resources, Ontario sought support from other provinces. Quebec was an obvious ally. With its election of a Liberal government under Jean Lesage in June 1960, committed to autonomy within the federal system and the development of a modern provincial bureaucratic complex, Quebec, like Ontario, wanted greater access to income and corporate taxes. On one exceptional occasion when Quebec was tempted by a federal offer of higher equalization payments in exchange for lower tax revenues, Ontario was there to remind it of the greater issue that was at stake. In stressing the importance of tax revenue, George Gathercole suggested to a Quebec official that Quebec, with its growing industrial structure and unlimited resources, might be sacrificing its long-term interests for the sake of a short-term equalization gain.[36] Quebec rarely needed to be reminded of where its interests lay, but as the Diefenbaker government continued to isolate Quebec, as it had been doing since it swept the province in 1958, Ontario became an increasingly important interpreter of the Quebec position for the federal government.

The two largest provinces shared an aversion to federal encroachment on provincial power, so their alliance was neither surprising nor new. It was, however, more than

---

32   *Globe and Mail*, 26 July 1960.

33   John T. Saywell (ed.), *Canadian Annual Review for 1960* (Toronto: University of Toronto Press, 1961), 42-43.

34   AO, RG 6-116, box 23, file: Statement concerning a new basis… "A Statement Concerning a New Basis of Tax Sharing Between Canada and the Provinces and the Advantages that are Apparent in Making a Redivision of Tax Sources over the Imposition of Retail Sales Taxes by the Provinces to Meet Their Needs," 6 May 1960.

35   DCC, Diefenbaker Papers, reel M-7936, file 364 B Provincial Governments B Ontario B 1957-1962. "A Report to the People from the Hon. Leslie M. Frost," 4 May 1959.

36   AO, RG 6-115, box 16, file: Federal-Provincial Conference, 1960 — 11th Continuing Committee, September 1960, George Gathercole to Leslie Frost, 22 September 1960.

a mere marriage of convenience. The Diefenbaker government had made two errors in the eyes of Ontario Conservatives, who were prepared to take advantage of the opportunities that had been created. First, Diefenbaker had not lived up to his promises of greater provincial autonomy, at least in the area of tax sharing. Second, he had compounded this failure by not establishing a coherent policy of national development; his economic measures were piecemeal, designed to solve specific rather than general problems. In the area of social policies, where there had traditionally been considerable cooperation between the two levels of government, Diefenbaker had made only negligible progress. Thus, Ontario now began to articulate economic policies that would be both national in scope and beneficial to Ontario.

Most of the debating and positioning in federal-provincial conferences occurred behind closed doors. Frost's normal tack would be to reiterate Ontario's constitutional rights to at least 50 percent of the direct tax fields, and underline the overall loss Ontario experienced under the existing equalization agreements. Treating intergovernmental conferences as an opportunity to explain the position of other provinces to Diefenbaker, he would then explain to his provincial colleagues how the Ontario plan would benefit them.[37] His officials followed a similar approach. George Gathercole, for example, argued that "the illogicality of ... the present [equalization] formula was turning one province against each other [sic]," and that "the provinces should raise and spend their own monies but that there should be opportunities for the provinces to enter into tax collection agency agreements with the Federal Government." Although federal Finance Minister Donald Fleming tended to agree with Gathercole, and only Saskatchewan and Manitoba were opposed, no decision was reached.[38] On the other hand, most Premiers were not predisposed to accept Ontario's "cost of growth" argument. As the *Winnipeg Free Press* noted sarcastically, the time had come "for all good Westerners and Maritimers to break out their handkerchiefs and join the Toronto *Globe and Mail* in weeping over the parlous financial plight of the province of Ontario."[39]

If the other provinces were hesitant to accept Ontario's version of the best fiscal arrangements for the nation, Ottawa seemed prepared to go part way toward meeting Ontario's demands. At the 1960 fiscal conference, Diefenbaker proposed to partially vacate the direct tax fields and freeze equalization payments. The national response was not positive, as Ontario's feeble complaints about the changes not amounting to a substantial increase in tax room were drowned out by the sharper cries of a return to "what's in it for me" fiscal policy. Some observers suggested that Diefenbaker's proposal "was a bluff, designed to restore the initiative to the federal government and place the provinces, divided amongst themselves, on the defensive," as they realized that they "could not afford to operate without the largesse of the Federal Government."[40] Whether or not this was an attempt to regain the initiative, it was a

---

37   For example, at an in-camera session of the July 1960 federal-provincial conference, Frost noted that "Ontario was prepared to approach everyone's problems with reason," and then proceeded to dominate the discussion by explaining various economic problems to Diefenbaker, pressing the issue of sharing tax fields and offering support for regional adjustments once the fiscal fields were sorted out. See ibid., notes on in-camera proceedings of federal-provincial conference of 25-27 July 1960.

38   Ibid., Gathercole to Frost, 22 September 1960.

39   *Winnipeg Free Press*, 14 June 1960.

40   Saywell, *Canadian Annual Review for 1960*, 45; DCC, Diefenbaker Papers, reel M-7834, file 306.1 B government B federal-provincial relations B federal-provincial fiscal arrangements, 1961, Senator

position from which Ottawa would partially retreat the following year in announcing increases to equalization, a stabilization formula, and the replacement of the tax rental system with one of tax sharing.[41] Although Ontario was disappointed with these eventual changes, it indicated that it viewed "the new arrangement as a substantial improvement."[42]

While Diefenbaker was Prime Minister, Frost consistently argued in favour of a renegotiation of the tax rental agreements, insisting that the short-term arrangements that had characterized the postwar period had been meant only as band-aid solutions. When the federal government failed both to respond to the call for a new basis for fiscal federalism and to provide effective national leadership, Ontario began to argue that its proposal was not merely offered to further its own interest, but would serve the national interest more effectively than the existing system. Ottawa hesitantly accepted some of Ontario's arguments, as witnessed in the new 1962 tax collection agreement, but Ontario had by this time adopted its new strategy of appealing to other provinces. Attempts to influence the actions of the federal government directly were essentially discarded in favour of working around Ottawa and appealing to the provinces affected by intergovernmental arrangements. In the meantime, Leslie Frost had retired as Premier of Ontario, and had been succeeded by John Robarts.[43]

Diefenbaker had liked Frost, and felt some obligation toward him for his support in the 1957 and 1958 elections. Frost's retirement speech gave some indication of the direction in which the province was going. Instead of emphasizing Ontario's development, he had a grander vision: "We must have clear, positive, vigorous ideas of Canada's place and opportunities — in other words, what kind of country Canada should be with the very great opportunities she has."[44] Diefenbaker, too, spoke of the important national role Ontario had played in extending "the hand of fellowship to other Canadians by added [sic] grants to the Atlantic provinces … [at] the expressed desire of Premier Frost," but his praise for Ontario's support in the 1958 federal election came too little and too late.[45] The selection of John Robarts to lead the Ontario party signalled changes to come. Not only did Robarts and Diefenbaker share nothing in the way of organization, but Robarts disliked Diefenbaker and was clearly not disposed to cooperate with him.

The fiscal relationship through 1967 had been set by the time Robarts came to power, so there was little room for debate in this area. That there was no love lost between the Prime Minister and the new Premier of Ontario, however, was evident in other areas. Diefenbaker moved quickly to alter the form of address used in

Harold Connolly to Diefenbaker, 31 January 1961.

41   AO, RG 6-115, box 17, file: Federal-Provincial Finances, 61 B Federal-Provincial memoranda, 1961. Diefenbaker to Premiers, 16 June 1961; *Proceedings of the Dominion-Provincial Conference*, Ottawa, 23-24 February 1961.

42   AO, RG 6-115, box 18, file 93, "An Address to the Canadian Tax Foundation on Federal-Provincial Tax Arrangements by G.E. Gathercole, Ontario Deputy Minister of Economics, Montreal, November 22, 1961."

43   Interview, Dalton Camp, 19 February 1997.

44   AO, John Robarts Papers, Series F-15-4-3, MU 7998, file: Frost, Leslie, speech at the leadership convention of the Progressive Conservative Party of Ontario, 23 October 1961.

45   AO, Hugh Latimer Papers, MU 4543, Minutes of the Ontario Progressive Conservative Leadership Convention, October 23rd, 24th and 25th, 1961, Diefenbaker, pp. 69-70.

correspondence with Robarts; all Premiers were to be called "Premier of…" in official correspondence, a change aimed at putting both Ontario and Quebec in their place, as these two provinces had for the past hundred years officially referred to their leaders as Prime Minister or Premier ministre.[46] For his part, Robarts played a limited role in the 1962 federal election. Despite being asked "specifically and urgently to take part in the federal campaign," and despite Robarts's claim that "there is no wish on my part to give the impression of not supporting Mr. Diefenbaker," it was clear that the two were working at more than arm's length.[47] When Diefenbaker was reduced to a minority government in 1962, it was deemed to have been because "John Robarts, not a particularly well-known man at the time, was chosen to lead the Ontario Conservative Party as well as the Ontario Conservative Government."[48] It was also clear that the Conservatives had lost the support of urban and professional voters, who composed a large part of the Ontario electorate.[49] When Diefenbaker was ousted from office in the spring of 1963, the greatest concern for Ontario Conservatives was to "dissociate ourselves from this association" with Diefenbaker.[50]

Instead of working in concert with Diefenbaker, Robarts pursued the policy tentatively begun by Frost of devising programs that would serve the national interest while at the same time protecting Ontario's enviable position within the federation. As the Premier commented to his Minister of Mines: "we, in the Province of Ontario, have always assumed that what was good for us was good for the whole country."[51] In addition to continuing the work of the Portable Pension Commission established by Frost, Robarts also investigated the best way to introduce full health insurance. Both moves were designed to determine social policies for Ontario, but the expectation was that they would provide a sound basis for the development of parallel national programs. Robarts, however, did not trouble the Prime Minister with these projects. By 1962, the only connection Diefenbaker had with Ontario was through occasional correspondence with the retired Premier Frost.[52] Thus, it was to the leader of the Liberal Opposition, Lester Pearson, that Robarts turned in support of the extension of Ontario's social policy. "I learn with much pleasure," he wrote, "of your proposals to develop a contributory social security scheme for the aged…. May I say, therefore, that the government of Ontario would concur in and facilitate proper and reasonable plans by your government resulting in a contributory social insurance program

46   DCC, Diefenbaker Papers, reel M-7935, file 360 B Provincial Governments, General, 1959-1962, memo to file, Derek Bedson, 21 November 1961.

47   AO, Robarts Papers, Series F-15-4-3, box 10, MU 8006, file: PC Party of Canada, 1962-1963, Senator Joseph Sullivan to Robarts, 16 May 1962 and Robarts to Rev. Smyth, 28 March 1962.

48   NA, Progressive Conservative Party Papers, MG 28 IV 2, vol. 390, file: election, 1963, Hyndman, Peter, speech by Joel Aldred to the PC Nominating Convention, Sudbury, 2 March 1963.

49   Ibid., vol. 336, file: Diefenbaker, general (June-July 1962), Roy Faibish to John Fisher, 25 June 1962.

50   AO, Robarts Papers, series F-15-4-3, box 8, MU 8004, file: Ontario PC Party B election, George Hogan to Robarts, 11 April 1963.

51   Ibid., Series 4-1, MU 7959, letter books, 1961-1962, Robarts to George Wardrope, 17 October 1961.

52   Frost continued to try to educate Diefenbaker on financial issues. In early 1962, for example, he wrote: "The re-examination of our whole tax structure should be undertaken in Canada with a view to reducing the impediments thrown on industry and aimed at stimulating the willingness and, indeed, the ability of our people to work and save." He was nothing if not consistent. See AO, Frost Papers, new series, F 4345, container 1, file: Diefenbaker, 1962, Frost to Diefenbaker, 19 February 1962.

becoming a reality."[53] It was an odd comment to make to the as yet unelected Prime Minister leading a party of a different partisan stripe, but it underscores the fact that Diefenbaker and Robarts did not work well together, and that Robarts continued to pursue and support national policies in the tradition Frost had established.

Ontario's relations with Ottawa during the years of Conservative government at both levels were more problematic than was anticipated. Despite Leslie Frost's support of Diefenbaker's bid for the leadership, the support of the Ontario Conservatives in the elections of 1957 and 1958, and Frost's willingness to agree to policies such as the Atlantic Adjustment Grants that benefited less prosperous regions, Diefenbaker moved too slowly for Ottawa's liking in the direction of a more equitable division of tax revenues. Ontario had expected more from a Conservative Prime Minister. Diefenbaker's failure to respond to Ontario's most pressing demand, coupled with his own leadership problems, pushed Ontario into a position of essentially by-passing the federal government. Frost, who remained reasonably close to the Prime Minister throughout his tenure in office, made only subtle and private forays into articulating the national interest. Robarts, unhampered by any pre-existing allegiance to Diefenbaker, moved more explicitly in the direction of designing policies for implementation on a national scale. Perhaps his most important national role was in attempting to find a comfortable place for Quebec within the federation through the Confederation of Tomorrow Conference in 1967, but his early years as Premier suggested that he more generally saw a role for Ontario in the design of national social policies. If the province's relations with the federal government between 1957 and 1963 were not marked by bitter confrontation, they nevertheless seem to have been driven by a growing sense of the centrality of Ontario's place in the nation. Not prepared to attack Diefenbaker directly when his policies failed to meet the expectations of the Ontario administration, Premiers Frost and Robarts opted instead for the presentation of plans that would prove that "what is good for the province is good for the nation."

Note

The author gratefully acknowledges the support of the Social Sciences and Humanities Research Council, as well as Susan Precious for her research assistance.

---

53   Queen's University Archives, Tom Kent Papers, box 2, file: Correspondence June 1963, Robarts to Pearson, 6 February 1962.

DIEFENBAKER AND THE PRESS:
A CASE STUDY OF *MACLEAN'S*, 1958-1963

Patrick H. Brennan

At the outset of the 1962 election campaign, as he boarded the Diefenbaker aircraft, reporter Val Sears joked: "To work, gentlemen, we have a government to overthrow!" No one seemed to doubt that he spoke for the majority of his fellow journalists.[1] The Prime Minister believed that he and his government had been cursed by a vindictive and "servile press" beholden to dark — presumably Liberal party — interests.[2] Among historians, it is a point of departure that one of the greatest disasters to befall the Diefenbaker prime ministership was the progressive deterioration of his relationship with the press. Nor is there any doubt that the press had constituted the most effective "opposition" the government had faced, or that a great many journalists, having lost faith in the Conservatives' capacity to govern and the Prime Minister's capacity to lead, had accepted and even embraced this role. The question for historians, then, is not whether an antagonistic and critical press helped indirectly to undermine the Diefenbaker government — this seems self-evident — but whether the partisan sympathies of the press shaped their coverage of public affairs in ways intended to damage Diefenbaker and his government, or whether the Prime Minister and his government suffered chiefly from self-inflicted wounds, with the journalists' role merely one of keeping Canadians informed of their government's current state of self-destruction.

Maclean's magazine, which targeted a better-educated middle- and upper-income audience during the 1950s and early 1960s, had the largest readership of any Canadian general news and commentary magazine, and unquestionably helped shape the opinions of Canadians.[3] Because of its bi-weekly publication, and lead times of as much as six weeks for feature stories, *Maclean's* emphasized commentary and

---

1   As quoted in Peter C. Newman, *Renegade in Power: The Diefenbaker Years* (Toronto: McClelland and Stewart, 1973 [Carleton Library reprint]), 246.

2   Ibid., 246, 244-45.

3   *Maclean's* bi-weekly circulation during the late 1950s and early 1960s hovered around the half-million mark. It was 525,000 in 1961. Archives of Ontario (AO), Maclean-Hunter Papers, vol. 29, *Annual Report*, 1961; ibid., vol. 4, Minutes of Board of Directors, 20 March 1962.

background rather than hard news. Its principal political commentators, Blair Fraser and Peter Newman, were among the most respected, widely read, and, thanks to regular CBC radio and television exposure, widely listened to and watched authorities on public affairs during this period, reaching a national audience. While Prime Minister Diefenbaker did not list *Maclean's* (or its sister publication, the *Financial Post*) among those he read regularly to gauge the media's portrayal of his government, he was fully apprised of what the magazine was saying, and considered it "unfriendly."[4] Thus, examining the coverage of the Diefenbaker government in *Maclean's* provides valuable insights into both the attitudes and the performance of an important element of the English-language press.

Despite the impeccable Bay Street links of its senior management, Conservatives had long considered Maclean-Hunter Publishing to be sympathetic to the Liberals. Officially, *Maclean's* had no editorial slant when it came to national politics; as proof, its leading political columnist claimed that he never had to rewrite any material to fit a preconceived Maclean-Hunter editorial line.[5] The journalistic culture of *Maclean's*, dating back to the editorial policy of Arthur Irwin in the 1940s, gave its writers as free a hand as possible in commenting on national politics, with a powerful editor fending off management whenever it proved necessary. It was a policy to which Irwin's able replacement, Ralph Allen, adamantly adhered.[6] In practice, however, the magazine had exhibited a sort of "government party" sympathy for the Liberals during the latter King and then St. Laurent years. Outright criticism of the St. Laurent government on philosophical lines had certainly been rare in *Maclean's*, at least until Liberal fortunes began to unravel during the pipeline fiasco of 1956. It was an editorial position that most of the writing staff found congenial.[7]

The magazine's leading personalities did little to assuage Conservative party fears. A majority of Conservatives dismissed Blair Fraser — author of the most popular feature in *Maclean's*, "Backstage at Ottawa" — as a Liberal insider whose long-standing friendship with Lester (Mike) Pearson fatally compromised his objectivity. While it was true that Fraser had become an establishment journalist during the 1950s and remained a close friend of Pearson, he was less a Liberal by sympathy than an unabashed admirer (and promoter) of the postwar mandarins' view of Canada. During the Liberal locust years, however, it had been understandably difficult for many among the perpetually marginalized Conservatives to detect such nuances of commitment. Moreover, Fraser's record had been forever blotted by the famous June 1957 "post-election" editorial in *Maclean's* in which Ralph Allen, harassed by deadlines, had made the assumption that the Liberals would be returned to office and roundly chastised Canadian voters for re-electing them. Partisan Conservatives promptly attributed the contents to Fraser, and felt vindicated for having assumed the worst about him and his magazine for so many years.[8]

---

4   Ibid., vol. 59, file: McEachern-Chalmers 1958 and before, Chalmers memo re: meeting with Diefenbaker, 18 October 1958; Newman, *Renegade in Power*, 241; and interview with Alvin Hamilton.

5   AO, Maclean-Hunter Papers, vol. 21, file: D.G. Campbell — Royal Commission Publications "Hearings," memo, 14 December 1960. The journalist was Fraser.

6   Patrick Brennan, *Reporting the Nation's Business: Press-Government Relations during the Liberal Years, 1935-1957* (Toronto: University of Toronto Press, 1994), 102-5.

7   Interviews with Pierre Berton and Peter Gzowski.

8   Brennan, *Reporting the Nation's Business*, 144 and 166; and National Archives (NA), Gordon Churchill Papers, vol. 105, file: Personal 1968-74, Churchill memo to Melville, 23 July 1970. Interviews with

Blair Fraser doing a television news report from Parliament Hill for CBC TV, c. 1957 (courtesy Graham Fraser).

Fraser, in turn, was suspicious of the Conservatives in general and Diefenbaker in particular. Like many of his generation and intellectual bent, he suffered from having experienced Conservative government first-hand during the Depression, and had then watched the party as Opposition wallow in self-pity, engage in endless internecine conflicts, and generally oppose for more than two decades what he approvingly saw as the achievement of Canadian nationhood. The anti-French Canada, anti-social welfare, anti-bureaucratic, and anti-internationalist tone of many Conservatives had both depressed and alarmed him, and in his mind effectively rendered the party unfit to govern. While he was impressed by the party's apparent embrace of more moderate positions, especially under Diefenbaker's leadership, he still did not trust them. Moreover, the individual Conservatives he respected — the brighter, more "civilized," and generally less partisan ones such as David Fulton, George Nowlan, and James Macdonnell — seemed to him to be the exceptions that simply proved the rule.[9] Such sympathy as he could muster for the Conservatives in 1957 was predicated on his growing disgust with Liberal arrogance rather than any conviction that the Conservatives would govern well. As for Diefenbaker personally, Fraser admired his obvious commitment to individual liberties and his socially progressive instincts, but his populism and "outsider" mentality did not endear, nor did his pomposity, vanity, and occasional vindictiveness. The thought of Diefenbaker as Prime Minister rather than lonely Opposition critic was disturbing. That the Conservatives he knew intimately,

---

Roy Faibish, Davie Fulton, Alvin Hamilton, Charles Lynch, and Frank Peers. Not surprisingly, extreme partisans such as Churchill set out to make sure that Fraser was reminded of his past and ongoing sins in none too subtle ways — interviews with Escott Reid, Roy Faibish, and Charles King.

9   Interviews with Graham Fraser, Frank Peers, and Gordon Robertson.

such as fellow Nova Scotian and Acadia University alumnus George Nowlan, had deep reservations about their leader simply confirmed his doubts.[10] Finally, from Fraser's perspective, the new Prime Minister had committed an unpardonable offence by making partisan use of a secret economic report authored by Mitchell Sharp, then Deputy Minister of Trade and Commerce and a highly respected public servant. As a political move, it effectively cut the ground out from under the Liberals' economic criticisms. For Fraser, however, there was a larger issue; namely, the harm being done both to the public's perception of civil service impartiality and the tradition of confidentiality in civil service-Cabinet dealings.[11] There was no Liberal partisanship here, however; for proof, one need look no further than Fraser's confrontation of an embarrassed and clearly irritated Lester Pearson on "Press Conference," where he ridiculed the Liberals' self-righteous indignation by pointing out that they had kept the report secret and failed to act on its warnings while they were still in government.[12]

March 1958 brought another election, but this time Ralph Allen confined his editorial comments to platitudes. Fraser had so despaired of both parties that he was considering voting CCF, he confided to a friend, to avoid "having to choose between the two old trollops again."[13] Nevertheless, covering the election on CBC television, he did not hide his disappointment at the magnitude of the Conservative sweep, at one point labelling it a "disaster for Canada." While he quickly explained to viewers that he had meant the lack of an adequate Opposition, co-anchor Charles Lynch always thought his comments had been part Freudian slip.[14]

The traditional media honeymoon was remarkably short-lived in the case of the Diefenbaker government. Nonetheless, little hard criticism appeared in Fraser's "Backstage" columns, feature articles, or broadcasts during the months immediately following the Conservative sweep. In one article tackling the already sensitive issue of Diefenbaker's supposed "one-man rule," for instance, he concluded that the stories were much exaggerated.[15] Editorially, *Maclean's* supported the government's "common-sense" decision to suspend work on the costly Avro Arrow jet fighter in the fall of 1958, and broadly sided with the interventionist, spending side of the Conservative Cabinet in its deepening debate over the priority to be given inflation versus employment policies.[16] Some months later, in "The Government's Second Birthday:

10   Blair Fraser, *The Search for Identity: Canada, Postwar to Present* (Toronto: Doubleday, 1967), 163. James Macdonnell was another. During the 1957 campaign, he had confidentially dismissed Diefenbaker as a "horse's ass" to one colleague, and his populism as so much "BS" to another. Interviews with Charles King and Robert Fulford, respectively. Interview with Graham Fraser.

11   Brennan, *Reporting the Nation's Business*, 169. Gordon Churchill, one of the most suspicious and partisan of Diefenbaker's ministers, was convinced that Fraser sought revenge against the government over the "mistreatment" of Sharp, a close friend of the journalist. See Peter Stursberg, *Diefenbaker: Leadership Gained, 1956-62* (Toronto: University of Toronto Press, 1975), 151-52.

12   CBC TV, Cartographic and Audio-Visual Archives, 160380, "Press Conference," 21 January 1958.

13   NA, Frank Scott Papers, vol. 25, file: Personal Correspondence, January-June 1958, Fraser to Scott, 28 January 1958; "Editorial: The real issues in the election," *Maclean's*, 1 March 1958. Ibid., 15 February 1958.

14   Interview with Charles Lynch.

15   "Is Diefenbaker Running a One-Man Government?" *Maclean's*, 14 March 1959; Denis Smith, *Rogue Tory: The Life and Legend of John G. Diefenbaker* (Toronto: Macfarlane Walter and Ross, 1995), 327-28.

16   "Editorial: Let's not let inflation blind us to unemployment," *Maclean's*, 14 March 1959; "Editorial: Tight money or inflation: we have to take our choice," ibid., 24 October 1959.

A quick inventory of the pros and cons," Fraser gave the government passing grades, but pointed, quite rightly, to growing questions of competence, especially on economic and defence matters.[17]

Evidence of the growing suspicion between press and government, and the excessive sensitivity of the Prime Minister and many of his colleagues to media criticism, was dramatically presented in June 1959 with the "Preview Commentary" affair. "Preview Commentary" was a daily morning radio analysis by members of the press gallery of current goings-on in the House of Commons. Diefenbaker was known to be a regular, if increasingly critical, listener. The program was abruptly cancelled under suspicious circumstances by senior CBC management on 15 June 1955, and just as abruptly re-instated a little more than a week later after the threatened mass resignations of most of the network's talks and public affairs staff. Rumours of political interference by a thin-skinned government suffering its first wave of troubles circulated around Ottawa.[18] Fraser discussed the affair in "Backstage," and while carefully avoiding implicating the Prime Minister in the uttering of any threat, he pointed out that Diefenbaker's well-known aversion to media criticism had given the suggestions of political interference credibility.[19] The "Preview Commentary" affair helped confirm the perception held by many Conservatives that the CBC had been and continued to be a supporter of the Liberal Party. While "Preview Commentary" was seen as a victory for CBC editorial freedom, a chill had descended on the broadcaster, one of the consequences of which was the noticeably less frequent use of Blair Fraser as a freelancer.[20] During the latter months of 1959, as the economy stagnated and the government seemed without solutions, Conservative fortunes declined steadily, and it was hard for Fraser not to comment on the obvious.[21]

The spring of 1960 saw Fraser reluctantly assume the editorship of *Maclean's*. The first attempt to find a successor for Ralph Allen had been botched by management, who now fell back on their remaining "star," with Allen agreeing to stay on informally for three years as a sort of editorial advisor. Fraser had been their "Ottawa man" for sixteen years, and only his loyalty to the magazine and the promise of a posting in London after two years at the editor's desk in Toronto had pried him loose from the

---

17   "Backstage at Ottawa," *Maclean's*, 4 July 1959; "Editorial: It takes no courage to drop the Arrow — just common sense," ibid., 25 October 1958; "Editorial: Time for Ottawa to stop fighting the last election," ibid., 28 February 1959. See also CBC TV, V1 8209-0091, "Press Conference," 22 March 1959. Fraser referred to the government's defence policy as a "fog" in one broadcast. See CBC TV, V1 8605-0115, "Newsmagazine," 13 December 1959.

18   Frank Peers, *The Public Eye: Television and the Politics of Broadcasting, 1952-1968* (Toronto: University of Toronto Press, 1979), 194-200. See also Newman, *Renegade in Power*, 234-37 and Smith, *Rogue Tory*, 333-34. On deteriorating press relations and Diefenbaker's reaction to criticism, see Charles Lynch, *The Lynch Mob: Stringing Up Our Prime Ministers* (Toronto: Key Porter, 1988), 54-55; and David Taras, *The Newsmakers: The Media's Influence on Canadian Politics* (Toronto: Nelson, 1990), 133, 136-37.

19   "Backstage at Ottawa," *Maclean's*, 1 August 1959. Later in the fall, Fraser confronted Nowlan, the minister responsible for the CBC, on the question of political interference in the corporation's public affairs programming. See CBC TV, NFA-75-4-21, "Press Conference," 11 November 1959.

20   NA, CBC, acc. 86-7/031, box 174, file 18-15-0-9, Taylor to Gillingham, 6 April 1959. Interviews with Tom Earle , Frank Peers, and Peter Dempson, *Assignment Ottawa: Seventeen Years in the Press Gallery* (Toronto: General Publishing, 1968), 238-39. See NA, CBC, PG 10-17, pt. 2, re: Patrick Nicholson letter, memo, 1 September 1959; NA, Lester Pearson Papers, N2 Series, vol. 35, file 391.6.3 — publicity, memo to Pickersgill, 10 July 1959.

21   "Backstage at Ottawa," *Maclean's*, 26 September and 21 November 1959; "The Political Outlook," ibid., 7 November 1959.

Blair Fraser (centre) with Ralph Allen (right) and an unidentified staff member in the editorial offices of Maclean's, *1960 (courtesy Maclean-Hunter).*

capital. In terms of political sympathies, Allen had actually been more of a Conservative than a Liberal, though not a Diefenbaker Conservative, and he had always insisted on keeping the political commentary in *Maclean's* objective.[22] In contrast, most Conservatives viewed Fraser as an establishment Liberal, plain and simple. The Prime Minister, government insiders insisted, saw Fraser's appointment as a hostile act, and repeatedly telephoned Floyd Chalmers, head of the magazine division at Maclean-Hunter, to demand Fraser's dismissal.[23] As it turned out, Fraser, though a brilliant writer and reporter, was a disinterested administrator, and did little to put his own mark on the magazine. The principal change for both *Maclean's* readers and the Diefenbaker government was the appointment of Peter Newman as Fraser's "Backstage" replacement — and, at least some of the magazine's staff thought, a weakening of the editorial desk's "no partisanship" resolve.[24]

Newman had worked with Fraser in Ottawa since 1957, and before that with the *Financial Post.* Able and ambitious, he felt himself as much an outsider in Ottawa as his predecessor had felt himself an insider. Like Fraser, however, he had developed excellent contacts in the capital; in particular, he had gained the confidence of several Cabinet ministers and senior assistants, which proved a tremendous advantage once he set about exposing the Prime Minister's "feet of clay."[25] He also represented

22   Interviews with Robert Fulford and Peter Gzowski. Blair Fraser Papers, private collection, Irwin to Fraser, 16 July 1960.

23   Interview with Charles Lynch.

24   Interview with Sidney Katz; interview with Pierre Berton.

25   Interviews with Joyce Fairbairn, Robert Fulford, and Bill Wilson.

a more confrontational style of journalism which was new to the gallery. Over the coming months, Newman led the way for an increasingly adversarial press corps in bringing the Diefenbaker government's deficiencies to the attention of the voters, and in the process supplanted even Blair Fraser in the Conservative pantheon of journalistic demons. The Prime Minister bestowed on the new "Backstage" editor one of his singular honours of disapproval, referring to him disparagingly as "Noy-man" — an offensive reference (or so it was certainly taken) to Newman's Jewish heritage. The two men soon despised one another openly.[26]

Newman's early columns were inoffensive enough. Many did not even deal with the government, *per se*, and those that did were generally favourable in a backhanded sort of way, as when he observed that "John Diefenbaker's ministry has finally snapped out of the inertia that weighed it down during much of the last parliament." Newman followed this up with a rather sympathetic account of Diefenbaker's ongoing twenty-year struggle "with the reactionaries of his party" to reorient toward the Canadian political centre the Conservatives' economic, social, racial, and ideological principles.[27] Sandwiched between these columns, however, was a positive portrayal of Lester Pearson's transformation from diplomat to political leader, so any goodwill was undoubtedly dissipated.[28]

The apparent failure of *Maclean's* to report more critically on the Diefenbaker government perplexed some of the magazine's admirers and the government's critics. Maclean-Hunter executives, while nominally subscribing to Horace Hunter's dictum that publishers should publish and editors edit, faced a sticky problem. Cynical observers suggested that one of the reasons the company had been broadly sympathetic to the Liberals during their long run in office was the need to gain favourable tax and other legislation for Canadian magazine publishers, and, in particular, restrictions on the operation of American magazines in the Canadian market. By keeping the financially marginal *Maclean's* afloat — it was never a money-maker, unlike its sister publication, the *Financial Post* — the company was able to boast that it spent more to promote Canadian spiritual and literary values than the Canada Council.[29] *Maclean's* provided an intellectual cachet for Maclean-Hunter, but it also firmly established the company's nationalist credentials in any negotiations with Ottawa. Circumstances would be more difficult with a Diefenbaker government, as Chalmers had quickly found out in the fall of 1958 when presenting the company's case for the first time. The Prime Minister, a chastened Chalmers later reported, furiously denounced the *Financial Post* for "vicious pressure propaganda at its worst" over the government's Arrow policy. Chalmers's reply that *Maclean's* had been strongly supportive of the government failed to appease him. Dismissing Diefenbaker as a "small town lawyer" with all the petty prejudices and insecurities thereof, Chalmers lamented that "obviously he looks only at criticism and takes favourable comment for granted."[30] Though impressed by the Prime Minister's knowledge of the difficulties

---

26   Interviews with Tom Earle, Alvin Hamilton, and Charles King; interview with Davie Fulton. On Fraser's and Newman's mutual despising of Diefenbaker, see Robert Fulford, *Best Seat in the House: Memoirs of a Lucky Man* (Toronto: Key Porter, 1988), 4-55.

27   "Backstage at Ottawa," *Maclean's*, 17 December 1960, and ibid., 10 September 1960.

28   Ibid., 22 October 1960.

29   AO, Maclean-Hunter Papers, vol. 59, file: McEachern — Chalmers 1958 and before, Chalmers memo to McEachern, 18 October 1958.

30   Ibid.; Brennan, *Reporting the Nation's Business*, 103.

that Canadian publishers faced, he was anything but hopeful of immediate government assistance. Donald Hunter, the normally low-key president of the company, had the true Bay Streeter's visceral contempt for Diefenbaker, but as a realist argued that the company's publications had no choice but to go lightly on the government in order to win its support on more vital matters. "Is there any way out other than for you to state bluntly to Allen, Fraser, [the *Financial Post*'s Ronald] McEachern and [Michael] Barkway that you very much hope we can give the government no offence unless it is on a matter of [the] greatest urgency and on matters where it has been clearly established that serious principles are involved?" he inquired of Chalmers.[31]

Chalmers was unlikely to have much overt success in persuading Allen to tone down criticisms of the government's failings,[32] while McEachern, ruthlessly ambitious and a company loyalist, would accept the necessity of tempering criticism at the *Post*.[33] Chalmers fretted himself over the dangers of offending the Conservatives, and he was particularly worried about radio and television appearances by Fraser and Newman, whose views, he feared, would likely be mistaken for the magazine's. Justified or not, by the winter of 1960-61 rumours abounded in Ottawa that Fraser had been the victim of a "soft-on-Diefenbaker" policy dictated by his cowering employers. The ever-suspicious McEachern, who disliked the recently appointed editor of *Maclean's*[34] anyway, and quite possibly saw some personal advantage in discrediting him in management's eyes, suggested to Chalmers that "Fraser [had] contributed to the canard on a television program when he was asked how he liked being an editor rather than a writer [and replied] something to this effect: 'They have put me in a corral where I can't be too troublesome... .' This was a very clear implication of what he said and unmistakable in its meaning to every half awake listener" — or at any rate to McEachern.[35] In the end, from the company's perspective, all depended on the government's implementation of the recommendations of the Royal Commission on Publications which, in the summer of 1961, had favoured tax and other changes long sought by Canadian magazine publishers. Their adoption, as Chalmers lectured his editors, would have to be "the highest priority for [the company]."[36] Despite relentless lobbying, with Maclean-Hunter in the forefront, the Cabinet delayed action, and before any legislation was passed the Diefenbaker government had fallen.

In 1961, more political woes greeted a government which was already wrestling with seemingly intractable unemployment, economic, and financial troubles. Often now, Newman portrayed a desperate administration in inexorable decline. Where, he asked, was the much-ballyhooed new vision? "The Diefenbaker government has attracted a surfeit of political strategists," he explained to his readers, "but it has failed

31   AO, Maclean-Hunter Papers, vol. 59, file: McEachern-Chalmers 1959. Hunter to Chalmers, n.d. Michael Barkway was the *Post*'s senior Ottawa correspondent.

32   Hunter certainly thought Chalmers had had no effect on Allen, as did Barkway. See ibid.

33   Ibid., file: McEachern-Chalmers 1960, McEachern to Chalmers, 5 July 1960; interview with Robert Fulford.

34   Fraser was appointed editor in the summer of 1960.

35   AO, Maclean-Hunter Papers, file: McEachern-Chalmers 1961. McEachern to Chalmers, 25 January 1961; ibid. 1960, Chalmers to McEachern, 26 April 1960. It is possible that Fraser was simply referring to his leaving Ottawa; as editor, his opportunities to write for the magazine, critically of the government or otherwise, were much reduced.

36   Ibid., file: McEachern B Chalmers 1961. Chalmers to McEachern, 15 August 1961; ibid., vol. 4, Minutes of Board of Directors Meetings, 20 March 1962.

to recruit the kind of brain trust that could produce dashingly original legislative proposals, [for] Conservative intellectuals, like Conservative businessmen, mistrust Diefenbaker."[37] By the spring, the government's budgetary pressures were increasingly evident. Newman alerted his readers to these, and to the dangerous deadlock between the "tight-money" policies advocated by the Bank of Canada and the expansionary policies favoured by most of the Cabinet. Objective though it was, Newman's report also served to reinforce the Liberal refrain that the Conservatives could not run the store. A subsequent "Backstage" column entitled, "Fleming's Double Gamble: Can he get the nation and his party out of hock?" continued the theme, though it was remarkably balanced in evenly attributing blame for the recent forced resignation of the Governor of the Bank of Canada — some to the government, but a good portion to James Coyne, too.[38]

While the Conservatives floundered, polls showed that Liberal fortunes were rising. Newman reported that, "until recently, Pearson thought that the acre of mocking Conservative faces in the House was a true reflection of the country's mood. Now, buoyed up by optimistic advisers, and trusting in his diagnosis of a national swing away from Diefenbaker, he feels that the federal Prime Ministership is within his grasp." Two months later, in a column titled "The Tory future: it looks a lot better than the past," Newman provided a more balanced look at the ideological triumph of John Diefenbaker, the progressive prairie radical, over the old line Bay Street gang.[39] But this was followed by a *Maclean's* "Special Report" on Canadian foreign policy contributed by freelancer Bruce Hutchison, a fervent admirer of Pearson and unabashed friend of the Liberal party, which pulled no punches on the failings of the Diefenbaker Conservatives, particularly in trade relations with the United States and Britain. Hutchison's underlying theme — lack of clear policy and indecision in equal measure — was one that was increasingly heard now among the government's critics.[40] As one of Pearson's key advisors put it, the voters were growing disillusioned with "a one-man show that doesn't get things done."[41]

For John Diefenbaker and his battered government, 1962 would be the year of electoral reckoning. "Conservative hopes, though still high, all hang on one man," wrote Newman in his "Backstage" overview of the impending campaign. For the Liberals, in contrast, it was the "Mike Pearson team." Newman's network of contacts in Ottawa seemed to keep him informed of every misstep and dispute within the government, and much of this intelligence made it into his "Backstage" columns, either overtly or by allusion, to the consternation of the Prime Minister. A good example of such embarrassing and harmful leaks were Newman's revelations of the infighting between the election-conscious Cabinet spenders and the government's last bulwark of fiscal prudence, Finance Minister Donald Fleming. The machinations within machinations recounted in "How Fleming lost his battle with the heavy spenders" hardly reflected well on Cabinet solidarity, and portrayed the Prime Minister himself as the central schemer.[42] The fact that Newman was long on getting

---

37   "Backstage at Ottawa," *Maclean's*, 28 January 1961.

38   Ibid., 15 July 1961 and 22 April 1961.

39   Ibid., 23 September 1961 and 26 August 1961.

40   "Special Report: Our risky place in the grand design for the Atlantic," *Maclean's*, 16 December 1961.

41   NA, Pearson Papers, N2 Series, vol. 22, file: T. Kent. Kent memo "campaign policies," 27 July 1961.

42   "Backstage in Ottawa," *Maclean's*, 27 January 1962. The column's title changed from "Backstage at Ottawa" to "Backstage in Ottawa" with the first issue of 1962.

the tone but not necessarily the facts right did not add to his reputation in the East Block.[43]

Of all Newman's columns, however, none can have cut deeper than the one outlining the unstated issue of the election, at least from the perspective of Conservative strategists: soured press relations. "By election eve, the feelings between the country's political press and the Prime Minister had deteriorated to such a degree that some Ottawa correspondents were convinced Diefenbaker was trying deliberately to goad reporters into intemperate criticism so that he could appeal to the electors' sympathy as the victim of a spiteful press that deliberately distorts all the good he has tried to do," wrote Newman in "Why Diefenbaker thinks the press is against him." The Prime Minister's efforts to improve his relations with the media had been only modestly successful, and contrasted sharply with the solid press relations some of his Cabinet ministers enjoyed. "The PM's sole criterion for measuring how he's going to respond to press criticism," one of Diefenbaker's close advisors had informed Newman, "is to put himself in the place of the man on the street and view its effects from that vantage point."[44] Under those circumstances, it would be hard to see any criticism as justified, let alone fair.

Newman's final pre-election column offered a general overview of the two main parties' campaign platforms, finding little to choose between the two. He pointedly concluded:

> Whether a Liberal government under Lester Pearson would be any more imaginative remains to be seen; that it would be calmer and managerially more efficient seems likely. Not only would a Pearson government receive full-out support from Ottawa's civil servants, but Pearson has been able to attract to his team men of high achievements in their own fields who might be expected to run this country with an independent authority that has seldom been granted to cabinet ministers under the personal kind of super-prime-ministership practised by John Diefenbaker.[45]

Blair Fraser's last editorial pointed to Conservative financial bungling — particularly the forced devaluation of the dollar and six consecutive budget deficits — and the inevitable austerity program that must come, then urged his readers to consider "which [government] will have the steadier hand on the helm through the storm that's plainly visible ahead."[46] On election night, the magnitude of the repudiation of the Diefenbaker government was only too clear: a loss of ninety-two seats reduced it to minority status. Watching CBC election night coverage would have been painful enough for Conservative loyalists without having to endure Fraser's analysis, although, given the election results, merely doing his job would have been incriminating. When political scientist John Irving asserted that Pearson had led the Liberals to defeat, Fraser reacted almost angrily. Pearson had brought the Liberals back from near ruin to almost becoming the government, "and I don't see how that performance would in any way be considered defeat," he lectured the startled Irving, adding

43   Interviews with Joyce Fairbairn, Davie Fulton, and Charles Lynch.

44   "Backstage in Ottawa," *Maclean's*, 19 May 1962. See also Smith, *Rogue Tory*, 429. On the difficulty of trying to "manage" the Prime Minister's press relations, see Lynch, *The Lynch Mob*, 54-55 and Taras, *The Newsmakers*, 137.

45   "Backstage in Ottawa," *Maclean's*, 16 June 1962.

46   "Editorial: The only issue: Are Canada's affairs in competent hands?" *Maclean's*, 16 June 1962.

that the Conservative government was coming back "pretty clearly to me with the mark of death on it."[47] Newman later summed up the election result:

> The agonizing indecisive outcome of the election campaign was a direct result of John Diefenbaker's failure to overcome the peccadilloes of his past. In trying to prolong the term in office of his party — which shouldn't have been difficult for a Prime Minister going into the election with seventy seats more than he needed for an absolute majority — he was severely hampered by a personal background that weakened his appeal to the voters.
>
> His career as an eloquent and often underpaid defender of the underdog in the courtrooms of dusty prairie towns fitted him ideally for the 1957 and 1958 contests, when he cast himself as the angry avenger of Liberal insolence. But 1962 was not 1958, and Diefenbaker was stuck playing the backwoods attorney, propounding his personal testament before the voters. As a result, his message aroused nearly as much ridicule as admiration.[48]

The vote revealed clearly enough that Diefenbaker had simply alienated too many voters over the past four years; for them, his message was now either insincere or not credible, or so Newman saw it. Diefenbaker supporters cannot have missed Newman's brief critique of Pearson in the same "Backstage" column: "the campaign left little doubt about Lester Pearson's concern and understanding of Canada's domestic problems [but] also proved that his view of life — tempered by twenty years as a career diplomat — was still that of an intellectual who looks upon politics as something if not alien, at least imposed upon his nature." Fraser rubbed salt in Conservative wounds in a post-election feature with the engaging title, "What Pearson Won By Losing: Luck left the Liberals out of office while crash measures against the money crisis are sealing the Conservatives' defeat." In the same issue, Newman's cold dissection of the Conservative collapse in "Why Diefenbaker Lost Canada" attributed the government's repudiation entirely to the failings of its leader.[49]

Plunged into a financial crisis during the campaign which forced the politically devastating devaluation of the dollar, the Diefenbaker government had little choice but to embark on an austerity campaign a week after its re-election, just as Fraser had forecast. Newman, who had never approved of the Conservatives' free-spending ways, was suspicious of whether Diefenbaker and Fleming would really follow through with the tough measures needed to put the country's economic house in order. "Whatever the Conservative Cabinet finally decides to do in its efforts to balance the national budget will be painful for a government whose leader repeatedly boasted during the recent election campaign that he had reduced the tax burden on eighty-five percent of Canadians since taking office. But eating words he spoke on the hustings has in recent weeks become a necessary part of the Prime Minister's diet."[50] As Diefenbaker and his besieged Cabinet struggled with the country's finances during the coming months, they would receive little sympathy in the pages of *Maclean's*.

At almost the same time as the Conservatives were confronting political reality as a minority government, *Maclean's* underwent another transition. Blair Fraser's two-year commitment had expired, and he took up his promised London post late that

---

47   CBC TV, V4 8210-0002 (2 to 4), -0003 and -0004 (1 and 2), "Election Night Coverage," 18 June 1962; NA, CBC Papers, acc. 86-7/031, box 193, file 18-19-5-8-28, "Draft schedule for election night."

48   "Backstage in Ottawa," *Maclean's*, 14 July 1962.

49   *Maclean's*, 28 July 1962.

50   "Backstage in Ottawa," *Maclean's*, 11 August 1962.

summer, where he continued to add to the government's media woes as a foreign policy critic. A successor had been groomed, Fraser's dynamic young managing editor, Ken Lefolii. The elevation of Lefolii to the editorship, and with him Peter Gzowski as managing editor, marked a shift in power to a more journalistically as well as politically radical generation of journalists at *Maclean's*. While both men respected Fraser's competence as a reporter, neither particularly admired his style. He had been too close to the Liberals, of course, but he also clung to the old notion that a responsible press had an explanatory role to perform; he was ill at ease with adopting the now-favoured probing and attacking role of journalists who deemed themselves to be in a permanent state of conflict with the government. In contrast, Newman, whose prestige was soaring both at the magazine and nationally, had been successfully putting his own mark on "Backstage" by embracing just such adversarial journalism, and so encountered no difficulty in adapting to the new, more critical and confrontational role set for *Maclean's*.[51] Unless management was more successful in restraining Lefolii than it appeared to have been with his predecessors, the editorial changes at *Maclean's* did not bode well for the struggling Conservatives and their leader.

Considering the magnitude of the June election losses, the Prime Minister's post-election Cabinet shuffle was surprisingly modest, and Newman's pen showed no mercy:

> Although he lost more votes on June 18 than any other Prime Minister in Canadian history, John Diefenbaker's recent cabinet transfiguration was far from the kind of drastic reconstruction which might have been expected from a party leader anxious to rebuild national confidence in his ministry.... .

> Diefenbaker obviously rejected all suggestions which might have infringed on his control over the party and the government. As in the past, he will be the silent partner in every Cabinet Minister's office, operating his administration through personal pressures rather than the normal distribution of authority...[52]

Writing from London, Fraser added to the government's woes. In his report on the Prime Minister's performance at that fall's Commonwealth Conference, Fraser referred to Diefenbaker's 1957 promise to divert an additional 15 percent of Canadian trade to the United Kingdom, noting that the British had "made the pardonable error of assuming this meant that he intended some change in Canadian trading policy," and concluding that "Canada's prestige has never quite recovered from this initial disillusion." That the relationship between Canada and the UK had progressively deteriorated, Fraser opined, was almost entirely attributable to the Diefenbaker government's assorted blunders. He left his readers to ponder whether "this historical background may explain the reaction in London, which ranges from contemptuous to openly hostile, to the so-called Diefenbaker 'plan' for Commonwealth trade."[53] A subsequent column and "Capital Report" broadcast were just as damning.

---

51   Interviews with Roy Faibish and Graham Fraser; interviews with Robert Fulford and Bill Wilson.

52   "Backstage in Ottawa," *Maclean's*, 8 September 1962. Newman was not alone in his surprise that the Cabinet was not thoroughly revamped. See Smith, *Rogue Tory*, 446-48.

53   "Overseas Report," *Maclean's*, 6 October 1962; ibid., 20 October 1962; NA, CBC, acc. 86-7/031, box 50, file: "Capital Report" September B October 1962, transcript, 9 September 1962. A newcomer to London, Fraser was doubtless influenced in part by the British officials' hostile briefings of the press; Smith, *Rogue Tory*, 450. Certainly he was despairing of Diefenbaker's foreign policy competence. See NA, Fraser Papers, Blair Fraser memo, 18 September 1962.

In the aftermath of the election, Peter Newman soon identified the Diefenbaker government's Achilles' heel, the acquisition of American nuclear weapons for the Canadian armed forces. Dismissing the Cabinet's indecision as political pandering, he pointed out that with the weapons now in place, "the government ... has only two choices: to scrap $685 million worth of military hardware and thereby publicly renege on our obligations under NORAD and NATO; or to accept joint US nuclear warheads under a system of joint control. Despite Prime Minister Diefenbaker's hints that there are other possibilities, no other choice in fact exists."[54]

The remainder of the column was a scathing exposé of the sorry state of Canadian defences in the absence of the warheads the weaponry had always been known to require. Interestingly, in the fall of 1960, when the nuclear genie of Canadian politics was just beginning to escape from its bottle, Fraser had written a strongly worded editorial answering the question of whether Canada should have nuclear weapons with "a flat unqualified no [under] any circumstances whatever." He had gone on to commend Pearson and other political figures — including, he hinted, some members of the Diefenbaker Cabinet — for changing their views from pro- to anti-nuclear weapons.[55] As recently as January 1962, Fraser had reiterated the magazine's opposition to Canadian acceptance of nuclear warheads, while emphasizing the gravity of the decision to be made and the indefensibility of continuing to postpone the decision simply to avoid the domestic and international political reckoning.[56]

In his last "Backstage" column of 1962, Newman highlighted another issue which must have caused the blood pressure of Conservatives to soar: the growth of anti-Diefenbaker sentiment within the party. "One of the most hallowed customs of Canadian Conservatives is to undermine — fatally, if possible — a federal leader who gets into difficulties," he reminded his readers. "In Ottawa, and around the country these days, Conservative functionaries are observing the tradition of revolution from within, with gusto [and] it is not a pleasant process to watch." According to Newman, and his story was correct in its essentials, the Conservatives were a badly divided party with two clearly identifiable factions, the prairie radicals and the Bay Street traditionalists. This, coupled with "a Prime Minister weighed down by a reluctance to make decisions," had paralyzed the government. Now a third faction was emerging which eschewed these ideological extremes and was even prepared to accept a temporary spell on the Opposition benches if it meant the end of "the Chief." Newman concluded that "there seems little doubt left that within his own party decisions are being made that will bring the political career of John Diefenbaker to a close."[57]

Ironically, even praise for individual Conservatives could be taken as — and certainly opened the opportunity for — criticism of the Prime Minister, as when Davie Fulton, a seventeen-year veteran of the House and one of the best and brightest of Diefenbaker's ministers, announced that he was leaving Parliament to lead the British Columbia Conservatives. Newman admired Fulton, both as a man and a politician, while possessing little respect for Diefenbaker on either score. Toward the end of what he openly titled a tribute to Fulton, Newman pointed out:

---

54   "Backstage in Ottawa," *Maclean's*, 20 October 1962.

55   "Editorial: Let's not let politics distort the issue of nuclear weapons," *Maclean's*, 10 September 1960. See also "Editorial: We can refuse nuclear arms and also keep faith with NATO," ibid., 22 April 1961.

56   "Editorial: Even in an election year, we should make some decisions," *Maclean's*, 27 January 1962.

57   "Backstage in Ottawa," *Maclean's*, 15 December 1962; Smith, *Rogue Tory*, 451-52.

although John Diefenbaker once regarded young Davie as something of a protégé, the two men broke over the 1956 leadership convention which Fulton contested against Diefenbaker's wishes. Despite the strained relations between them, Fulton (unlike many other Conservative ministers) never allowed anyone in his office to speak badly of "The Old Man." But when Diefenbaker humiliated him last summer by demoting him [from Justice] to the Public Works portfolio, the last incentive for Fulton to remain in Ottawa disappeared.[58]

The winter of 1962-63 was, indeed, the winter of discontent for the Diefenbaker government. Ideologically riven, as Newman had accurately described it, and now openly riven by the nuclear weapons issue, it clung to power amid a deepening sense of crisis. Never could the Prime Minister's dark allusions to a "conspiracy of interests" against him have seemed more real. Side by side with his endless criticisms of Diefenbaker's political opportunism and pathological inability to make up his mind on difficult issues, Newman's sympathetic accounting of the Liberals' recent opportunistic switch to the nuclear option after years of staunchly opposing it must have left a bitter taste.[59] Maclean's, which had praised Pearson for his earlier embrace of the non-nuclear option, failed to comment on this latest evolution of his nuclear thought. Instead, the magazine — this time in an editorial signed by Fraser — straightforwardly called for an election to clear the air and provide Canadians with the government they needed; namely, a majority government that could make decisions.[60]

The Diefenbaker government was defeated on a non-confidence vote in early February and an election was called for 8 April. In a column titled "Trouble at the Top," Newman accurately sketched the outlines of the cabinet putsch that had nearly toppled Diefenbaker, and then described in hopeless terms the Conservatives' re-election prospects. Those prospects were bleak, but they were not helped by the "foregone-conclusion" tone prevalent in most publications and epitomized by Maclean's. Indeed, all reporting of the Diefenbaker campaign in Maclean's exuded a grim air. A subsequent Newman editorial strongly criticized the Conservatives and especially their leader for gratuitous anti-Americanism on the hustings. Meanwhile, an extended editorial entitled "The Nuclear Mess," which appeared in mid-campaign, savaged the Conservatives' defence muddling, though not the non-nuclear option that appeared to be Diefenbaker's definitive policy.[61] As the Conservatives' re-election chances — and hence the prospect of their authoring any magazine legislation — melted like the March snows, even company management must have lost interest in maintaining a balance. "The powerful gifts and glaring flaws of John Diefenbaker," was a fair but, to say the least, unflattering characterization of the man, complete with a glowering portrait in a Newman feature article[62] (Maclean's never seemed to encounter the slightest trouble finding pictures of a beaming, bow-tied Pearson). A later column, written on the Prime Minister's whistle-stop tour of the Prairies,

---

58   "Backstage in Ottawa," Maclean's, 5 January 1963.

59   Ibid., 9 March 1963.

60   "Editorial: If what was true in '58 is true in '63 (and it is), we need an election now," Maclean's, 5 January 1963.

61   "Editorial: The nuclear mess," ibid., 9 March 1963; ibid., "Editorial: Some of our best friends are Americans. Let's keep it that way during the campaign."

62   Neither columnists nor feature writers had the final say in the titles chosen by the editorial staff, and the same was true of illustrations.

acknowledged that the campaigning had gone well, but Newman's concluding lines still betrayed his view of both the style and the substance of the campaigner's message:

> Everywhere the train halted, Diefenbaker seemed almost desperately anxious to make an urgent point: that he had tried his mightiest to improve the lot of the average Canadian during his time in office, and that if he had failed it was not because of his own shortcomings but because of the opposition of those never-defined evil powers he lumped together angrily as *they*. This is the message that John Diefenbaker is determined to leave behind him, if it's the last thing he does as Prime Minister. And it may very well be.[63]

In a final editorial, Ken Lefolii raised the spectre of Quebec separatism and elevated nation building, particularly the ability to reach out constructively to Quebec — an unquestioned commitment of the anglophones at *Maclean's* — as a prime requirement for the new national government. Given John Diefenbaker's well-known attitude toward the problems posed by the new Quebec, this might have been taken as a none-too-subtle suggestion to vote Liberal.[64] Meanwhile, Pierre Berton, a former managing editor under Allen and no admirer of the Prime Minister, provided his own summation of "The Real Issues of the Election" in a brilliantly written polemic. Describing the Progressive Conservatives' policy on defence as "positively unbelievable," Berton credited the NDP and the Liberals with at least having clear positions for the voters on the real issue of the campaign: our place in the world and within the Western partnership. The NDP's "noble if difficult isolationism" he dismissed as looking too much like the pious moralizing which had become the Canadian way of late. The alternative, unpalatable though it might be, was unavoidable, namely the Liberals' "committed and equally difficult internationalism," which meant Canada finally shouldering its responsibilities in the Western alliance and particularly in its crucial partnership with the Americans. As Berton bluntly phrased it: "We must stop the pretence, the indecision, the fence straddling, the welshing and the double-dealing which have characterized our relations with our partners."[65]

The 1963 election completed the work begun the previous year by reducing the Conservatives from minority government to official Opposition status. For those who had remained loyal to Diefenbaker, it had to be an embittering result. His prime ministerial career, begun with such promise less than six years earlier, was over. Newman, in his post-election survey, offered an unemotional analysis:

> Lester Pearson counted on common sense to create a separation between the people's material aspirations and his appeal for the strong, stable government we so desperately need. The urban voters responded to him, because he was outlining the kind of wide, sophisticated world which might further their own ambitions. But the rural electorate stayed with John Diefenbaker: unlike Pearson, Diefenbaker was an eloquent spokesman for *their* world, with all its frustrations, hardships and futile attempts to get something from the economic establishment.... .
>
> That there was no logic or structure to his appeal, no sense of reality beyond that of a man trying to vindicate himself, was certainly not due to any lack of self-confidence on Diefenbaker's part. But to the unsympathetic, no

---

63   "A Reporter's Election Diary," *Maclean's*, 6 April 1963 and 23 March 1963.

64   Ibid., "Editorial: The hidden issue of 1963 is the decisive one: do we put Confederation back together?"

65   Ibid., "Pierre Berton's Page: The real issues of the election."

matter how eloquent or impassioned he became, he sounded like a man asking to be rescued by the voters, rather than a leader willing and able to come to aid *them* in facing the uncomfortable facts of the atomic age.

This appeal for sympathy pervaded his every appearance. He ranted against the powerful interests arrayed against him — against the Americans, the generals, *Newsweek*, the "press barons," and even his own advisors... . Once he had established his claim to martyrdom, Diefenbaker could not purge himself of it, and on April 8th more voters decided to tie themselves to the less tarnished star of Lester Pearson. And so the Liberals almost won the election, though Diefenbaker won the campaign... . John Diefenbaker floundered for a very special reason of his own. He had given the people a leadership cult without leadership.[66]

During the 1963 campaign, Diefenbaker would point toward any group of journalists he happened to see and sneer: "There they are, the Liberal press."[67] Nothing could have been more revealing. He never understood the role of the press, not least because he could not accept criticism as other than personal, unfair, and partisan, and most of his ministers and back-benchers clearly felt the same way. Nor did he or they appreciate the difference between press impartiality and press objectivity, with the inevitable result that any manifestations of the absence of the latter brought into question the presence of the former.[68] "To read the press for the period of my government," Diefenbaker observed in his memoirs, "is often to read the opposite of what actually took place."[69] With respect to the leading journalists of *Maclean's* magazine, this was simply not the case. Readers demanded an examination of the government, not the Opposition. Indeed, criticism of the Opposition is precisely what the Conservatives had so often complained made their Liberal predecessors shine. It was understandable and inevitable that press coverage focussed on the Conservatives, and that the steady decline of a government and its leader was hard to portray favourably. Coverage and commentary in *Maclean's*, however, remained quite balanced, at least until 1962. And impartiality was maintained, for the most part, even if objectivity suffered with the temper of the times. Certainly, Blair Fraser had always had to struggle to write objectively about Diefenbaker,[70] and the same was surely true of Newman, Allen, Lefolii and, one might add, a host of other journalists throughout the country. Whether Fraser and Newman merely reciprocated in print the Prime Minister's vindictiveness toward them remains unclear.[71] Certainly, simply exposing what was going on in Ottawa — and coverage in *Maclean's* had focussed on the dominating issues of economic management, defence policy, and of course leadership — could not help but favour the Liberals. What is clear is that Fraser and Newman shaped their critiques of the Diefenbaker government independently of any partisan Liberal interests. If anything, pressure came from their publishers not to alienate the Diefenbaker forces unnecessarily.

---

66   "Backstage in Ottawa," *Maclean's*, 4 May 1963.

67   Interview with Tom Earle.

68   Interview with Roy Faibish and Newman, *Renegade in Power*, 232.

69   As quoted from his memoirs in Allan Levine, *Scrum Wars: The Prime Ministers and the Media* (Toronto: Dundurn Press, 1993), 209.

70   Interview with Gordon Robertson.

71   The journalists interviewed by the author denied vindictiveness was widespread, while Diefenbaker's most thorough biographer argues otherwise. See Smith, *Rogue Tory*, 429.

There seemed little that journalists at *Maclean's* could do to convince Diefenbaker of their impartiality, for practically everything written or said was deemed by him to be poisoned at the source. If the Prime Minister could dismiss his home-town newspaper and its editor, an unabashed admirer, because of the publication of a single critical letter, what hope was there for those who dared to doubt or question?[72] The larger reality is that public affairs journalism was changing in Canada during this period, and there was more adversarialism and editorializing as the media eagerly assumed the mantle of the "unofficial opposition." The evidence indicates that *Maclean's* and its leading journalists carried out no partisan witch hunt on either the government or the Prime Minister. They did not approve of the direction of the government and its leadership, but they said so by recounting the facts.

In the end, the greater part of the responsibility for the deterioration in the relationship between press and government must be laid at the feet of John Diefenbaker and like-minded members of his government and party, not the press.[73] From the outset, Newman and Fraser and a host of others were dismissed as mouthpieces for the Liberal party, and their publications as partisan broadsheets, in the process angering and disillusioning a broad spectrum of opinion, including more moderate voices in the Progressive Conservative party.[74] This was the response of a man who believed he was destined to do great things for ordinary Canadians and was opposed by a sinister conspiracy led by Liberals, supported by Bay Street, aided by the media, and planned by the Americans.[75] In the end, policy and personality undermined Canadians' faith in the Diefenbaker government. Newman, Fraser, and most other journalists were not displeased with the result, and doubtless contributed to it in their way, but in the end John Diefenbaker and his government expired largely from a contracted illness made worse by "the times." From 1958 through 1963, *Maclean's*, though not overly solicitous of the patient's well-being, simply reported the symptoms and charted its declining state of health.

Reporting the symptoms of a government in decline had become the natural course for Canadian journalists during the Diefenbaker years. Their transformation to out-and-out adversarialism in the 1960s, which remains with us to this day, was certainly accelerated by Diefenbaker's unhealthy perceptions of, and attitudes toward, the media. But there were other catalysts, not the least being the influences of American journalism and the advent of television as the pre-eminent medium for covering public affairs. In retrospect, one thing is certain: by 1963, adversarial journalism had become a fixture of the Canadian political scene. After his own brief honeymoon with journalists, Lester Pearson, for whom the press in earlier times had often been a virtual cheering section, would endure almost as severe a testing from the fourth estate as his predecessor. It is ironic that the journalistic exposé style of Peter Newman, which proved so effective in tormenting the Diefenbaker government and heartening the Pearson Liberals, would play such a central role in their own subsequent fall from media grace.

---

72   NA, Progressive Conservative Party Papers, vol. 347, file: Newspapers 1957-59, Roy Thomson to Grosart, 13 May 1957. See also Newman, *Renegade in Power*, 232.

73   Interviews with Tom Earle, Joyce Fairbairn, Bill Wilson, and Christopher Young.

74   Interview with Davie Fulton.

75   Levine, *Scrum Wars*, 210.

BUREAUCRATS AND POLITICIANS IN THE DIEFENBAKER ERA: A LEGACY OF MISTRUST

Ken Rasmussen

It is generally acknowledged that, having spent most of his political career in opposition, John Diefenbaker had an abiding distrust and dislike of the Ottawa civil service, which he saw as little more than a "local branch of the Liberal Party."[1] His attitude was understandable, given the role the federal Liberal party played in building up the senior civil service in the two decades following World War II.[2] In fact, it is only natural for any incoming political executive to be suspicious of the senior civil service.

Yet the curious fact about John Diefenbaker's distrust of these officials was that he did not act to replace them, or make any structural adjustments to supplement their "Liberal" advice. Both R.B. Bennett before him and Joe Clark after him made more changes at the deputy minister level and to the machinery of government than John Diefenbaker did during his entire time in office.[3] The explanation for Diefenbaker's inaction regarding the senior civil service appears to be that his administrative thinking was shaped by his acceptance of certain aspects of the "Whitehall model" of political-bureaucratic relations. In Diefenbaker's understanding, the Whitehall model meant that there was a clear line between politics and administration: policy making was the prerogative of politicians, implementation the duty of public servants. If the public service had drifted too close to policy making under the Liberals, this would have to change. In short, John Diefenbaker reasserted the notion of a political/administrative dichotomy, and wanted to bring about the proper division of labour between Cabinet and the senior civil service.

Diefenbaker's feelings toward the civil service were mixed. Indeed, at times he

1   Denis Smith, *Rogue Tory: The Life and Legend of John G. Diefenbaker* (Toronto: Macfarlane, Walter and Ross, 1995), 250.

2   J.L. Granatstein, *The Ottawa Men: The Civil Service Mandarins, 1935-1957* (Toronto: Oxford University Press, 1982).

3   Sharon L. Sutherland and G. Bruce Doern, *Bureaucracy in Canada: Control and Reform* (Toronto: University of Toronto, Press, 1985), 166.

Political cartoon: "One Man Band: Those Cabinet Pickin' Blues," 1959 (courtesy the Diefenbaker Centre).

suggested that he received no partisan advice from public servants; they were always professional and responsible. At other times, he regarded the bureaucracy as a fifth column of Liberals — at best, waiting for him to leave; at worse, plotting his downfall. This dichotomy in his thinking is an indication of his belief that the civil service should be respected and its administrative ability and grasp of the facts acknowledged, but that it had no proper role in providing a government with policy advice. If the civil service confined itself to administering policy and offering technical support, and the Cabinet concentrated on making policy, then in Diefenbaker's mind the proper relationship between politicians and bureaucrats would have been established — or, more precisely, re-established. Thus, in the end, and despite his distrust and fear of the senior civil service, he engaged in no purge or major alterations in the senior administrative cadre or to the machinery of government, because he believed the bureaucracy could be tamed with the proper division of responsibilities.

It appears, however, that Diefenbaker missed some of the subtleties that made the Whitehall model effective in Britain. The key to the model's success was an acceptance by politicians that the senior civil service had an important role in the policy-making process. While civil servants were of course the constitutional servants of ministers, they also fulfilled an important function in educating and guiding those ministers. Even more important than this, civil servants played a critical role in interest mediation, and because of their knowledge of both program details and specific concerns relevant to the organized interests, they were required to conduct small-scale policy adaptations on a continuous basis.[4] For these reasons, the Whitehall model always conceived of a partnership between the civil service and the ruling party.[5] As one British political scientist noted, there may have been one tiller on the modern state, but there were two hands on the tiller.[6] Diefenbaker chose to send the crew below deck and steer the ship himself. Unfortunately, those he sent below were the very people who might have kept the ship from the rough and unknown waters toward which it inexorably sailed.

4   Joel D. Aberbach and Bert A. Rockman, "Image IV Revisited: Executive and Political Roles," *Governance* 1 (January 1988): 1-25, 4.

5   Hugh Heclo and Aaron Wildavsky, *The Private Government of Public Money: Community and Policy Inside British Politics* (Berkeley: University of California Press, 1974).

6   Richard Rose, "Steering the Ship of State: One Tiller But Two Pairs of Hands," *British Journal of Political Science* 17 (1987): 409-53.

On a broader level, Diefenbaker ignored the changes that were occurring in the relationship between politicians and bureaucrats as a consequence of the expansion of the administrative state. Since at least World War II there had been a movement toward a model that we now know as "political administration."[7] This model is based upon the concept of shared responsibility, mutual reliance, and, above all, personal trust between senior bureaucrats and politicians.[8] While it was possible to distinguish between politicians and bureaucrats in the policy process, together they formed a policy-making community which was in touch and worked within a shared framework. J.E. Hodgetts noted the ongoing importance of the civil service in the area of policy formation as early as the mid-1950s.[9] Yet Diefenbaker misinterpreted the model of political administration as a Liberal aberration to be rejected, rather than an inevitable aspect of the growth of government and of the peculiarities of Canadian administrative practice. This model needed to be adapted to his circumstances and his brand of politics, for what Diefenbaker interpreted as the Liberalization of the bureaucracy was just as much the bureaucratization of the Liberals. In rejecting the model of political administration, Diefenbaker was also rejecting the notion that a policy-sensitive bureaucracy involved in interest mediation was an important aspect of Canadian governance. He would try to terminate the model, but in the end he succeeded only in hastening the emergence of a more aggressive version under the administration of Pierre Trudeau.[10]

Diefenbaker's decision to reject this movement toward political administration no doubt stemmed from a combination of his well-documented lack of interest in administrative matters, a feeling that the bureaucracy was too "red," and a personal leadership style which demanded that he stay in touch with the "people" without any mediating structures. He felt that the close connections between the Liberal party and the bureaucracy was one of the reasons the Liberals had grown out of touch with the average Canadian, and he wanted to avoid this mistake. Senior officials recognized Diefenbaker's attitudes, and watched as he tried to govern Canada without their counsel. As Peter C. Newman noted: "Their absence, it turned out, was a crucial factor in the succession of reason that eventually brought about the downfall of the Diefenbaker ministry."[11]

While relations between bureaucrats and politicians changed with the arrival of John Diefenbaker, the public service as an institution was undergoing a more general transformation. It was becoming a much more technical institution, in which management ability, analytical skill, and a technocratic education were coming to be prized over the generalist skills associated with the older mandarins. The bureaucracy was coming to have a much more analytical orientation in regard to policy making, and was developing a perspective on management as a science. The public service as a whole was becoming a more autonomous institution. No longer wishing to be

---

7   Joel D. Aberbach, Robert D. Putnam, and Bert Rockman, *Bureaucrats and Politicians in Western Democracies* (Cambridge, MA: Harvard University Press, 1981).

8   Michael M. Atkinson and William D. Coleman, "Bureaucrats and Politicians in Canada: An Examination of the Political Administration Model," *Comparative Political Studies* 18 (April 1985): 58-80.

9   J.E. Hodgetts, "The Civil Service and Policy Formation," *Canadian Journal of Economics and Political Science* 23 (November, 1957): 467-79.

10   Colin Campbell and George J. Szablowski, *The Super-Bureaucrats* (Toronto: Macmillan, 1979).

11   Peter C. Newman, *Renegade in Power: The Diefenbaker Years* (Toronto: McClelland and Stewart, 1973), 91.

patronized by government or Parliament, the rank-and-file employees were demanding collective bargaining and political rights which they were shortly to receive. There were also growing pressures from Quebec to ensure a fairer representation of francophones throughout the bureaucracy. Pressure groups, too, were demanding access to policy making through their bureaucratic champions, and they were less inclined to be ignored than they had been during the Liberal decades. In short, the growth of government and the elaboration of specialized bureaucracies were to bring about a spectacular diffusion of power all down the bureaucratic hierarchy.[12] This would normally require a more conscious effort at control from above, but the opposite occurred instead; few innovative overhead control mechanisms were instituted, resulting in a general policy drift.

Diefenbaker presided over a public service that was responding to the pressures of increased size, new technology, the Cold War, and social and cultural forces that were transforming it from a close-knit, clubby, Anglo-Canadian structure in which decisions were based on the long acquaintance of the individuals involved to a more managerial institution, one that was acquiring more power relative both to the legislature and to the executive. Diefenbaker tried to contain the myriad of forces that were pushing the old model aside, but the systems of public administration and policy making he chose were inadequate to deal with the changes that were occurring. His legacy in this regard was the lesson to observers of public administration in Canada that, rather than fighting political administration, a successful politician needs to harness this movement in the service of his or her own goals.

THE DIEFENBAKER MACHINE:
POLICY COMPETENCE VS. PARTISAN RESPONSIVENESS

Establishing the correct balance between policy competence and partisan responsiveness is something all chief executives strive to achieve — and the literature on what happens to those in Canada who do not do this is growing.[13] In the modern administrative state that emerged after World War II, establishing this balance involved the skilful deployment of career civil servants who could manage in the executive-bureaucratic arena. John Diefenbaker never successfully gained control of the bureaucratic establishment, which meant that his government lacked policy competence. Many in Diefenbaker's retinue, and Diefenbaker himself on occasion, came to blame a fifth column of Liberal bureaucrats who subverted their agenda. Yet it is much more likely that Diefenbaker was simply too concerned with retaining partisan responsiveness. Consequently, he failed to make good use of skilled career civil servants; he made no attempt to bring in talented administrative outsiders with the ability to carry forward the successful integration and implementation of his policy objectives; nor did he establish a structure of countervailing advice that would have helped him deal with the resultant problems.

John Diefenbaker unambiguously wanted to reduce the importance of civil servants and consciously avoided using them in policy making in order to ensure that his government remained responsive to partisan pressures. He abandoned the practice of having deputy ministers attend Cabinet meetings to make presentations

---

12   A. Paul Pross, *Group Politics and Public Policy* (Toronto: Oxford University Press, 1986), 46.

13   See Jeffrey Simpson, *The Discipline of Power: The Conservative Interlude and the Liberal Restoration* (Toronto: Macmillan, 1984).

Diefenbaker and his first Cabinet, with Governor General Vincent Massey, on the steps outside Rideau Hall after swearing in ceremony, 21 June 1957 (courtesy the Diefenbaker Centre, MG01/XVII/JGD 401).

to Cabinet. Indeed, as Donald Fleming notes in his memoirs, only once did a public servant attend a Cabinet meeting, and that was when A.D.P. Heeney went to Cabinet to explain his report on the reform of the civil service; Fleming writes that this was "a tribute not only to the importance attached to the report but also to the Prime Minister's confidence in the author."[14] Clearly, however, opportunities to bring in individuals with administrative expertise and sensitivity to the subtleties of existing policies to help Cabinet in its deliberations were foregone. Under Pierre Trudeau, in contrast, public servants frequently advised Cabinet, and often represented their ministers at Cabinet committee meetings.

Diefenbaker's Cabinet decision-making structure was another reflection of his belief that policy should be the sole prerogative of Cabinet. Throughout his time in office, the Prime Minister operated Cabinet as a committee of the whole. He understood well enough that, in a country such as Canada, Cabinet must serve not only as a decision-making body but also as a regional, linguistic, cultural, and sectorally representative body. However, he seems to have been less well acquainted with the dilemma — recognized by other Canadian Prime Ministers — that, as the representational role of Cabinet increases, its ability to function as an effective decision-making body diminishes. This dilemma had been overcome in the past by appointing a series of Cabinet committees that would serve to overcome the diseconomies of a large Cabinet. Yet Diefenbaker chose to institute only the occasional *ad hoc* committee of Cabinet, relying instead almost exclusively on full Cabinet to make decisions on public policy.

---

14   Donald Fleming, *So Very Near: The Summit Years* (Toronto: McClelland and Stewart, 1985), 91.

While abandoning Cabinet committees, Diefenbaker also abandoned Cabinet secretariats. In addition, he put an end to the practice of having committees or groups of deputy ministers who would provide important integrating and coordination functions. Departments were now on their own, and interdepartmental coordination was severely weakened. In the past, noteworthy committees such as the Interdepartmental Committee on External Trade Policy, created in 1949, had been a crucial resource for the Cabinet Committee on Economic Policy; as Granatstein notes, this body of deputies "began to assume coordinative functions taking in virtually the entire compass of government." Under Diefenbaker, these types of committees atrophied or were abandoned, with predictable consequences for government coordination of policy activities.

Adding to the burdens of government was Diefenbaker's insistence that Cabinet come to a consensus before proceeding on any matter. This had a clear impact on the efficiency of the machinery of government, which saw Cabinet becoming bogged down in cumbersome processes and in too many details to be effective. Granatstein notes: "So heavy was the agenda, so frequent the meetings that many ministers could barely keep abreast of their own portfolios."[15] It might not have been so onerous a burden had Diefenbaker not been notoriously indecisive: "He carried the principle of collective decision-making to its extreme, and was reluctant to recommend any course of action that did not have unanimous Cabinet approval."[16] The problem was that the desire for Cabinet unanimity and the insistence that the political aspects of every problem be minutely considered meant that "the efficiency of the policy-making process was sharply reduced, so that the Cabinet reached almost a state of immobilism, and in time Mr. Diefenbaker lost control of his Cabinet."[17]

If this were not enough, there is strong evidence that Diefenbaker tried to dominate government — not only decision making within Cabinet, but the administration of departments as well.[18] His methods tended to be clumsy, and worked against the feelings of loyalty that are necessary for a Prime Minister to inspire in his colleagues.[19] Similarly, he was hostile to the notion that a minister might develop a close relationship with the members of his bureaucracy. In describing the ideal relationship between the deputy and his minister, for instance, Diefenbaker noted that "the most important consideration is to have ministers who do not allow themselves to be led around by their deputies, and who are not cowed by their deputy's superior command of relevant data. The Civil Service is there to advise on, but not to determine, policy. A minister is there to see that government policy is carried out within his department, or to know the reason why." This is hardly the notion of a shared community of interest, each bringing various forms of knowledge to a decision but ultimately existing within a shared framework. In Diefenbaker's mind, bureaucrats dealt in facts and politicians dealt in values. This fact/value distinction is a notoriously slippery notion. In short, Diefenbaker had a combination

15   J.L. Granatstein, *Canada, 1957-1967: The Years of Uncertainty and Innovation* (Toronto: McClelland and Stewart, 1986), 31.

16   R.M. Punnett, *The Prime Minister in Canadian Government and Politics* (Toronto: Macmillian, 1977), 96.

17   W.A. Matheson, *The Prime Minister and the Cabinet* (Toronto: Methuen, 1976), 163.

18   Ibid., 160.

19   Ibid., 161.

of a keen political consciousness and a lack of appreciation for administration which caused him serious and ongoing problems as Prime Minister.[20]

The comparison between Diefenbaker's style of Cabinet decision making and the Trudeau style of rationalism has often been made. Diefenbaker is cast as the non-rationalist, or incrementalist, Trudeau as a rational, systematic thinker. There is a good deal of truth to this characterization. Diefenbaker essentially implemented policies that were intended to patch up the regional and group grievances that had been festering for years, rather than deal with their underlying causes. His policy-making style reflected "an instinctive broker-incrementalist response to the griev-ances of particular groups and regions which had helped put him in power."[21] The brokerage character of early Diefenbaker decisions is further revealed by the fact that so many of them resulted in handouts rather than programs. This was owing not only to Diefenbaker's personal policy style, but also because the central machinery did not think or operate in program terms.[22]

It is worth noting that others recognized the problems Diefenbaker was experi-encing and offered good advice. One of the Glassco Commission's study groups working on the structure of government management suggested to the Diefenbaker government that it create, under the Privy Council Office (PCO), a large central staff support mechanism that would have combined, under one roof, the roles of the PCO and the Treasury Board.[23] This recommendation would have to wait for the Trudeau government of the late 1960s before it emerged as the centre of a new structure of policy coordination.

THE SENIOR PUBLIC SERVICE: FROM MANDARINS TO MANAGERS

As noted above, the changeover from Liberal to Conservative government did not result in a major change in the senior civil service. The noted mandarin A.D.P. Heeney commented, with some understatement, that "the changeover from Liberal to Conservative rule in Ottawa was accomplished with extraordinarily little adminis-trative disturbance and surprisingly little fuss."[24] As late as the end of 1959, all but one deputy minister had been appointed by the previous Liberal government.[25] In that same year, Peter Newman notes, there were forty-seven vacant senior federal appointments, all of them the prerogative of the Prime Minister to fill. All of this occurred despite strong feelings by some Cabinet ministers and by the *Globe and Mail* that a thorough house cleaning was in order, and that the government had a right and a duty to dismantle the existing bureaucratic establishment.[26]

Despite Diefenbaker's inaction, 1957 is the date most often chosen to signal the end of the mandarin era. Its end, then, was not due to a deliberate dismantling of a

---

20   Ibid., 160.

21   G. Bruce Doern, "The Development of Policy Organizations in the Executive Arena," in G. Bruce Doern and Peter Aucoin (eds.), *The Structures of Policy-Making in Canada* (Toronto: Macmillian, 1971), 45.

22   Ibid.

23   Ibid., 46.

24   A.D.P. Heeney, "Traditions and Trends in Canada's Public Service," The Empire Club of Canada, *Addresses*, 1957-58, p. 177.

25   Parliament of Canada, *Parliamentary Guide* (Ottawa: Queen's Printer, 1959).

26   Granatstein, *The Ottawa Men*, 267.

core of entrenched bureaucrats, but rather a natural conclusion to an informal experiment with a Canadian version of the British two-tier administrative structure. Since it had been reformed in 1918, the civil service of Canada had opted for an "American" system of rigid position classification.[27] However, members of English Canada's intellectual élite had pressed long and hard for a two-tier civil service, in which the highest ranks would be reserved for those with a good humanist education, preferably acquired in one of the great British universities. The opportunity to institute such a system informally came during the period of extended Liberal rule. In 1946 it was even recommended by a royal commission headed by Walter Gordon that the best way to ensure a steady supply of senior administrative talent was to "bring in yearly an appropriate number of the best products of the universities, selected not because of some special aptitude, but on grounds of general intelligence and capacity."[28] What was really at the core of these plans was a kind of nostalgic conservative nationalism which demanded that the core of government be peopled with those who were well above average, who respected the institutions and traditions of government, and who could provide mature guidance to a democracy in need of leadership.

The pressures for this kind of élitism were slowly giving way to the demand for a more specialist orientation within the civil service, which itself reflected the highly differentiated nature of Canada's federal bureaucracy. The end of this experiment with a mandarin structure was an end to the idea of talented generalists occupying the highest positions in the bureaucracy. After the early 1950s, there was a recognition of the advantages of the "job" civil service which regularly recruited experts and specialists into senior positions. While many Canadian intellectual leaders may have sentimentally favoured the British model, equal numbers acknowledged the demand for specialist knowledge that the positive state was forcing on governments.[29]

A combination of generational change, social pressures for more francophones in the public service, and the increasing importance of technical knowledge all conspired to end the mandarin era. What was beginning to replace this generation of talented generalists was the more faceless era of the expert; the "men with computers and flowcharts" were coming on the scene. Bureaucracies were getting so large that the personalized kind of direction associated with the mandarins was simply no longer practicable. "A new generation of technocrats, whose claim to involvement in the solutions of public problems lay in their formal training and substantive expertise rather than in seniority and experiences, saw in the planning movement an ideal instrument to speed the supplant of the mandarinate and their own succession to power."[30] Decision making at the bureaucratic level was coming to mean analytical capacity based on formal education rather than judgement based on experience.

There was clearly emerging a new type of bureaucratic career during the Diefenbaker era. This was to bring about a profound change in the norms, prestige

---

27   Alasdair Roberts, *So-Called Experts: How American Consultants Remade the Canadian Civil Service 1918-21* (Toronto: IPAC, 1996).

28   Canada, Royal Commission on Administrative Classification in the Public Service, *Report* (Ottawa: King's Printer, 1946), 15.

29   Alexander Brady, "The Training and Development of Public Servants," *University of Toronto Quarterly* 22 (April 1953): 217-29.

30   Richard D. French, *How Ottawa Decides* (Toronto: Lorimer, 1984), 21.

structure, and career patterns of the federal civil service. Where once program management and broad experience were the sole qualifications of any significance, a new parallel, and in many ways more attractive career path in policy, planning, and analysis was opening up.[31] A changing role for the social scientist in Canada was being developed at this time. Indeed, members of all disciplines, but particularly economics, were dominating the enormous number of royal commissions Diefenbaker initiated.[32] The complexity of government was, then, leading to an explosion in the activity of the social sciences. The analysis of public problems was coming to require specialties and expertise; such problems did not lend themselves to solution over lunch at the Chateau Laurier. "There was enormous optimism about the knowledge emerging from these forms of analysis and about its potential effectiveness in the solution of public problems."[33] This knowledge was available to Diefenbaker, but he was not inclined to listen to the advice of bureaucratic "experts."

Adding to the pressures bringing about the end of the mandarin era was the fact that there was a breakdown in the consensus among the bureaucracy over some fundamental issues concerning the nature of the economy and the responses that should be made by the state. The old mandarins maintained a consensus on the need of federal government involvement in social welfare, the management of the economy, and the need for freer trade and closer economic links with the United States. All these notions were being challenged, both from outside and from within the senior ranks of the civil service, as early as the mid-1950s. There were, for example, growing concerns about Canada's economic dependence on the United States. Mitchell Sharp has noted that the underlying consensus among politicians and their senior advisers about the direction of economic and social policy was clearly disappearing at this time.[34]

Despite the turmoil around him, Diefenbaker remained quite proud of his handling of the senior cadre in the civil service, noting in his memoirs: "Appointments at the deputy-minister level also received my fullest consideration, after consultation with the appropriate ministers. When a government had been in power as long as the Liberals, it was natural that many public officials absorbed the political faith of the government, which in their opinion seemed destined to endure forever."[35] Yet, given his obvious feelings about the nature of bureaucratic advice being given to the government, he was proud to admit that only a few senior civil servants were dismissed. And while he felt that "perhaps there were a number of high-ranking public servants who should have been dismissed without delay when we took office," he also noted that "I was one who was extremely reluctant to remove civil servants on the sole ground that they had served another administration."[36] Diefenbaker appeared trapped in his own administrative thinking. Unwilling to dismiss those who had worked for another administration, but not trusting their advice, he could

---

31   Ibid., 26.

32   See Stephen Brooks and Alain G. Gagnon, *Social Scientists and Politics in Canada* (Montreal: McGill-Queen's University Press, 1988).

33   French, *How Ottawa Decides*, 19.

34   Mitchell Sharp, *Which Reminds Me... A Memoir* (Toronto: University of Toronto Press, 1994), 78.

35   John G. Diefenbaker, *One Canada: The Years of Achievement, 1957-1962* (Toronto: Macmillan of Canada, 1976), 52.

36   Ibid., 53.

conceive of no other way of, nor even the need for, getting alternative forms of advice or new ways of managing his decision-making apparatus. As opposed to Pierre Trudeau, who recognized the changing nature of public administration and harnessed these changes in the service of his agenda, Diefenbaker could not conceive of either a new structure or an alternative source of advice.

POLICY VS. POLITICS: THE ROLE OF ADVICE

Diefenbaker did not really see a difference between policy as a neutral activity with its own dynamics, institutions, and interest groups, and policy as a means of advancing partisan interests. Because in his mind politics and policy were intimately connected, he was reluctant to listen to the advice of bureaucrats on anything but administrative matters. Given this distrust of the bureaucracy and its advice, a natural course of action would have been to find another mechanism of countervailing advice. Such a course was taken by Pierre Trudeau, who had an equal distrust of the advice he would receive from the bureaucracy. Trudeau realized that he would have to create an alternative structure to ensure that he would not have to rely on what was coming out of the bureaucracy, which he thought was lacking in imagination and mostly interested in preserving the status quo. In response, he greatly increased the size of the PMO and the PCO and turned both of them into active policy units. It was evident to Trudeau that the changes in the nature of the administrative state since the Second World War meant that a "modern Prime Minister requires a large machine and support staff merely to maintain his relative position within the machinery of government"[37]

Diefenbaker clearly did not maintain his relative position within the machinery of government. In an interview in the 1970s, he noted that "the growth of the Prime Minister's Office under Prime Minister Trudeau is the biggest hoax that has ever been created. It indicates first a complete lack of knowledge of Parliament and of the Prime Minister's responsibilities.... I operated the Prime Minister's Office on $50,000 a year, now it costs almost a million."[38] In point of fact, Diefenbaker operated a sort of fused PCO/PMO with Robert Bryce, one of the last of the classic mandarins, at its head. Diefenbaker's system focussed decision making on Cabinet and the collegial process, but he personally got very little by way of high quality advice, either of a partisan or of an expert nature. Instead, the PCO maintained the classic roles of dealing with the organizational, secretarial, and coordinating functions of Cabinet, and the PMO dealt with the Prime Minister's correspondence and appointments. The PCO did not function as a secretariat for Cabinet, nor did it supplement the policy advice that was coming from departments. Most scholars would agree with Bruce Doern's droll assessment that the PCO's role was "rather passive during the Diefenbaker era."[39] The only kind of advice that Diefenbaker really sought was the "political advice" of a few close, trusted, but generally untalented advisors.

The one source of non-partisan expert advice that John Diefenbaker did turn to came from royal commissions, which he was very fond of establishing. While the use of royal commissions may have had the virtue of delaying any action at all, they were

---

37   Punnet, *The Prime Minister*, 81.

38   Thomas A. Hockin, *Apex of Power: The Prime Minister and Political Leadership in Canada* (Scarborough: Prentice-Hall, 1971), 189.

39   Doern, "Policy Organization in the Executive Arena."

Diefenbaker with Jules Léger (left), then of External Affairs, and R.B. Bryce (right), Clerk of the Privy Council, 1957 (courtesy the Diefenbaker Centre, MG01/XVII/JGD 3966).

clearly a source of advice independent of the civil service. Eleven of the sixteen royal commissions established by the Diefenbaker government were functioning by 1960. As V. Seymour Wilson notes: "This interesting fact gives some credence to Mr. Diefenbaker's reputed mistrust of the Ottawa bureaucracy, and his initial attempts to rely on expert advice for policy-making from outside the confines of the federal civil service."[40]

Diefenbaker established sixteen royal commissions, including the Glassco Commission on Government Organization, the Borden Commission on Energy, the Carter Commission on Taxation, the McPherson Commission on Transportation, the Hall Commission on Health Services, and the Porter Commission on Banking and Services, to name the more prominent ones. Lester Pearson, and later Pierre Trudeau, wanted to bring bold, imaginative new ideas into the decision-making process, but rarely resorted to the ponderous, independent machinery of the royal commission. Instead, they chose to make use of task forces, which were much more nimble and more closely connected to executive government.

While much of the advice of Diefenbaker's royal commissions came too late to be of much use to his government, they had one indirect benefit: they gave a number of young, talented, educated, and ambitious individuals experience in policy analysis and government operations. In a few short years, many of these people would be

---

40   V. Seymour Wilson, "The Role of Royal Commissions and Task Forces," in G. Bruce Doern and Peter Aucoin (eds.), *The Structures of Policy-Making in Canada* (Toronto: Macmillan of Canada, 1971).

incorporated in the senior positions of the government. Michael Pitfield, from the Royal Commission on Magazines and Other Periodicals, and Douglas Hartle, who was with the Carter Commission, are just two examples of the people Diefenbaker "trained" and who would later occupy key positions in the Pearson government, or play a role in the Trudeau experiments of the late 1960s and early 1970s.

In the final analysis, Diefenbaker held firm to the belief that policy advice should come from Cabinet and not from experts. Indeed, he did not want his Cabinet colleagues to get too close to the bureaucrats and the experts, and those such as Donald Fleming who did get close to their officials he came to distrust.[41] He had an aversion to anything that separated the Prime Minister from the ordinary people and, as such, he had no functionaries of the quality of Tom Kent or Tom Axworthy in his office. He was, in fact, quite critical of individuals such as these who were attached to the Prime Minister. Of course, this had consequences. Whereas under Louis St. Laurent the policy process was decisive and efficient, with the bureaucracy the major source of input, under Diefenbaker the policy process lacked precision. The bureaucracy was not without ideas, but they would only turn up later during the Pearson and Trudeau years.[42]

CONCLUSION

During the Diefenbaker era, relations between bureaucrats and politicians underwent a transformation. The system of collaboration between the bureaucracy and politicians in the formation of public policy that had developed under the Liberals was considered an aberration to be set right. What is now clear is that this collaborative system was a response to the new demands of the administrative state and the pressures of the myriad of interest groups that had come by the late 1950s to depend on it. Diefenbaker was not inclined to accommodate these demands in a way that would have allowed his government to make use of the policy competence contained in the bureaucracy, while remaining responsive to the people. Instead, he tried to return to a system that kept a clear line between the responsibilities of officials to provide facts and the responsibilities of politicians to provide values. What subsequent political leaders have come to realize is that it is quite legitimate to impose one's will on the administrative state in a number of ways, but it is fatal to ignore it.

Diefenbaker's failing was not that he saw policy as an activity that belonged to the political realm. Most of the neo-conservative politicians of the 1980s felt just as strongly that policy was the prerogative of politicians.[43] Thatcher, Reagan, and Mulroney all wanted control of the policy agenda, and tried to force public servants to act as managers rather than policy advisors. They all took steps to weaken the policy role traditionally played by career officials, just as Diefenbaker had. However, they also took steps to gain control of the policy-making process. As Savoie has noted: "Thatcher sought to centralize policy advice in her own office; Reagan went further than any president in fifty years in making sure that appointees and even senior career

---

41   Fleming, *So Very Near*, 88.

42   See, for example, Rodney Haddow, *Poverty Reform in Canada, 1958-1978* (Montreal: McGill-Queen's University Press, 1993).

43   Donald Savoie, *Thatcher, Regan, Mulroney: In Search of a New Bureaucracy* (Toronto: University of Toronto Press, 1994).

officials shared his political views; and Mulroney appointed political and policy 'commissars' to all ministerial offices."[44]

But neo-conservative attempts to alter the location of policy making have also come to be seen as failures. Even with their extraordinary efforts to gain control of the bureaucracy, they have come up against the reality that there are few effective substitutes for the expertise and knowledge of the bureaucracy. In the end, political leaders in the 1980s created a great deal of long-term harm by gutting the policy capacity of government. "The fear of strengthening the policy role of officials prevented the political leadership from reforming the government machinery for policy formation, co-ordination, and evaluation."[45] This same debility affected Diefenbaker. So strong was his desire to control the policy agenda that he ultimately left his government with little policy capacity. The lesson of Diefenbaker, which is yet to be fully appreciated by politicians even today, is that a political leader must accept the legitimate policy role of civil servants. The art of political leadership in the era of the administrative state involves harnessing the policy capacity of the bureaucracy so that it works toward a partisan agenda.

---

44   Ibid., 276.

45   B. Guy Peters and Donald J. Savoie, "Civil Service Reform: Misdiagnosing the Patient," *Public Administration Review* 54 (September/October 1994): 418-25, 424.

Contributors

ROBERT M. BELLIVEAU graduated with a BA (Honours) in History from Dalhousie University and an MA in Political Studies from the University of Saskatchewan. The subject of his MA thesis was John Diefenbaker and the Bill of Rights. Mr. Belliveau is now Executive Vice-President, External Affairs, with the London Telecom Group Inc., a telecommunications company based in southwestern Ontario.

PATRICK H. BRENNAN is an Assistant Professor in the Department of History, University of Calgary. He holds a Ph.D. in History from York University. In 1996 he published *Reporting the Nation's Business: Press-Government Relations during the Liberal Years, 1935-1957.*

P.E. BRYDEN is an Assistant Professor in the Department of History at Mount Allison University. She received a Ph.D. from York University in 1994. In 1997 she published *Planners and Politicians: Liberal Politics and Social Policy, 1957-1968* and was co-author of *The Welfare State in Canada: Past, Present, Future.*

KEVIN J. GLOIN is a Ph.D. student with the Department of History, Ohio University. His major field of study is US foreign relations.

WENDY GREEN-FINLAY is a Ph.D. student at Queen's University, Kingston.

ANN FLANAGAN is a Ph.D. student with the Department of History, University of Toronto.

RUSSELL ISINGER graduated with a BA (Honours) and an MA in Political Studies from the University of Saskatchewan where he is currently employed as a Research Assistant with the College of Law. In recent years he has been a Guest Curator with the Diefenbaker Canada Centre and the National Aviation Museum, Ottawa, where he worked on an Avro Arrow exhibit and a Website/CD-ROM respectively. He has published several articles, including "Paradigm's Lost: German Federal and Electoral Solutions to Canada's Constitutional Problems," *Constitutional Forum* (Winter 1995).

PATRICK KYBA is a Professor with the Department of Political Studies, University of Guelph. He holds a Ph.D. from the London School of Economics and Political Science. In 1989, he published *Alvin: A Biography of the Honourable Alvin Hamilton, P.C.* He is currently working on a history of the Conservative party in Saskatchewan.

CHRISTOPHER MACLENNAN is a Social Policy Analyst with Human Resources and Development Canada. He holds a Ph.D. in History from the University of Western Ontario. In 1996 he presented a paper, "Canada and Universal Human Rights: International Influences and the Evolution of Human Rights in Canada, 1944-1968," at the Annual Conference of the Association of Canadian Studies.

KEN RASMUSSEN is an Associate Professor in the Faculty of Administration, University of Regina and holds a Ph.D. in Political Science from the University of Toronto. He is the co-author of *Privatizing a Province: The New Right in Saskatchewan.*

R. BRUCE SHEPARD is a graduate of the Universities of Regina and Saskatoon. He is the author of *Deemed Unsuitable: An Examination of the African-American Migration to the Canadian Plains.* He is currently the Director of the Diefenbaker Canada Centre, University of Saskatchewan.

RICHARD SIGURDSON is Acting Dean of Arts, University College of the Cariboo, Kamloops, B.C. He has published articles in the *Canadian Journal of Political Science*, the *International Journal of Canadian Studies* and other journals. He is currently finishing a book for Broadview Press on citizenship and nationalism in Canada.

ERIKA SIMPSON is an Assistant Professor with the Department of Political Science at the University of Western Ontario. She is the author of various studies concerning Canada's NATO commitments, and co-authored the original proposals to establish the Lester B. Pearson Peacekeeping Training Centre.

DAVID K. STEWART is an Associate Professor with the Department of Political Science, University of Alberta. He holds a Ph.D. from the University of British Columbia. His recent publications include "Parties and Party Systems," in Christopher Dunn (ed.), *Canadian Provincial Politics* and "The Changing Leadership Electorate," in the *Canadian Journal of Political Science*.

DONALD C. STORY is an Associate Professor with the Department of Political Studies, University of Saskatchewan. He holds a Ph.D. from the University of Toronto. In 1993, he edited *The Canadian Foreign Service in Transition*.